WORKING TOWARD FREEDOM

To the Memory of Christopher Lasch

WORKING TOWARD

∽ FREEDOM ∽

Slave Society and Domestic Economy
in the American South

Edited by

Larry E. Hudson Jr.

University of Rochester Press

First published 1994
University of Rochester Press
34-36 Administration Building, University of Rochester
Rochester, New York, 14627, USA
and at PO Box 9, Woodbridge, Suffolk IP12 3DF, UK

Library of Congress Cataloging-in-Publication Data

Working toward freedom : slave society and domestic economy in the
American South / edited by Larry E. Hudson Jr.
    p.   cm.
  Includes bibliographical references and index.
  ISBN 1–878822–37–3 (alk. paper) : —ISBN 1–878822–38–1 (pbk.) :
  1. Slaves—Southern States—Economic conditions. 2. Home economics—
Southern States—History. 3. Plantation life—Southern States—History.
4. Slavery—Economic aspects—Southern States. 5. Southern States—
Economic conditions.   I. Hudson, Larry E., 1952– .
E443.W675   1994
306.3′62′0975—dc20   94–31998

British Library Cataloguing-in-Publication Data

A catalogue record for this book is available from the British Library

This publication is printed on acid-free paper
Printed in the United States of America
Designed and Typeset by Cornerstone Composition Services

~

CONTENTS

∼

INTRODUCTION

The work and productive activities performed by slaves for themselves rather than for their masters provided a foundation on which they built their domestic life and community. Work patterns shaped the social structure of slave society and provided a material basis for the slaves' distinctive culture. The papers presented at the Work and Culture conference held at the University of Rochester in the Spring 1993 investigated the intimate areas of slave life—their family organization, value systems, and cultural practices.[1] The Conference achieved much more than the sum of these provocative papers because the presenters, commentators, and the diverse audience,[2] combined to address several difficult and abiding questions about slavery, slaves, slave life, and the continued effects on African-American life. As always, there was insufficient time to address all questions that grew out of our collaborative efforts, and few of them were answered in a way that satisfied everyone present. That participants raised many new, as well as old, questions about the lives of slaves testifies both to the timeliness of the conference and to the still prickly nature of the subject of slavery: there remains some uneasiness with the "stories" of slavery that becomes more acute when the subject is about the slaves themselves.

What new insights did we gain at the Rochester Work and Culture Conference? We were reminded that the slaves and their world retain a near impenetrable shield; that any conclusion derived from one particular glimpse into the private world of the slave is often quickly countered by an opposite "picture"; and that much of what is said about slaves has repercussions that reach beyond the academy. Accordingly, the authors have worked hard to present their findings in a sensitive manner, particularly those whose work moves the discussion into new directions, or who diverge from traditional interpretations. These essays provide conclusions that challenge earlier presentations about slavery and raise new questions that demand an analysis of new sources as well as traditional sources in novel ways.

Given the subject material, the relatively sparse documentation on the slave past, and the difficult, if not impossible, task of gauging accurately the psychological makeup of a people who recorded little of their private thoughts, it is to be expected that these innovative studies tend toward the impressionistic and the speculative. Nevertheless *Working Toward Freedom* marshals the disciplines of history, sociology, and anthropology, in search of more accurate "pictures" of slave life. The common theme throughout this volume is an attempt to better understand people who were slaves and who, armed with few if any choices regarding the broader structures of their lives, took advantage of available opportunities to determine and shape its "inner contours" in an effort to make lives of their own while working toward freedom.

By the eighteenth century, masters and slaves knew what they could expect from one another and from the world around them. The broader patterns first established in the Chesapeake would change little over the next century or so. Essentially, masters would endeavor, or be forced, to provide their slaves with life's basic necessities. In return, they would expect a full day's work and good behavior from their slaves. The more personal relationship between master and slaves, on the other hand, was never static but characterized by both continuity and change: a complex process of social interaction that was in a constant state of flux. The slaves' familiarity with their landscape, its flora and fauna, as well as its diseased environment, gave them certain advantages over newcomers without such knowledge—be they black or white. The masters' growing familiarity with their slaves permitted a reduction in the use of physical force and an extension of the use of incentives to bring about their desired ends. These shifts, sometimes subtle, allowed the slaves greater control over their own lives. Therefore, relationships between masters and their slaves that appear to be peculiar to the antebellum period had their origins in the early eighteenth century.

Working Toward Freedom examines the ways in which work and property accumulation facilitated an ever-widening social and economic space between masters and slaves. The essays included here recall the lives of slaves who, like the vast majority, worked hard to accumulate some property in an attempt to make a better life for themselves under slavery. They describe some of the mechanisms slaves used to eke out an existence for themselves and to create some social space wherein they could articulate, practice, and institutionalize their own values and customs. The essays tell the story of slaves who were neither oblivious to the world around them, nor passive participants who accepted their enslavement on their masters' terms. Although always disadvantaged, slaves did not give up their social and spiritual individuality, thereby conceding to their owners all of the legally protected privileges of slave ownership. The arrangements worked out between slaves and their owners on farms, plantations, and in urban households were seldom determined by the formal rule of law. Neither were their negotiations conducted between people who were absolutely powerful on the one hand, and abject and powerless on the other. Masters, mistresses, and their slaves "battled" for dominance and control: sometimes violently, yet at times with mutually expressed good feelings. Moreover, the terrain on which these "battles" took place occasionally rendered the slaves far more powerful than has been imagined. Of course, there was a great deal masters could safely concede to their slaves without losing their advantage; nevertheless, for slaves the opportunity and ability to compete at all, constituted a significant victory.

By the antebellum period, slaveowners were finding it increasingly difficult to protect their terrain. Slaves, particularly those in urban areas, pursued a variety of non-violent means to loosen the bonds of slavery by enhancing their control of important areas of their lives. Those more firmly ensconced in rural areas on farms and plantations sought to make-over their less public world and construct more satisfactory and manageable internal structures. There, despite the attempt (and success) to distance themselves from the white world, their practices were not wholly European, African, Native American, but a combination of all three and numerous other influences.

There were, however, cultural practices within the slave quarters that maintained a direct and clear continuity with West African cultural forms, but the social structure in the slave quarter community was not immune to, and was sometimes decisively shaped by, outside influences.

In Part One, Lorena Walsh's "A 'Place in Time Regained': A Fuller History of Colonial Chesapeake Slavery Through Group Biography," addresses the difficulty of recapturing the early African American past. To gather information is tough enough, but without painstaking effort, and novel means, the "stuff of history" that will reveal the "stories" about slave life will remain buried in the distant past. Walsh digs deep into early Virginian history and unearths a fascinating picture of the construction and re-construction of slave quarter communities. Her study reveals the essential vulnerability of the slaves and their dependence upon the master for provision of the crucial "outer contours" of life. The slightest attack on the structure of the master's family could have dire consequences for the slaves, their families, and their community. Therefore, the fortunes of the slaveowning family could not be separated from those of the slave family. However much space slaves were able to create for themselves, the slave world could not remain immune or too distant from that of the white world.

Just as slaves could not prevent white intrusion into their world, slave masters were not always able to ignore external intrusions into their private domain. They never really enjoyed as much control over their slaves as they would have liked. Robert Olwell's " 'A Reckoning of Accounts': Patriarchy, Market Relations, and Control on Henry Laurens's Lowcountry Plantations, 1762-1785" discusses an example of the struggle between masters and slaves for control of important areas of life. These master and slave confrontations did not always end with a conclusion satisfactory to the owner. The parameters of their struggle, as Olwell points out, revolved around the relationship the master wished to have with his slaves: that of the patriarch whose every material concession to his slaves was seen as an act of paternalism—gifts or rewards to deserving, hardworking dependents; or that of the "factor" who pays his slaves for the goods and services they produce in the time allotted to them after completing their master's work. In the latter case, the slaves' work would constitute a direct source of monetary gain, and lead to property accumulation, and increased autonomy. While Laurens, like most masters, would have happily retained a paternalistic relationship, the slaves sought to locate their economic activities more firmly in the "impersonal and transitory cash nexus of market relations."

As well as market forces, the formal law could also protrude into the slaveholders' private domain limiting their ability to act as freely as they wished, and frustrating their efforts to respond effectively to their slaves' demands for additional social and economic space. Slaveowners were willing to concede a great deal to their slaves as long as these concessions did not seriously reduce the master's authority, and contributed to the economic well-being and good order of the plantation. John Campbell's " 'My Constant Companion': Slaves and their Dogs in the Antebellum South," investigates the several roles of slave dogs in a slave community and the private and public responses to what came to be seen as a public nuisance. It reveals some of the ways in which masters, slaves, and public laws influenced the structure of master/slave relations, and the continued effort by the slaves to carve out some niche under slavery for themselves and their families. In so doing, Campbell also provides a glimpse into the social organization of the slave quarters and the important emotional and intrinsic services that dogs provided the slaves—from loving and obedient pets, to primary weapons in the crucial activity of hunting for food.

With or without dogs, South Carolina's slaves were able to exploit the available opportunities to increase their income and control areas of their lives. Their work activities for themselves on land assigned to them by their masters were sufficient to help them accumulate surplus provisions which could then be sold to the master for cash or bartered with fellow slaves for other goods. In " 'All that Cash': Work and Status in the Slave Quarters" Larry Hudson examines the impact of the growing prevalence of money in the slave quarter community where, at least in theory, the slaves, being property themselves, could neither accumulate, nor legally dispense property of their own. The time to work for themselves after they had completed their masters' work assignments facilitated the accumulation of such amounts of property that there developed noticeably different attitudes toward the accumulation and uses of money among slaves and, consequently, clear social distinctions between slaves began to appear. These different and sometimes conflicting values in the slave quarters reveal an ever-growing willingness on the part of slaves to work hard and to exploit their opportunities to the fullest—if only to maintain a standard of living above that typical of slaves who depended upon their masters for most if not all the basic necessities of life. Those slaves best able to provide extra goods and services for themselves and their families were revered in the quarters and often dominated its social, economic, and political order.

Kenneth Brown's paper, "Material Culture and Community Structure: The Slave and Tenant Community at Levi Jordan's Plantation, 1848-1892," shifts our focus from the deep South and into eastern Texas where, using the skills of the archaeologist, he tracks the material development of an African-American community through slavery and into freedom. Through a close examination of retrieved artifacts, Brown presents an interpretation of the economic, political, and ritual life and adoption within a black community from 1848 to 1892. His documentation of the Jordan people's experience reveals the type of continuity that might be expected when slaves were able to remain on the same plantation for two or more generations.

Part Two of this volume emphasizes family, gender, and social order under slavery. It examines additional benefits that resulted from an increase in social and economic autonomy made possible by the small victories won by the slaves. Never with any guarantee of success, slaves worked hard to maintain the integrity of their families: from the provisions of extra goods and services, to the socialization of children, and even to self-purchase.

The stories told by Cheryll Ann Cody in "Sale and Separation: Four Crises for Enslaved Women on the Ball Plantations, 1764-1854," best exemplify the efforts made by individual slaves to interpose themselves between their masters and other forces hostile to slave family unity. At crucial junctures, slave women used a variety of strategies (with varying degrees of success) to modify or reduce the worst effects of the sale and separation of family members.

Mary Beth Corrigan's "It's a family Affair: Buying Freedom in the District of Columbia, 1850-1860," looks at family attempts to bring about a similar end. She focuses on an urban rather than a rural setting and looks closely at the more ambitious, but economically feasible realm of self-purchase. More often than not, these urban slaves had to do more than accumulate money in order to purchase themselves or family members; they also had to engage in complex and frequently unsatisfactory bargaining strategies with unscrupulous masters.

The trials and tribulations faced by slave parents is attested to by the tensions revealed in the stories recounted by Wilma King in " 'Rais your children up rite': Parental Guidance and Child Rearing Practices Among Slaves in the Nineteenth-Century South." Parents were often caught in a terrible dilemma when it came to teaching their children how to behave both in the public world dominated by the rules of the white master and in the private world coded by rules largely determined by the slaves themselves. Here, where the two worlds frequently met, the struggle between masters and slave parents for dominance over slave children, often led to confusion and heartache for the children and frustration and sadness for the parents.

In "Symbol, Memory, and Service: Resistance and Family Formation in Nineteenth-Century African America" Sharon Holt embarks upon a theoretical excursion that argues for a subtle shift in the primary focus of slave families between the antebellum and post-bellum periods. In the former, given a prevalence of family separation through sale and wide geographical dispersion, slaves could sometimes do no more than hold on to their family through the emotional and spiritual mechanism of what she terms a "defiant memory." While a slaveowner could physically wrench apart slave families, he could not affect their continued existence in the slaves' memory. Constituting defiance on the slaves' part, such behavior was thus an act of resistance. In the post Civil War period where former masters attempted to deny former slaves access to the economic opportunities that freedom promised (and the former slaves desperately needed to exploit), resistance was expressed primarily through their provision of goods and services. Within the more localized, post-bellum family arrangements, membership was determined less by symbolic memory than by the provision of goods and services.

Josephine Beoku-Betts' " 'She Make Funny Flat Cake Call Saraka': Gullah Women and Food Practices Under Slavery," follows a similar path in her examination of African-American cultural practices: in this case, those of African derived food practices. She first locates her research in 1990s Georgia and then connects her findings there with the antebellum period, which, in turn, she links with a more distant West African past.

In sum, all these articles reveal the existence of some cultural space (never as much as slaves wanted but almost always more than masters willingly conceded) wherein slaves could take steps toward making their world over in shapes and forms that most closely reflected their particular situation, and aspirations. Through their exploitation of the opportunities that came their way, these slaves were better able to cope with the demands of their enslavement while working for that "Day of Jubilee" that few ever doubted would one day arrive.

～
NOTES

1. I would like to extend my appreciation to all those who took part in the conference, and to those who made it possible: Radio WDKX, Aenon Baptist Church, Provost Brian J. Thompson, the Departments of Economics, English, History, Religion and Classics, the Graduate School of Education and Human Development, the Interfaith Chapel, and Kitabu Kingdom Bookstore. Thanks also to the following university offices and student organization for their support: Multicultural Committee, Outside Speakers Committee, Office of the Dean, CAS, Student Activities/Wilson Commons, and University and Community Affairs. And special thanks to the New York Council for the Humanities, Frederick Douglass Institute for African and African-American Studies, Office of Minority Students Affairs, and the Susan B. Anthony Center for Women's Studies, without whose financial assistance the conference would not have taken place: heartfelt thanks to Patricia Neill. To all the commentators and participants in the Sunday Roundtable–Robert Baum, Stanley Engerman, Veronica Gerald, Graham Hodges, Karen Fields, Charles Joyner, Daniel Littlefield, Roderick McDonald, Philip Morgan, and Margaret Washington–a special word of gratitude.
2. A special thanks to the Reverend James Cherry of Aenon Baptist Church who hosted the second full day of the conference. Aenon Baptist is an historical African-American church, and the participation of its members in the organization, and conduct of the conference was invaluable. The opportunity to bring together members of the academic community and those of the wider community, provided an additional dimension that is all too often absent from the deliberations.
3. In 1989 a conference was held at the University of Maryland under the heading "Cultivation and Culture: Labor and Shaping Slave Life in the Americas." Scholars there investigated the process of production and their influence the lives of the men and women who tended the New World's major staple crops. See *The Slaves' Economy: Independent Production by Slaves in the Americas*, eds. Ira Berlin and Philip D. Morgan (London: Frank Cass, 1991).

~

A "PLACE IN TIME" REGAINED
A Fuller History Of Colonial Chesapeake Slavery Through Group Biography

Lorena S. Walsh

The history of Chesapeake plantations and especially of those plantations that have become public museums has traditionally been the history of the great planters who developed them.[1] Only very recently have we begun to think about the history of individual plantations as also the history of the African Americans whose labor as enslaved workers made great houses and good lives possible for a few.[2] And, while most regional museums have begun to incorporate material from generalized studies of Chesapeake slavery into their interpretative programs, the preconception remains that little or nothing of the history of individual groups of slaves has survived to retell.

To redress this imbalance, Colonial Williamsburg has made a start with the reconstructed slave quarter at Carter's Grove plantation. Initially it seemed that almost all of the slaves' particular history was irretrievably lost. Surviving plantation account books dating from the mid- to late-eighteenth century yielded little more than an incomplete list of names and a much smaller list of occupations. These documents revealed almost nothing about where the slaves lived or about family histories. Thus the only option appeared that of peopling the reconstructed quarter with historically justifiable but hypothetical residents and of interpreting their lives as a composite of the generic experience of slaves in tidewater Virginia. In addition, the decision to focus the interpretation on one point in time—circa 1770—muted the relevance of earlier events; and, if

1

so little could be recovered for the later eighteenth century, presumably almost nothing could be learned about the preceding century.

Unfortunately, as a recent critique has noted, it is exceedingly difficult if not impossible to present a seemingly authoritative interpretation or to evoke the same imaginative responses through a recounting of the probable experiences of hypothetical men, women, and children with a generic history as it is from a recounting of the histories of known individuals living at a given place in a given time, however sketchy the evidence.[3] This challenged me to reinvestigate the evidence available for the Carter's Grove slaves, with unexpected results.

It remains the case that we are unlikely ever to be able to trace family trees or to recover much of anything of the life stories of individual Carter's Grove slaves. Yet, if we phrase the question just a little differently–do the Carter's Grove slaves *as a group* have a recoverable history?–the answer is a resounding *"yes."* The general outline, of necessity, had to come first. Only with the pioneering work of Russell Menard and Allan Kulikoff on colonial Chesapeake slave demography and slave society could we grasp the significance of previously available materials.[4] That it has taken so long after the appearance of these works to frame new approaches for the study of specific slave groups shows that we all have blind spots when thinking about the history of African Americans.

The core materials for this project are the standard deeds, wills, and inventories that scholars have long used to trace the title histories of large plantations. We can pose similar questions for most other plantation museums. The potential for developing more fully informed and more concrete interpretations of slave plantation life from documentary sources is truly exciting. So too are the implications for archaeology at many Chesapeake slave sites. Armed with more precise information about the people who lived on particular places at particular times, we can perhaps learn more from the material record as well.

At Carter's Grove, two distinct groups of African Americans were united into one "work force" at the home plantation and its associated quarters in 1738, when, for the first time, there was a white planter family in residence. One group was composed of recently enslaved Africans who had lived, after their forced removal from the Old World, only at Carter's Grove; the others were mostly first or second generation native-born Virginians with older and wider roots in the colony. It is with the latter group that the Carter's Grove slaves' story begins.

THE YORK/GLOUCESTER BRANCH

The longer-established branch of the Carter's Grove slaves were members or descendants of the bound work force assembled by planter Lewis Burwell II

(c. 1646–1710) of Fairfield, Gloucester County, grandfather of the first resident owner of Carter's Grove. The first of the family born in Virginia, Lewis developed a sizeable estate in the last quarter of the seventeenth century. The Burwell slaves came in turn from four separate sources.

First were the roughly twenty slaves, plus their children, that Lewis Burwell II purchased himself between 1667 and his death in 1710. (Burwell's father, the first of the family in Virginia, accumulated several thousand acres of land by importing white indentured servants; there is no evidence that he bought any slaves.)[5] The majority of the Burwell slaves became Lewis's property through inheritance from his first wife, Abigail Smith, whom he married by 1674. Abigail was niece and principal heir of Nathaniel Bacon of York County, president of the Virginia Council, and cousin to the more famous rebel of that name. Bacon willed the slaves to Lewis and Abigail during their lifetimes, leaving it to them to divide the slaves among their seven surviving children as they saw fit. The Bacon group numbered forty individuals of whom Lewis gained control in 1694.[6]

By 1695 Lewis had taken a second wife, the widow Martha Lear Cole, and through her added to his "work force" slaves who had been attached to two other estates. The first consisted of an unknown number of individuals whom Martha Burwell's father, John Lear of Nansemond County, willed to her in 1695. Nansemond Sarah, mentioned in Lewis's 1710 will, was one of them. Eight more came from Martha's first husband, planter William Cole of York County. Lewis and his executors managed these people in trust for a minor Cole son who did not reach majority until 1713.[7]

Who were these blacks who themselves or their children ended up at Carter's Grove in 1738? From surviving Burwell and Bacon records, we can identify eighty-nine individuals who were present in one of the estates at some time between 1692 and 1710. The following discussion draws on a composite profile of the whole group.[8] These slaves' roots in Virginia stretch back at least to 1666, when Nathaniel Bacon patented land using headrights he had acquired for importing nine negroes.[9] From both headright entries and York County probate records, we can identify a surge in slave imports into that colony circa 1657 to 1666; it is likely that the first Bacon slaves arrived during these years.[10] Some of the grandparents of the Carter's Grove slaves were probably among these anonymous early forced migrants.

Other of the Bacon slaves were Africans who may either have come via the West Indies or who had been transported directly to Virginia beginning in the 1680s. These included the men Yaddo, Cuffy, Colly, and Denbo who appeared in Bacon's 1694 inventory; Bungey, apparently a teenager, who may have been transported as a child; the unidentified parents of a small child, Cumbo; and

Harry, the most highly valued slave on Bacon's estate, who named one of his sons Corajo. If Bacon followed the custom of other large planters of the period, he bought slaves in small numbers throughout the 1670s, '80s, and '90s, and may have acquired others through his second wife, Elizabeth Kingsmill.[11] These slaves likely embarked from various ports in West Africa and included members of several different ethnic groups.

The demographic makeup of the eighty-nine early Bacon/Burwell slaves suggests that they may have been healthier than more recent arrivals, and that they may have suffered somewhat less trauma (or have put that trauma further behind) than those who endured the full horrors of the Middle Passage on large slave ships in the early eighteenth century. As one would expect, given planters' labor preferences, there were half again as many men as women overall, so not all the men were able to find mates, at least on their own plantations. On the other hand, both among the earlier 1694 Bacon slaves and among the 1710 Burwell group, there were two children for every adult woman, a relatively high level of childbearing compared with Virginia and Maryland slaves overall at that time. Doubtless some of these women were native-born Virginians who began having children at earlier ages than did most women brought from Africa.[12] A few of the slaves had long-established unions, especially Harry and Sue who had had at least three children by 1710.

Immediately upon arrival, the Bacon slaves had been set to work raising tobacco and corn at the home plantation on King's Creek or on at least one nearby quarter. At first they likely shared dwellings and worked alongside white indentured servants (mostly men) whom Bacon also regularly purchased in the 1660s, '70s, and '80s. There was also the occasional Native American in the work force; Bacon had at least two Indian servants, one acquired in 1666 and one in 1689.[13] We know much less about the laborers Lewis Burwell II bought in his own right, but one can suppose a similar acquisition pattern. Burwell bought some of his slaves in ones, twos, and threes from area planters, and also purchased indentured servants through the 1690s.[14] Interracial work groups would have been the norm into the 1680s, but increasingly less frequent thereafter; fewer white servants immigrated to the York basin after the early 1680s, and those who did were more likely to be skilled artisans who probably did not share quarters or work closely with slaves.[15]

Since servants would have at first outnumbered slaves in the various work forces, and since no special system of "slave management" had yet developed, the initial customs of the plantation governing work and leisure were those prevailing for white servants. The slaves were made to work as hard as, but likely no harder than, the servants, and they probably shared such customary privileges as free Saturday afternoons and no labor after sundown. Although all worked together at agricultural tasks for which there was a time constraint—setting out and harvesting tobacco, for example, and, in winter, stripping and packing the crop in favorable weather—individual rather than group tasks were often the norm. There is no evidence that planters or overseers were attempting to set up any system of intense, highly regimented labor. The slaves surely took whatever advantage they could from the white servants' often tenacious insistence on customary privileges and resistance to "unreasonable" work requirements.[16] And, as Mechal Sobel has suggested, they may also have brought to bear "experience with both 'proper' slave behavior and the 'rights' of slaves" prevailing in West African societies.[17]

Shared work and living arrangements in the early years, when racial prejudices were less highly developed, encouraged cultural melding. The documentary record speaks largely of the extent to which the slaves assimilated Anglo-American culture; however, there is every reason to suppose that the exchange went both ways, and indeed some confirmation that this was so. First are the naming patterns. Generally the slaves' various owners had selected and imposed English names; however at least five of the men retained African names, two couples chose an African name for one of their children, and several of the men went by names—Will Colly, Jack Sunto, and Jack Toath—that appear to be either cultural amalgams or successful assertions of traditional practices. Among some West African peoples, the father's first name became the son's second name. Will Colly, for example, was apparently the son of Colly, an African-born artisan.[18]

Second, some of the blacks and whites developed close personal relationships. At least thirteen (15 percent) of the 1692–1710 group were the offspring of interracial encounters. These included Billy, born about 1704, the son of a black man and white woman (probably an indentured servant) who was to serve to age thirty-two, and twelve mulatto slaves, children or grandchildren of slave women and white men. The fathers were probably indentured or recently freed servants. Some of the slave women may of course have been sexually exploited by white men. However, so long as black and white bound laborers shared quarters and work and working conditions, relationships based on mutual affection were not uncommon. In the seventeenth century when whites accorded slaves an English surname, as was the case with some of the Bacon/Burwell group, these were usually the offspring of consensual pairings in which the white father had publically acknowledged the children. Unions of slave men and white women were almost invariably consensual.[19]

There is no information about how the slaves communicated with each other upon arrival, or about when and how well the adult Bacon/Burwell slaves learned English, but we can suppose that by 1710 many were exceptionally fluent in the language. Children born in Virginia of course absorbed English at an early age. This is pure conjecture, but it does seem likely that some of the slaves arriving in the second half of the seventeenth century gained a wider command of English more quickly than did many Africans who came later. Since almost all shared work and living quarters with white laborers, they had both greater need and more opportunity for picking up the language. And, if the slaves came from different groups who spoke unrelated languages, some form of English may have provided the quickest escape from relative verbal isolation. (In contrast, there was a greater chance that some of the Africans arriving in the first third of the eighteenth century lived with or near others who spoke similar languages. These slaves likely retained more elements of African speech. At the same time, intimate contacts with whites diminished.) It was surely one thing to learn a new language from fellow unfree workers, and in some cases, from lovers, and quite another for those whose main English-speaking contact was a hated and feared overseer.[20]

Another indication of the slaves' relatively high level of acculturation is their occupations. By 1694 Nathaniel Bacon had but three indentured servants, one of them a woman domestic. Although Bacon could have hired free white craftsmen to supply plantation needs, it is likely that some of his slaves were already doing much of the coopering and rough carpentry required on a large plantation. By 1710 the artisans on the Burwell quarters were slaves, not servants. Lewis II had at least four highly valued slave carpenters as well as other unspecified "tradesmen." In contrast, on most Chesapeake estates, few slaves were trained as artisans until the middle of the century.[21]

The Bacon/Burwell materials also demonstrate that almost from the outset these slaveowners established a color-based social and occupational hierarchy among their work forces. They chose mulatto women and girls as domestics, and selected mostly mulatto men as craftsmen. The men were often able to transmit skills and status from one generation to the next. Mulatto carpenter Old Tom, for example, mentioned in Lewis Burwell's 1710 will, had already trained his son, Young Tom, in his craft. Mulatto Jack Parrat, owned first by Bacon and then by Burwell, had no stated craft, but his son Billy, born in 1713, became a cooper, and in 1746 was the most highly valued slave on Lewis's grandson, Nathaniel Bacon Burwell's, York plantations. The situation of the mulatto women and girls is more problematic. From the records it is unclear whether daughters were able to translate domestic skills learned from their mixed-race mothers into preferential work assignments for themselves. One woman, Mulatto Kate, benefitted from her background. She was likely a domestic in the Bacon household and, respecting the wishes of his deceased wife, Elizabeth Kingsmill, Bacon freed her in 1692, the only slave the Bacon/Burwell tribe manumitted before the Revolution. On the other hand, mulatto girls were often chosen as appropriate gifts for Burwell daughters; such girls stood a high risk of being separated from their families upon the death of the master. Burwell willed Jack and Sue Parrat's daughter Mary, for example, to one of his daughters.

It is misleading, however, to think of these slaves as a single group for purposes other than demographic comparison. Lewis Burwell II's slaves never lived together. Fairfield, the Burwell home farm, lay on the north side of the York River. Some of the slaves whom Lewis bought and some coming from his second marriage lived there, while most of the Bacon slaves remained on Bacon's dwelling plantation near King's Creek and on at least two other quarters that Lewis owned on the south side of York River, directly opposite Fairfield. After 1694 Lewis maintained two residences, one at Fairfield and one at Bacon's former home plantation, and split his time between the two farms.[22]

While we cannot be certain how the slaves thought of and used the York River—whether it obstructed movement or instead offered an easy avenue for communication—clearly the river presented no insurmountable barrier, and it may have facilitated rather than precluded connections between the more mobile African Americans.[23] Burwell slaves transported supplies from one plantation to another, and frequently ferried their owners and guests back and forth across the river. Three bits of evidence suggest that some slaves were quite familiar both with the river itself and with the neighborhoods on either bank. First, when Robert "King" Carter needed to deliver an urgent letter from his home on the Rappahannock to the governor in Williamsburg in 1724, he instructed his coachman, Charles, who carried the letter, to stop at Rosewell, the Gloucester County home of a son-in-law, near Burwell's Fairfield. Charles did not know the south side of the York, but Ned, one of Page's slaves, did. Carter assumed that Ned, who was "better acquainted" with Williamsburg, could cross the river, make his way on foot to Burwell's New Quarter on Queen's Creek, and there borrow a horse to ride into town and deliver the letter.[24] Second, when two men, Cuffee and Essex, ran off from Lewis Burwell's grandson's plantation on King's Creek in 1736 in "a clinsch-work yawl to row with 4 oars," this was doubtless far from their first voyage on the river, since they eluded capture for some time.[25] Finally, in 1766 three Gloucester County Burwell slaves, Will, Ned, and Zacharias, crossed the river in order to raid James Burwell II's smokehouse at King's Creek, making off with twenty pieces of bacon, a crime for which Will and Ned were sentenced to hang.[26] While Ned, Cuffee, Essex, Will, Ned, and Zacharias doubtless enjoyed greater mobility than most area slaves, there remains the possibility that the slaves commanded a superior knowledge of the waterways and accompanying freedom of movement, licensed or unlicensed, that such knowledge conferred.

Over the next fifty years, Burwell family slaves increased in numbers and most continued to live in the neighborhood. Chart 1 outlines the various slaves groups, and Map 1 locates the home farms and quarters. That some of the Burwells chose to entail slaves as well as land in the male line, and to attach groups of slaves to particular tracts, allowed the Burwell slaves more generational continuity and more settled places of residence than was often the case among Virginia slaveholders.[27]

Lewis Burwell II divided most of his slaves between his sons Nathaniel (1680–1721), James (1689–1718), and Lewis III (c. 1699–1744). James inherited the Bacon lands in York County near King's Creek, and many of the Bacon slaves. Some of the slaves living at King's Creek in 1710 appear in the 1746 inventory of James' son Nathaniel Bacon Burwell, and several direct descendants in the 1775 inventory of grandson James II, and in the 1791 inventory of great grandson Nathaniel Junior. Others were sent west to a quarter in distant Frederick County in the 1770s, and by 1792 those remaining in York were divided among various heirs and permanently dispersed.[28]

A second third of the Bacon/Burwell slaves ended up at Kingsmill plantation adjoining King's Creek on the north, but fronting on the James River side of the York peninsula. Ownership of these people passed from Lewis II to his son Lewis III, and grandson Lewis IV (1716–1784). The group was augmented by twenty-seven slaves living on adjacent Utopia Quarter, of whom Lewis IV gained control through marriage to the widow of a neighboring planter.[29]

Finally, we return to tracing the slaves who eventually lived at Carter's Grove. Lewis II's eldest son Nathaniel had married and set up housekeeping at the family home across the York River at Fairfield in 1709, the year before his father died. When Nathaniel married, Lewis apparently transferred some Gloucester slaves to him, probably including artisans, as part of a marriage settlement with the bride's father, Robert "King" Carter. To round out Nathaniel's share, Lewis left him twelve additional adult field hands. Nathaniel also got any children living in Gloucester that Lewis had not specifically willed to other heirs; additionally, he inherited Harry and Sue's children Corajo, Jemy, and Betty in trust for his son Lewis. At least one member of the Parrot family remained at Fairfield, since a John Parrot was baptized there in 1753.

Aside from this, we know little about Nathaniel's work force, although it seems safe to assume that they were similar to the other, better-documented Burwell slaves. Nathaniel inherited between twenty-five and thirty slaves from

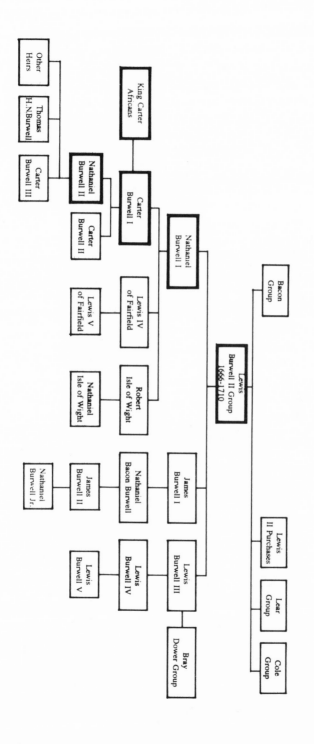

CHART 1. THE CARTER'S GROVE SLAVE COMMUNITY

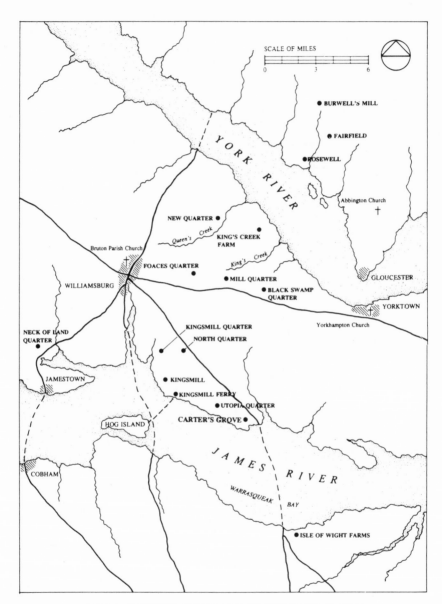

MAP 1. CARTER'S GROVE AND VICINITY CIRCA 1750

his father, and purchased at least one mulatto woman and her child from a local widow in 1706.[30] As eldest son, Nathaniel assumed management of his own slaves and farms and of those of his minor brothers James and Lewis. He employed white overseers to run each of the quarters, and, as had his father, a general manager to oversee all the Burwell concerns. The preceding generation, in effect, took care of three of the four children he and his wife, Elizabeth Carter, had between 1709 and 1721. His father intended that the Gloucester plantations go to their first-born, Lewis (1710–1754). His father-in-law, Robert "King" Carter, bought Merchant's Hundred (later Carter's Grove) plantation across the river in James City County—and slaves to work it—for the second son, Carter (1716–1756). Upon the death of his brother James, Nathaniel also acquired reversionary rights to Bacon land in Isle of Wight County; this he set aside for the third son, Robert (1720–1777). Nathaniel himself had then only to provide for his daughter Elizabeth.

That time was not far off, for Nathaniel died in 1721. At first, property divisions were of more concern to the slaveowners than to the slaves, for most of them stayed wherever they had been living in Lewis II's lifetime. Except for the artisans, they were to "be kept together where they are now," until the Burwell sons came of age, unless the executors decided to seat new plantations.[31] Elizabeth got her dower life interest in a third of the slaves. A few domestics moved into Williamsburg upon her second marriage to a town resident in 1724, but most of the dower slaves continued to work at Fairfield. All would have returned there upon Elizabeth's death ten years later.[32] The home Gloucester farm and its workers went to the couple's eldest son Lewis (1710–1754). When he died in 1754 they were transferred to his eldest son of the same name who also inherited the home farm and remained there until he died in 1779.[33]

Nathaniel's executors may have sent the slaves allotted to Robert, the youngest son, to work one of three plantations on Warrasqueak Bay on the Isle of Wight land Robert was to inherit. Alternatively Robert may have moved them there when he came of age in 1741. Although removed to the south bank of the James River, even this group was not entirely isolated, for a public ferry ran from Robert's plantation to Trebell's Landing adjoining Carter's Grove. This afforded them a line of communication to kin in York County, and through them, back to Fairfield. To his only daughter Elizabeth, Nathaniel left £1,000 sterling; her legacy involved no transfer of slaves.

Nathaniel's second son Carter (1716–1756) inherited Merchant's Hundred from maternal grandfather Robert Carter and other York County land on Queen's Creek that Lewis Burwell II had acquired. Prior to 1721 Lewis II or Nathaniel established an auxiliary farm there called New Quarter. To this was added a second plantation (Foace's) between Queen's and King's Creek, purchased in the early eighteenth century. Carter Burwell moved all his slaves to York County when he set up housekeeping at Merchant's Hundred–subsequently called Carter's Grove–in 1738.

The relevance of this convoluted Burwell family history for Carter's Grove slaves becomes clear when we turn to the layout of the land upon which these slaves lived and worked as seen on Map 1. If we use a compass to delineate a five-mile radius around Carter's Grove circa 1750, we find first Carter Burwell's home house, along with his ancillary quarters at Foace's, New Quarter, Black Swamp, and Abraham's. Also within the circle is the home house of his cousin Lewis Burwell IV at Kingsmill, the adjacent Kingsmill and North Quarters, and the former Bray quarter at Utopia, as well as the King's Creek plantation (and probably other quarters) of cousin Nathaniel Bacon Burwell, and the Lightfoot quarter on the same creek. Opposite, on the north bank of the York, we find his older brother's Fairfield, and just across the James, brother Robert's farms in Isle of Wight.

Juxtaposed, this handful of Burwell plantations translates into a much larger resident community of somewhere over three hundred African Americans, some of whom shared family connections equally as close as those of the Burwell clan on whose land they lived and labored. The cabins and work areas at Carter's Grove (other than the main house) were part of the slaves' domain, and wooded ravines adjacent to the slave quarters afforded secluded places where slaves might go to get away from white supervisors or to gather in leisure moments. In addition, as Dell Upton has put it, "Slaves formed neighborhoods, black landscapes that combined elements of the white landscape and of the quarters in a way that was peculiar to them and that existed outside the official articulated processional landscape of the great planter and his lesser neighbors."[34] Every time Carter's Grove slaves drove horse or ox carts laden with goods to the ancillary quarters, or else carted wheat, corn, fodder, straw, meat, butter, milk, cider, or firewood into Williamsburg, they likely encountered kinsmen during their journeys. Gloucester slaves, ferrying whites across the river, maintained at least a tenuous link with the York/James City County slaves and their kinspeople at Fairfield, as did Isle of Wight slaves crossing the James. At night, Carter's Grove slaves, when they could summon the energy to make a one to two hour's walk to an adjacent Burwell plantation and back home again, could have visited a variety of kin. Come Saturday nights and Sundays, when the slaves had command over their own time, this neighborhood may have been much more Bacon/Burwell slave territory than it was Burwell property.

While no written evidence survives to prove that these York and Gloucester slaves maintained a strong sense of kinship and passed a knowledge of family history from one generation to another, this was likely the case. The Butler family of southern Maryland provides a model. Unlike most slave genealogies, this family's oral history did become part of the written record as a result of a series of freedom suits in the later eighteenth century. By the 1760s, between 120 and 300 southern Maryland slaves could trace their origins back to the union in the 1680s of an African man and an indentured servant woman, and by 1789 as many as 750 claimed descent. Over the years the original couple and their offspring had been parcelled out among numerous white family members in two southern Maryland counties. Although slave families were often split, they still lived close enough together that many of the slaves could visit back and forth. Even those sold out of the family to more distant places kept their family history alive in their new homes, and the core group of slaves kept track of the whereabouts of separated kinsfolk.[35] Here the enabling conditions for preserving and transmitting the family history were first, that most of the slaves remained in the original owner's family, and second, that most continued to live no more than twenty miles apart, and many, much closer. The Burwell slaves certainly shared these enabling circumstances.

THE AFRICANS

Although already complicated, the history of the Carter's Grove slaves across the eighteenth century would be comparatively straightforward if most of its members had arrived in the third quarter of the seventeenth century. As it is, theirs is only part of the story.

The focus now shifts to African slaves acquired by Virginia's richest planter of the period, Robert "King" Carter. Sometime between his daughter Elizabeth's marriage to Nathaniel Burwell in 1709 (and probably after the birth of their first child in 1710) and 1721, Carter purchased Merchant's Hundred plantation. He quickly bought new African slaves to work it, intending that the profits of their labor go to his daughter during her lifetime, and then to one of her sons; by 1727 he decided that this favored grandchild would be Carter Burwell.[36] By the terms of Carter's will, the numbers of working slaves and livestock were to be kept up to the number present at Carter's death. If some of the slaves died, his executors were to draw upon the proceeds of the tobacco crop to buy new hands.[37]

After son-in-law Nathaniel died, Robert Carter managed Merchant's Hundred himself, as current owner of the plantation and as guardian to his Burwell grandson who would eventually inherit. Carter disapproved of his daughter's remarriage to a Williamsburg doctor of questionable background, and made sure the new husband had nothing to do with the estate. Carter hired a white overseer to run the farm, and relied on the Burwell estate's general manager to handle day-to-day concerns. He also made frequent visits, as he had to travel within a few miles of the plantation whenever meetings of the colony Council or General Court called him to Williamsburg. Since the Merchant's Hundred slaves shared experiences similar to those of several hundred others who manned Carter quarters scattered throughout Virginia, for later 1720s and early 1730s, I will draw a composite description using evidence from all the Carter quarters.[38]

Shortly after a slave ship dropped anchor in the York or Rappahannock River, Robert Carter boarded the vessel and selected some of the most promising captives for Merchant's Hundred. Those debarking on the Rappahannock went first to Corotoman, while those coming ashore on the York went first to Fairfield, where Carter or the Burwell manager immediately issued them clothing and bedding.[39] Within a few days Carter evaluated the slaves and chose an English name for each. As he explained the process in 1717 "I nam'd them here [in this case at Corotoman] & by their names we can always know what sizes they are of & I am sure we repeated them so often to them that every one knew their names & would readily answer to them." Quarter overseers were then to "take care that the negros both men & women I sent you up last always go by ye names we gave them," and not allow them to revert to their African names.[40] Another letter makes clear that Carter did not turn over the critical initial training of names to underlings. Either Carter or one of his sons drilled the slaves themselves and the whites committed to memory at least a superficial perception of the individual. When, for example, an overseer reported that a shipment of clothing was missing a petticoat for the woman Grace, Carter retorted that "my sone Charles is very certain that he sent one before for her knowing her to be a large Woman & Cowkeeper. He was particularly carefull to choose a Petty ct for her and set her name upon it."[41]

Given the general pattern of the trans-Atlantic slave trade in the early eighteenth century, it is likely that most of the Merchant's Hundred slaves were Ibos, Ibibios, Efkins, or Mokos from the area of present-day Nigeria or adjacent Cameroon on the east. Sixty percent of Africans entering the York River between 1718 and 1726, years during which Robert Carter was buying slaves for the plantation, came from the Bight of Biafra.[42]

This suggests that, rather than being a heterogenous lot of individuals from varying ethnic and linguistic groups as the usual story goes, many of the Merchant's Hundred slaves arriving in the 1720s instead shared a similar cultural and linguistic background. Thus they may have experienced a less "rapid and thorough deculturation" than is generally supposed among Chesapeake slaves.[42]

Weakened and traumatized by the Middle Passage and unaccustomed to the Chesapeake disease environment, many of the slaves immediately fell sick. Some suffered from "scurveys, swellings, and other disorders" (likely the result of months of short and bad rations), others were "lame" in their knees, and still others sick with undiagnosible "strange distempers"; some died within a few days.[43] Most new hands who arrived in the spring also fell sick from malaria, endemic to the region, by early fall. In October 1729, for example, Carter reported "my new Hands are all down in their Seasoning Except one. I must wait with Patience till they recover their strength before I can send them [to a distant quarter]." Carter hoped adequate food and warm clothes and bedding would speed their recovery. Unfortunately, many who survived the summer did not live through their first winter in a colder climate, a season in which both whites and blacks often succumbed to respiratory diseases. Carter blamed "the carelessness and cruelty of the overseers in turning the people out in hard and bitter weather."[45]

Some of the strongest Africans tried immediately to escape their captors, as did seven men who took off from Corotoman in a canoe five days after their ship arrived, and who managed to elude recapture for a week.[46] Others, once they had regained strength and found an opportunity, took off into the woods. By the 1720s Carter had enough experience with newly arrived Africans to expect this, and for the first few months he ordered his overseers "to be kind to all the negros but especially to the new ones." Of one new Negro woman who had been hiding out in the neighborhood of one of the quarters, Carter observed that "now she hath tasted of the hardship of ye woods she will go near to stay at home where she can have her belly full."[47]

Eventually, however, Carter ran out of patience with Africans who refused to adapt to their new situation. Then he turned to brutal measures. For example, when, in 1727, Carter decided that chronic runaway Ballazore was an "incorrigeble rogue," he ordered the overseer to have the man's toes cut off; "nothing less than dismembring will reclaim him." This was not an isolated act of brutality, for Carter asserted "I have cured many a negro of running away by this means." A 1722 diary entry shows at least one other instance of a similar "cure." Other slaves who resisted in unspecified ways were alternatively whipped and branded.[48]

Part of Carter's strategy for forcing new Africans to become productive workers was to encourage them to form families as soon as possible. Married slaves were less likely to try to run away than were unattached individuals. Always attuned to the bottom line, Carter generally bought nearly twice as many men hands as women; but he did encourage as many as could find mates to marry at once. By 1733 almost no adult women on Carter quarters lived by themselves; most were either married in terms of whatever understanding they and Carter had negotiated, or else part of a household consisting of two or three other apparently unrelated men and women. Wherever possible, Carter kept husbands and wives together on the same plantation and allotted them a house to themselves. When spouses lived on another quarter or had died, mothers and their children, or, less often, fathers and their children lived together. Unattached and probably recently arrived men usually shared a cabin with one to three other males. Since no more than fifteen to twenty-five slaves shared living spaces on any individual quarter, there were no large concentrations of men living in barrack-like housing.[49]

Another of Carter's strategies for extracting work from the slaves was regimented gang labor. Rather than assigning individual tasks, overseers put all the laborers to work on one job at a time, keeping watch over all and forcing all to work at a similar pace. Carter's letters include repeated references to slave gangs. Whether it was planting, weeding, or harvesting corn or tobacco, gathering corn fodder, or digging a mill race, his slaves usually worked as a single unit. The overseers were "always to be with the people to keep them to their work."[50] Very likely Carter had hit upon this solution as the only way to control large numbers of new African slaves who understood little or no English, and whose main goal was to escape their captors. With the exception of artisans on the home plantation, Carter owned few white indentured servants. In earlier years, such servants might have served as an intermediating group; now their presence, on outlying quarters at least, would likely have complicated the imposition of radically "unEnglish" work regimens. Carter also usually mixed more acclimated slaves with the new Negroes on the various quarters, probably hoping to speed the assimilation process, but probably also aiming to gain more control over the recent arrivals through the mediation of more acculturated slaves.

Here, to the detriment of those who had a much longer history in Virginia, the immediate necessity of controlling large numbers of new, alienated workers became the overriding concern. Work rules for blacks and whites quickly diverged, and "old hands" were subjected to the increased regimentation that the continued influx of new arrivals required. Skilled white indentured servants did what they could to distance themselves from the increasingly disprivileged blacks. Those arriving in the 1720s and '30s refused to work, and did little but press complaints until they extracted current "customary" English workers' privileges, privileges that exceeded those allowed unskilled indentured servants at the turn of the century. And, unlike some of the mostly unskilled white servants who had arrived a few years earlier, the later white servants seem to have avoided contact with black women.[51]

Carter's third strategy for extracting work from new arrivals was to appoint a slave man on each quarter as foreman. Carter advanced the man certain privileges, including his own house even if he were single. In return he made the foreman responsible for keeping the other slaves in line and working at an acceptable pace. Some of the foremen had been enslaved for some time (several are described as "old"), and a few were creoles. There were not enough such men to go around, however, and Carter selected a number of Africans as foremen, including Ebo George at Totuskey, Ebo George at Head of the River, "King" Tom at Hamstead, and George at Forrest who had two wives.[52]

In contrast to the Burwell slaves, there is little evidence of a color-based occupational hierarchy on the Carter plantations. For one thing, African immigrants greatly outnumbered creoles who reached working age early in the century, and for another, so far as we can tell, only a handful of the Carter slaves were of mixed race. The family apparently put little stock on country birth or mixed blood; with recent arrivals predominating, the Carters distinguished only between "old" and "new" hands. In addition, not many of the Carter slaves worked as craftsmen or domestics. For artisans, Carter relied primarily on white indentured servants; most of the scattering of slave carpenters and coopers were creoles, but only one was identified as a mulatto. Most of the privileged slaves were either foremen or sailors, and many of these were African immigrants. Given the unprecedented scale of the Carter operations—in a Chesapeake context—contemporary Caribbean plantations may provide the best models for better understanding conditions on the Carter plantations in the 1720s and 1730s.

We can get some impression of living arrangements at Merchant's Hundred from inventories of forty-seven of Robert Carter's quarters taken in 1733. Then the Merchant's Hundred slaves likely numbered between fifteen and twenty-five. Fifteen was both the mean and median number of people on the inventoried quarters, and Carter considered this the optimal size work force for seating outlying units.[53] The largest of Carter's quarters (with the exception of his home quarter) housed no more than twenty-six men, women, and children. Fifteen was apparently the most slaves ordinary overseers could control, and twenty-five the maximum. Tobacco production at Merchant's Hundred—between ten and seventeen hogsheads a year from 1723 to 1731—also suggests fifteen- to twenty-odd hands.[54]

Assuming the Merchant's Hundred work force in the early 1730s was like those on other Carter quarters, there were almost twice as many men as women. Young adults would have predominated. Only four percent of the inventoried slaves had survived long enough to be classified as "old." The immigrant women were also slow to have children. Only half of the slave households on Carter's quarters included any children at all, and the ratio of children aged under one year to fifteen to adult women was lower than that in the Bacon/Burwell group in both 1694 and 1710. Other quarter households consisted of single men living together, of apparently unrelated households containing both sexes, or of only a husband and wife. Children aged five or under were less numerous than children aged between six and fifteen. Clearly some of the older children had come on the slave ships, and many of the others were the offspring of a small number of more acculturated slaves. Overall, the slaves on Robert Carter's quarters had had time to establish at best only rudimentary family connections and were less healthy and more alienated than African Americans who arrived earlier in Virginia.[55]

The Carter letterbooks and inventory also suggest something of the material conditions at Merchant's Hundred in the 1730s. Each slave was issued a new suit of winter clothing annually and some lighter summer wear, including, for the men, shirts, fustian jackets, and linen breeches, and for the women, shifts, petticoats, and aprons. Children got only a frock.[56] To complete their outfits, the adults had a pair of imported shoes, Irish stockings or plaid hose, and Kilmarnock milled caps.[57] Bed rugs and blankets or hair coverlets were replaced only when those first issued became threadbare. The Carters shipped new bedding to the quarters with "the names of every negro they are for" attached.[58] The Merchant's Hundred overseer collected the winter clothing at Fairfield each fall, checked the bundles to "see that everything is right," and then distributed the individually labelled garments. He had orders not to give out the winter clothes until the weather turned cold, as "some of ym would destroy [or, perhaps, trade] them before."[59]

Weekly owner-supplied rations consisted primarily of ground or unground maize. Meat rations were less frequent, with the overseers only occasionally killing an old steer or giving out some preserved pork "that they may have a bit now and then and the fat to grease their Homony."[60] In summer months, the slaves were expected to get by without meat; if poor whites could make do in hot weather with "Good Milk & Homony & Milk & Mush," Carter was sure the slaves could do so as well.[61] However, when some Merchant's Hundred slaves were sent to dig a mill race on another Carter plantation in York County in August of 1729, they got more regular issues of fresh pork or beef: "I would allow ye people (it is hard work if they follow it close) a pound a meat a man, one day if not two days in a week."[62]

Carter took some pains with housing for the slaves, wanting "very good Cabbins to be made for my people that their beds may lye a foot and a half from ye ground."[63] Other owner-supplied domestic equipment was scanty—wooden pails and other containers, an iron pestle, and iron pots and pothooks, and, if there was no gristmill nearby, a handmill for grinding corn. The main agricultural tools were hoes and axes, wedges for splitting timber, and a grindstone for sharpening tool edges. If someone had gotten around to planting fruit trees at the quarter, there might also be equipment for pressing cider. Otherwise, Carter supplied the white overseer with little more in the way of domestic goods than he did the slaves; nothing more than basic bedding, cooking pots, and usually, a gun. The quarter livestock consisted almost entirely of cattle and hogs, about fifty of each, and perhaps a horse for the overseer's use.

Carter hired doctors on annual contract to tend the slaves on the various quarters. One of the physicians, in Carter's opinion, neglected his charges, refusing to visit sick slaves when sent for. The man may well have been reaping a profit at the expense of the slaves, administering "pokes and other unwarrantable potions of his own Contrivance that cost him nothing in good and laudable medicines that comes out of England." A possible alternative is that the doctor was collaborating with the slaves in using herbal remedies.[64]

To supply other needs, the slaves had to rely largely on craft skills acquired in Africa—at least until they learned the lay of the neighborhood and developed contacts with local, primarily creole, slaves with whom they might barter goods.[65] Even bartering may have been rather limited, since it would take time for the slaves to find or fashion tradeables. With the overseer the only white on the plantation, and he probably a poor single man, there were few cast-offs or hand-me-downs to be had, and for that matter not much around that might be pilfered, aside from food and an occasional piece of clothing. Slave artisans, however, who came periodically to put up or fix cabins and tobacco barns, may have quickly taken advantage of the smallest openings that the underdeveloped local economy, both white and black, afforded. In 1731 the Carters suspected that a team of black carpenters and coopers, ostensibly building a barn and making containers and tools for an outlying quarter, "must spend a great deal of their Time in making pails & piggins & churns for merchandising," and that a slave blacksmith was working on the side on his own account for neighboring whites.[66]

Almost all the work the Carter slaves were forced to do was physically demanding and entirely manual. By 1729 Carter encouraged his overseers to train oxen to help with heavy hauling. However in the 1733 inventory there were working oxen on only six of the forty-seven quarters. Likely there were none at Merchant's Hundred. By Carter's own account, most of the slaves had to carry all fencing materials from the woods to the fields, tote firewood from wherever they cut it to their cabins, and haul corn and tobacco from field to barn either on their backs or, "African style," on their heads.[67] Robert's son Landon recollected in 1776 that his father had used no plows and had no more than twelve draft oxen on all the quarters. On quarters where Robert raised wheat, the slaves levelled the ground and chopped in the seed with hoes. They also rolled tobacco hogsheads to landings and loaded ships with thousands of bushels of wheat and corn entirely by hand.[68] The Merchant's Hundred Africans, then, were almost certainly forced to do extremely hard physical labor on scanty and monotonous fare, and had the comfort of few material goods during their first years in Virginia.

JOINING OF THE TWO GROUPS AT CARTER'S GROVE

Carter Burwell established a white family presence at Carter's Grove, heretofore lacking, when he and his new bride moved there in 1738. The situation in the slave quarters may have become tense indeed, and most unusual. Most area planters (like his uncle James who bought eighteen slaves, almost certainly all new African immigrants, over a period of seven years between 1711 and 1718), scattered the newcomers among their older, often creole, workers.[69] Instead, Carter Burwell moved the Gloucester hands that he inherited from his father and grandfather, surely by now almost all first- or second-generation Virginians, onto the immigrant Merchant's Hundred Africans' turf.

It is unclear just how many Gloucester slaves Carter brought, but they likely numbered about thirty, and the Africans at Merchant's Hundred numbered between twenty and twenty-five. Cultural conflicts may have been intense as the creole Gloucester slaves sought to maintain privileges and status advantages over the less acculturated Africans. Robert Carter had worried about the tendency for old hands to "crow over" new ones.[70] Such conflicts between old and new hands perhaps paled in comparison to ones that may have developed between skilled creole Burwell artisans and domestics and the African field workers. The shortage of women, especially among the Africans, may have fueled competition between unmarried African men and creole youths who may have been more successful than immigrants in finding mates.[71] On the other hand, some aspects of a shared African cultural heritage may have united the two groups, as did their shared condition of bondage and the need to survive and resist.

The records reveal almost nothing of the means young Carter Burwell employed to force the two groups of slaves to live and work together. He seems to have followed a "divide and conquer" strategy rather than housing the groups separately. His account book shows that between 1740 and 1745 "Glouster" Moll was assigned to Foaces quarter. Old Nan and Old Cato, probably Burwell family slaves, lived at Mill Quarter, while Old Moll resided at Black Swamp. At Carter's Grove carpenters Old Dick and the boy Dick (probably Old Dick's son), Sancho, Sam, and Jack, as well as shoemaker Jammey, were likely second-generation artisans, and given Burwell family predilections, probably also of mixed blood. The few house servants the Burwells would have employed, probably including "Gloster" Betty (likely the same woman as Betty "in the house") and Molly "in the Kitchen," were surely all former Gloucester hands, rather than Merchant's Hundred Africans of whom the whites would have known much less. On the other hand, Calabar at Carter's Grove was almost certainly one of the Africans whom Robert Carter had bought in the 1720s.[72]

In general, the Burwells had inherited all the workers they could readily employ on their existing quarters, and the family ceased buying new hands after the early 1740s. By then enough children were likely surviving into their teens and twenties to offset deaths among the older slaves. In 1745 Burwell bought an additional quarter, Neck of Land, just above Jamestown Island, and at least ten slaves who came with the land.[73] Otherwise he appears to have bought only two Africans, "new Negro Jammy" by 1743 and "new Negroe Tom" by 1745. These two men were housed at Carter's Grove where either he or his general manager could keep a close watch over them.[74]

Nor did many new slaves come to the other family quarters. Cousin Nathaniel Bacon Burwell purchased two young boys in 1737 and 1739, as did brother Robert in 1740,[75] and cousin Lewis at Kingsmill bought Jumper, a "very Black Mundingo Negro Man" in 1736. By the summer of 1738 Jumper spoke "pretty good English," and had learned enough about the neighborhood to escape from the plantation and elude capture for at least three weeks.[76] A man apprehended as a runaway in 1752 was perhaps the last newly imported slave one of the York County Burwells purchased. This African could not "speak English well or tell his name," although he apparently answered to the name Pompey, and told his Williamsburg jailers he belonged to "some of the Col. Burwell's."[77] By mid-century the Burwells had apparently become less diligent in their initial training of the few new immigrants they acquired than Robert Carter had been in the 1720s.

Also by mid-century, as creole children—of either the first or of the third or fourth generation—began to replace their elders, any conflicts resulting from the merging of the two groups of creole and African slaves faded, and the younger generation adopted more elements of white culture. As sex ratios began to even out, and native-born women to bear children at younger ages than their mothers, family life became possible for more of the slaves, and family size somewhat larger. Carter Burwell's work force grew from roughly fifty in 1738 to ninety-six at his death in 1756. Thirty years later the family slaves numbered at least 154, although not all were then living at Carter's Grove.[78]

The slaves' living standards at Carter's Grove also changed in small but significant ways after 1738. With the owner's family living on the plantation, and from 1755 living in a great house, there were simply more household goods, food, and livestock available on the plantation, some of which the slaves might have acquired as gifts, castoffs, or by pilfering. Indeed, as many European goods became cheaper and in greater supply, and as amenities such as ceramics, glassware, and mirrors became more widely distributed among white families, one would expect that these would begin appearing in slave households. At adjacent Kingsmill Quarter, for example, where slave housing (with the exception of that of domestic servants) remained similarly small and spartan across the eighteenth century, by the 1770s and '80s Burwell fieldhands had numerous ceramic tablewares including a surprising amount of Chinese porcelain. The archaeologist concluded: "House servants and fieldhands were equipped with, or equipped themselves with, a good representative sampling of whatever the owner had on hand."[79] Opportunities for making a little money from the sale of poultry or of produce raised in free time also increased. Both the Burwell family and the growing town of Williamsburg afforded slaves new customers for their produce and a greater variety of ways to acquire goods.[80]

Many of the Burwell slaves began to adopt–and surely also to adapt–the Anglican Christianity of their owners. The first converts came in the 1720s from the largely creole Gloucester branch at Fairfield; 122 individuals, mostly children but including some adults, were baptized in Abington Parish between 1721 and 1761. In addition, between 1747 and 1769, seventy-two of Lewis Burwell IV's slaves at Kingsmill, both adults and infants, were baptized at Bruton Parish Church, as were thirty-eight from Carter's Grove.[81] Going to Sunday services was an activity that brought together slaves from the various Burwell quarters.

MOVING WEST

Most of the Burwell slaves had the advantage of living in the same area for up to a century, and families were seldom separated by sales or estate divisions. But for all their apparent aversion to separating slave groups, the decision of more and more members of the Burwell clan to try their luck somewhere further west inevitably uprooted much of the extended Burwell slave community that had developed on the lower York peninsula between the 1660s and the 1770s. By the mid 1760s the whites began a process of forced westward migration that would result in the scattering of the great majority of the Burwell slaves throughout the state of Virginia in the 1790s.

Actions of King Carter, now long dead, determined where most of the slaves would eventually go. While proprietary agent for the Northern Neck, Carter patented thousands of acres for various children and grandchildren in present-day Fauquier, Loudoun, and Frederick Counties. As early as 1722 Carter seated a quarter at Bull Run for Nathaniel Burwell I's children, and by 1726 he was sending newly purchased African slaves there.[82] These farms and workers are seldom mentioned in surviving records, although Carter Burwell, for example, visited "my Negroes at Shenandoa" in 1745 and in his 1756 will, divided unseated lands at Bull Run and Shenandoah between sons Nathaniel II and Carter II.[83]

In 1765 Carter's executor, William Nelson, decided it was time to further improve these western lands with slaves from Carter's Grove. That year William Graves, the Burwell general manager, oversaw construction of a new quarter in Frederick County (near present-day Winchester, Virginia), hiring a wagon "to carry up the negroes and clothing" for the nearly 200–mile trip. The next year Nelson sent more slaves and two wagons of clothing to open a second quarter. When the next heir, Nathaniel II, came of age in 1771, he made two visits to his Shenandoah lands, taking with him on the second trip additional slaves. Nathaniel soon decided that future prospects were much brighter there than in the tidewater. By 1772 between one third up to one half of the Carter's Grove slaves were living far from the rest of their kin. Probably the slaves who moved west at first had greater control over work routines than those who remained in the east, since the only white on the plantations was the overseer. On the other hand, they had fewer chances for local trading and had lost the benefit of established kin networks.[84]

The slaves' only way of communicating with each other was through the twice-yearly visits two men made to take up a wagon-load of clothing and tools in spring and fall, or else through the twice-yearly visits of the executor or estate manager. Miserable at being separated from familiar places and kin, some ran away repeatedly trying to return home. Since the slaves from Carter's Grove had travelled cross-country overland, these runaways retraced that route. Slaves of other members of the Burwell clan went to Frederick by water, and tried to get back home on boats. Jack Dismal of Isle of Wight, for example, on his way to a Frederick plantation in 1773, ran off in Fredericksburg and apparently went back down the Rappahannock in some vessel in order to return to the south side of the James.[85]

The Revolution put a temporary stop to Nathaniel Burwell's plans for moving west, but not so his cousin Lewis IV at nearby Kingsmill. Lewis took some of the Kingsmill slaves west when he removed to Mecklenburg County in 1775, and sold others to cover his extensive debts. Still others remained at Kingsmill during the war, Lewis IV having turned that plantation over to his son Lewis V. This heir, who alienated most of his white neighbors by siding with the British, sold the home plantation in 1783. By 1787 he was living in Mecklenburg County with 172 slaves dispersed throughout four Southside counties.[86] Other Burwell kin also forced most of their slaves to go west. As mentioned above, Nathaniel's uncle Robert of Isle of Wight seated Frederick County lands with family slaves in the 1770s, as did cousin James II. James had a farm in Frederick County as early as 1775, although it is not certain that he had yet moved any slaves there. By 1791 James II's son, Nathaniel Junior, had sent twenty-seven of the slaves descending from the James Burwell I group to a Frederick quarter.[87]

After the Revolution, Nathaniel Burwell II spent more and more time and invested ever more capital in his Frederick County holdings, including several merchant mills and a distillery. In the 1790s Nathaniel built a second great house, Carter Hall, in Frederick and shortly brought most of his slaves there. Burwell removed most of the field hands from Carter's Grove in late 1796 or early 1797. Thereafter about fifteen adult workers remained at the Grove, just enough to keep the great house running, care for the livestock, maintain the garden and orchards, and perhaps to raise some small grains. Nathaniel turned the old home plantation over to his oldest son, Carter III (1773–1819), in 1804. Unlike his father, who had begun running his estate at majority, Carter had to wait until he was thirty-one before obtaining title to his inheritance, which included twelve adult slaves and perhaps as many children. The Burwell family had long relied on income from the adjacent quarters to maintain a high standard of living at the Grove, and with these eventually parcelled out among other family members, the 1135 acres and twelve taxable slaves attached to the home farm could not produce returns sufficient to maintain later heirs in the style of the father and grandfather. Carter III barely outlived his father. His widow, her second husband, and a series of administrators ran through most of the estate's assets; they hired out and eventually sold off the remaining slaves.[88]

Nathaniel intended for the York County quarters to descend to other of his children, but the estate was not fully settled until after his widow's death in 1843. Only at Foaces and New Quarters did significant numbers of the Burwell slave group remain together in the tidewater through the 1820s. These people, thirty-some adults along with younger children, continued to labor for the benefit of the Burwell family as a whole until 1829 when Nathaniel's youngest son, Thomas H. N. Burwell (1805–1841), turned twenty-one and returned to York County to manage one of the quarters. Thomas got title to half of the land and apparently all of the slaves. In 1834 most of them disappeared from the estate, bringing to an end any semblance of a Burwell slave community in the tidewater.[89]

After the mid-1790s, contacts between those slaves remaining in the east and the majority who went west became ever less frequent. Once Nathaniel's children inherited various family farms and slaves, they managed these as separate units, not as part of an integrated estate. The slaves had increasingly fewer opportunities for travel from one distant family plantation to another. Once the economic links were severed, the slaves' access to news of separated kinsfolk diminished proportionately. And, as the older generation died, children who grew up in both York and Frederick knew distant family members only through the stories the old people passed on.

Ironically, at the end of all this movement, several branches of the Burwell family slaves ended up living near one another once again in Frederick County. There too, the lands of various Burwells adjoined. This account ends with the dispersion of the Bacon/Burwell group and the Merchant's Hundred Africans and their descendants from the tidewater region. The groups' history in the west is for the present untraced, but likely not untraceable.

∼

NOTES

Note: This essay summarizes preliminary findings of a forthcoming manuscript on the Carter's Grove slave community.

1. Mary A. Stephenson, *Carter's Grove Plantation—A History* (Williamsburg: Colonial Williamsburg Foundation, 1964).
2. See, for example, Dorothy Spruill Redford, *Somerset Homecoming: Recovering a Lost Heritage* (New York: Doubleday, 1988).
3. Eric Gable, Richard Handler, and Anna Lawson, "On the uses of relativism: fact, conjecture, and black and white histories at Colonial Williamsburg," *American Ethnologist* 19 (Nov. 1992): 791-805.
4. Russell R. Menard, "The Maryland Slave Population, 1658 to 1730: A Demographic Profile of Blacks in Four Counties," *William and Mary Quarterly*, 32 (Jan. 1975): 29-54; Allan Kulikoff, "A 'Prolifick' People: Black Population Growth in the Chesapeake Colonies, 1700-1790," *Southern Studies*, 16 (Winter 1977): 391-428; Kulikoff, "The Origins of Afro-American Society in Tidewater Maryland and Virginia, 1700-1790," *William and Mary Quarterly*, 35 (Apr. 978): 226-59;

Kulikoff, *Tobacco and Slaves: The Development of Southern Cultures in the Chesapeake, 1680-1800* (Chapel Hill: University of North Carolina Press, 1986).

5. York County Project Biographical Files, Research Department, Colonial Williamsburg Foundation; York County Deeds, Orders, and Wills, 9, ff. 265, 291-92; 12, f. 437. MS, originals at the Virginia State Library, Richmond, microfilm, Colonial Williamsburg Foundation Library. (Hereafter York County DOW)

6. York County DOW, 9, f. 116 (will); 10, ff. 274-7 (inventory).

7. Lear's will is printed in *Virginia Magazine of History and Biography* 17 (1909): 228; York County DOW, 14, ff. 219, 225.

8. Bacon's will and inventory, York County DOW, 9, f. 116; 10, f. 274-7; Lewis Burwell II's will, York County DOW 14, ff. 60-64; James Burwell's will and inventory, York County DOW 15, ff. 329-36, 421-6, 435.

9. Nell M. Nugent, *Cavaliers and Pioneers: Abstracts of Virginia Land Patents and Grants, 1623-1800*, Volume I, 1623-1666 ([Richmond, 1934]; reprinted Baltimore: Genealogical Publishing Co., Inc., 1963), 547-8.

10. Wesley Frank Craven, *White, Red, and Black: The Seventeenth-Century Virginian* (New York: W. W. Norton, 1971), 83-7; Russell R. Menard, "From Servants to Slaves: The Transformation of the Chesapeake Labor System," *Southern Studies* 16 (Jan. 1977): 355-90.

11. Bacon's inventory lists slaves according to value, starting with prime adult men and then moving to adult women and finally children. Households or family relationships are not indicated.

12. Menard, "The Maryland Slave Population."

13. York County DOW, 4, ff. 141, 209, 372; 5, ff. 47, 139; 6, ff. 28, 67, 94, 299; 8, f. 261. For Indian servants see DOW, 4, f. 70; 8, f. 261.

14. York County DOW, 11, ff. 156, 189; 9, f. 265, 291-92.

15. Menard, "From Servants to Slaves."

16. Lois Green Carr and Lorena S. Walsh, "Economic Diversification and Labor Organization in the Chesapeake," in Stephen Innes, ed., *Work and Labor in Early America* (Chapel Hill: University of North Carolina Press, 1988), 144-88; Philip D. Morgan, "Task and Gang Systems: The Organization of Labor on New World Plantations," in *ibid.*, 199-201.

17. Mechal Sobel, *The World They Made Together; Black and White Values in Eighteenth-Century Virginia* (Princeton: Princeton University Press, 1987), 29.

18. For recent discussions of colonial Chesapeake slave naming patterns see Sobel, *The World They Made Together*, ch. 11; Darrett B. Rutman and Anita H. Rutman, *A Place in Time: Explicatus* (New York: W. W. Norton, 1984), ch. 7; and Kulikoff, *Tobacco and Slaves*, 325-6; In later eighteenth-century Burwell family inventories, (and for that matter, in most others), appraisers failed to record either English or amalgamated surnames for any of the slaves, nor did they distinguish mulattos from other slaves. For the West African naming patterns see A. J. H. Latham, *Old Calabar, 1600-1891; The Impact of the International Economy Upon a Traditional Society* (Oxford: Clarendon Press, 1973), 9-12, and John Thornton, "Central African

Names and African-American Naming Patterns," *William and Mary Quarterly*, 50 (Oct. 1993): 727-42.

19. The proportion of mulattos may have been smaller among all Burwell's slaves, since those whom he did not name were more likely to have been less skilled and less acculturated than those he mentioned in his will. We cannot be sure of this since we lack an inventory. (Colonial Gloucester County records do not survive.) On the other hand, mulattos from Lewis's estate, not named in his will, do appear in his son James's 1719 inventory.

20. Cf. Peter H. Wood, *Black Majority: Negroes in Colonial South Carolina from 1670 through the Stono Rebellion* (New York: W. W. Norton & Co., 1974), chap. 6.

21. Kulikoff, *Tobacco and Slaves*, 384-5.

22. York County DOW, 10, f. 483.

23. The work of Joyce Chaplin of Vanderbilt University and of Mart Stewart of Oregon State University has delineated the extent to which lowcountry South Carolina and Georgia slaves dominated their estuarine environments. Denser white populations in the tidewater Chesapeake precluded slaves the same degree of mastery; still it is worth thinking about Chesapeake waterways as affording overlapping but very different resources and opportunities for slaves and for various classes of whites.

24. Carter to [Page], 6 April 1714, Robert Carter Letterbook, 1723-24, Alderman Library, University of Virginia, f. 62.

25. *Virginia Gazette*, 17 December 1736.

26. York County Order Book, 1765-68, f. 52, MS, original at the Virginia State Library, Richmond, microfilm, Colonial Williamsburg Foundation Library.

27. Robert Carter, for example, annexed all the slaves he bequeathed to particular parcels of land, so that they might "descend as real estate according to our late Negro law." Will, Carter Papers, Virginia Historical Society. For a discussion of the legal complexities of entailing slaves, see Lewis Burwell and wife Frances v. Philip and Elizabeth Johnson, British Museum Additional Manuscripts, 36,318, pp. 138-143, microfilm 284, Colonial Williamsburg Foundation Library. The procedures for entailing slaves in eighteenth-century Virginia were then and are now poorly understood. The 1705 statute establishing slave entails was ambiguously drafted, and subsequent revisions to the law complicated rather than clarified the situation. Although an English chancery court eventually decided that slaves could be entailed only if they were attached to a particular parcel of land, in the intervening half century many Virginians thought slaves could be entailed without restrictions. Some testators did so entail slaves, and the bequests stood, especially if other potential heirs did not challenge the will. After the Revolution, entails in both land and slaves were abolished. See Marylynn Salmon, *Women and the Law of Property in Early America* (Chapel Hill: University of North Carolina Press, 1986), 152-6. The relevance of this seemingly arcane legal practice is that it served to keep groups of slaves together over long periods of time, often on the same tract of land.

28. York County Project Biographical Files; York County DOW 15, ff. 329-36; ff. 421-6, 435; York County Wills and Inventories, 20, ff. 148-51, 218; 22, ff.

348-51; 23, ff. 256-9, MS, original at the Virginia State Library, Richmond, microfilm, Colonial Williamsburg Foundation Library. York County Personal Property Tax records credit Nathaniel Burwell Jr. with thirty-three tithable slaves in 1790. Only nine were listed as belonging to the estate in 1791 (reflecting division of Nathaniel's inventoried slaves), and none were listed thereafter. MS, Virginia State Library, microfilm, Colonial Williamsburg Foundation Library.

29. Only one other child, a son Armistead (1718-54), apparently survived the parents. Armistead was a merchant in Williamsburg and seems to have owned very few slaves. York County Project Biographical Files. William M. Kelso, *Kingsmill Plantations, 1619-1800: Archaeology of Country Life in Colonial Virginia* (Orlando: Academic Press, 1984), 33-55; Ann Camille Wells, "Kingsmill Plantation, A Cultural Analysis" (M.A. thesis, University of Virginia, 1976).

30. York County DOW 12, 436.

31. Nathaniel's will, copy at the Virginia Historical Society, is transcribed in Stephenson, *Carter's Grove Plantation*, pp. 211-6.

32. These likely included the men Jemmy, Ben, and Peter. Robert Carter Diary, 1722-7, entries of 10 September 1723; 6, 15, 17, and 22 February, and 7 Oct 1724, MS, Alderman Library, microfilm M-113, Colonial Williamsburg Foundation Library.

33. Lewis also got other land in Richmond County that was probably part of Nathaniel's marriage settlement. If slaves accompanied the land, they were gifts from Robert Carter, and there is no information about them.

34. Upton, "White and Black Landscapes in Eighteenth Century Virginia," in Robert Blair St. George, ed., *Material Life in America, 1600-1860* (Boston: Northeastern University Press, 1988), 367.

35. Petition of Mary Butler v. Adam Craig, 1784, Papers of the General Court for the Western Shore, 1787; Papers of the Court of Appeals, 1791, Box C, MSS, Maryland State Archives, Annapolis. Court papers relating to the case have been assembled and analyzed by Phoebe Jacobsen, Archivist, Maryland State Archives. Robert Carter of Nomini estimated the number of Butler descendants in 1789. Entry of 17 September 1789, Robert Carter Letterbook, 1789-92, MS, Perkins Library, Duke University, microfilm M 26.3, Colonial Williamsburg Foundation Library.

36. Carter to Micajah Perry, 16 June 1723, f. 3, Robert Carter Letterbook, 1723-4, MS, Alderman Library; Carter to Perry, 31 July 1731, f. 19, Robert Carter Letterbook, 1731-32, MS, Alderman Library; (both on microfilm M-113, Colonial Williamsburg Foundation Library); Carter to John Falconer, 24 July 1727, f. 17, Robert Carter Letterbook, 1727-8, Carter Family Papers, Virginia Historical Society.

37. Will, f. 9, Carter Family Papers, Virginia Historical Society.

38. Sources include the Letterbooks and Diary cited above and the 1733 estate inventory, MS, Carter Family Papers, Virginia Historical Society. The home house slaves are not included in this analysis of quarters.

39. Entries of 7 October 1724, 22 May 1725, Robert Carter Diary.

40. Carter to Robert Jones, 10 October 1717, f. 72, Carter Letterbook, 1727-28, Alderman Library.

41. Carter to Robert Jones, 24 October 1729, f. 41, Carter Letterbook, 1728-30, Virginia Historical Society. Today it seems implausible that the Carters could have connected knowledge of over 500 slaves scattered throughout the colony as individual men, women, and children though a single proper, and to us, not very distinctive given name, but this seems to have been the case. While the family kept written lists of their human property, they apparently retained mental images of at least the adult slaves as well, and this was one reason for their insistence that the slaves use the English name they assigned them.

42. Kulikoff, *Tobacco and Slaves*, 321-2.

43. Michael Mullin, *Africa in America: Slave Acculturation and Resistance in the American South and the British Caribbean, 1736-1831* (Urbana: University of Illinois Press, 1992), chap. 1; quotation from p.19.

44. Carter to John Pemberton, 27 September 1727, f. 39, Carter Letterbook, 1727-28, Alderman Library; Carter to John Pemberton and Company 18 December 1727, f. 28; Carter to George Eskridge, 21 September 1727, f. 73, Carter Letterbook, 1727-8, Virginia Historical Society; Carter Diary, 2 August 1722.

45. Carter to Robert Jones, 24 October 1729, f. 41, Carter Letterbook, 1728-30, Virginia Historical Society. Carter Diary 8 November 1722; Carter to ?, partial letter of 1727 or 1728, f. 83, Carter Letterbook, 1727-8, Alderman Library.

46. Carter Diary, 12, 17, and 25 July 1727. For the general tendency of African slaves to try immediate escape, see Mullin, *Africa in America*, chap. 1.

47. Carter to Robert Jones, 10 October 1727, f. 72, Carter Letterbook, 1727-28, Alderman Library.

48. Ibid; Carter Diary 26 October 1722. If parts of this narrative appear a pale gloss upon the story of Kunta Kinte portrayed in Alex Haley, *Roots: The Story of an American Family* (New York: Doubleday & Co., 1976), I can only surmise that the Robert Carter letterbooks were among the sources upon which Haley drew. The Carter family papers are one of the most detailed sources that address the procedures whites used to acculturate recent African captives in the early eighteenth-century Chesapeake. Use of these materials is particularly appropriate for the Carter's Grove slaves since Robert Carter retained ownership of the plantation from initial purchase until his death, and assumed direct management of the farms between 1721 and 1732.

49. Carter Inventory, 1733, Virginia Historical Society. What either the slaves or Carter understood as a "proper" slave marriage is unclear. Presumably one of the Carters insisted on notification of the union or else they would not have provided separate housing. Otherwise, given the slaves' recent arrival in the colonies and the Carters' apparent indifference to converting them to Christianity, slave marriages were likely negotiated unions that included elements of both African and English expectations. In this inventory, slaves are listed by household and family relationships specified.

50. Carter to ? (torn) [1728] , f. 1; Carter to ? (torn) [1729], ff. 33-4; Carter to ? (torn), 27 Aug 1729, f. 36, Carter Letterbook 1728-30, Virginia Historical Society.

51. Carr and Walsh, "Economic Diversification"; Morgan, "Task and Gang Systems."

52. Polygyny was a common West African marital custom. Richer men often married as many wives as they could support, and the work of these women and their children further increased a complex household's wealth. Very few African slaves were able to re-establish the custom in the Chesapeake. Slaveowners did not allow men the right to accumulate the sorts of personal property with which they might have attracted or supported more than one wife, and in any case, most owners likely believed it their moral duty to enforce Christian concepts of monogamy among their slaves. In addition, the preponderance of men among forced African migrants made polygyny relatively impractical. Cf. Kulikoff, *Tobacco and Slaves*, 354-5.

53. See discussion of the new Rippon Hall plantation, Robert Carter Will. Carter also judged eighteen to twenty-five workers to be a suitable dowry for two of his daughters.(Provisions for Anne Harrison and Judith Page, Robert Carter Will).

54. In 1727 each adult fieldworker usually produced one hogshead per year. Carter to Hasewell and Brooks, 13 May 1727, f. 3, Carter Letterbook, 1727-8, Virginia Historical Society.

55. For another discussion of household structure on the Robert Carter plantations, see Kulikoff, *Tobacco and Slaves*, 353-8.

56. Entries of 2 and 24 August 1723, Carter Diary.

57. Carter to Micajah Perry, 13 February 1724, f. 43, Carter Letterbook, 1723-4, Alderman Library; Carter to John Stark, 27 September 1727, f. 40, Carter Letterbook, 1727-28, Alderman Library; Robert and John Carter to Alderman Perry, 16 June 1730, f. 74, Carter Letterbook, 1728-31, Alderman Library; Carter to Richard Oswald & Company, 27 July 1731, f. 12, and Robert and John Carter to Alderman Perry, 10 September 1731, f. 28, Carter Letterbook, 1731-2, Alderman Library; Carter to Robert Jones, 24 October 1729, f. 41, Carter Letterbook, 1728-30, Virginia Historical Society; Entry of 21 October 1722, Carter Diary. For a description of these items, see Linda Baumgarten, "'Clothes for the People': Slave Clothing in Early Virginia," *Journal of Early Southern Decorative Arts*, 14 (Nov. 1988): 26-70.

58. Carter to John Stark, 27 September 1727, f. 40, Carter Letterbook, 1727-8, Alderman Library; Carter to Richard Oswald & Co., 27 July 1731, f. 12, Carter Letterbook, 1731-32, Alderman Library; Carter to Robert Jones, 24 October 1729, f. 41, Carter Letterbook, 1728-30, Virginia Historical Society.

59. Carter to ? (torn), [1729], ff. 33-34; Carter to Robert Jones, 24 October 1729, f. 41, Carter Letterbook, 1728-30, Virginia Historical Society.

60. Carter to Robert Jones, 10 October 1727, f. 72, Carter Letterbook, 1727-8, Alderman Library.

61. Carter to Benjamin Grayson, 3 July 1731, f. 29; Carter to Nicholas Nicholas, 13 July 1731, f. 30, Carter Letterbook, 1728-31, Alderman Library.

62. Carter to ? (torn), 27 August 1729, f. 36, Carter Letterbook, 1728-1730, Virginia Historical Society.

63. Carter to Robert Jones, 10 October 1727, f. 72, Carter Letterbook, 1727-8, Alderman Library; Carter to ? (torn), [1728], f. 1, Carter Letterbook, 1728-30, Virginia Historical Society.

64. Carter to Richard Meeks, 30 June 1729, f. 11, Carter Letterbook, 1728-31, Alderman Library; Carter to ? (torn), [1728], f. 1, Carter Letterbook, 1728-1730, Virginia Historical Society. See also Todd L. Savitt, *Fevers, Agues, and Cures: Medical Life in Old Virginia* (Richmond: Virginia Historical Society, 1990), 46-8.

65. There are glimpses of the Carter slaves using traditional skills, for example, on one plantation they made "hollow gumbs" to store corn and salt. Carter to Robert Jones, 10 October 1727, f. 72, Carter Letterbook, 1727-8, Alderman Library.

66. Carter to Benjamin Grayson, 2 July 1731, f. 81, Carter Letterbook, 1731-2, Alderman Library.

67. Carter to Robert Jones, 24 October 1729, f. 41, Carter Letterbook, 1728-30, Virginia Historical Society.

68. Jack P. Greene, ed., *The Diary of Col. Landon Carter of Sabine Hall, 1752-1778 (Charlottesville: University Press of Virginia, 1965), 1038-9.*

69. York County DOW, 15, ff. 329-36, 421-6, 435. James also sent some of the newly purchased Africans along with some old hands to a quarter in King William; some of them were still there in 1749. The family retained this quarter through 1776. York County Wills and Inventories, 20, f. 218; 22, ff. 326-7.

70. Carter to ? (torn), [1728], f.1, Carter Letterbook, 1728-30, Virginia Historical Society.

71. Kulikoff, Tobacco and Slaves, 333-4.

72. Carter Burwell Account Book, 1738-55, MS, Colonial Williamsburg Foundation.

73. Burwell Account Book and Carter Burwell will, original, Virginia Historical Society, transcribed in Stephenson, Carter's Grove, 259-64. Neck of Land lies about ten miles from Carter's Grove; see map 1. The account books suggest that the Burwells did not visit the farm all that frequently, and that they left the newly purchased slaves, who were surely part of a different neighborhood network, on that quarter.

74. Carter Burwell Account Book, ff. 103-4.

75. York County Orders, Wills, and Inventories, 18, ff. 380, 515, 614.

76. *Virginia Gazette*, 21 April 1738.

77. *Virginia Gazette*, 7 August 1752.

78. For the 1756 total, see Thomas B. Griffin to [Edmund Berkeley], 10 October 1777, F. L. Berkeley Deposit, Edmund Berkeley Papers, Alderman Library (microfilm M-1816.2, Colonial Williamsburg Foundation Library). On changes in family life, see Kulikoff, *Tobacco and Slaves*, ch. 9. For 1786 see Jackson T. Main, "The One Hundred," *William and Mary Quarterly*, 11 (Jul. 1954): 354-84. Main credits Nathaniel with 179 slaves, but notes that twenty-five slaves in Mecklenburg County may have belonged to another Nathaniel Burwell. He was surely one of Lewis Burwell IV's descendants.

79. Kelso, *Kingsmill Plantation*, chap. 5 (quote, p. 205.) Some of these ideas are elaborated in Lorena S. Walsh, "Fettered Consumers: Slaves and the Anglo-

American 'Consumer Revolution'," Paper presented at the annual meeting of the Economic History Association, Boston, September 1992.

80. For changes in slave marketing opportunities, see Lorena S. Walsh, "Slave Life, Slave Society, and Tobacco Production in the Tidewater Chesapeake, 1620-1820," in *Cultivation and Culture: Labor and the Shaping of Slave Life in the Americas* eds. Ira Berlin and Philip D. Morgan (Charlottesville: University Press of Virginia, 1993), 170-99; and Walsh, "Work and Resistance in the New Republic: The Case of the Chesapeake, 1700-1820," in Mary Turner, ed., *Chattel Slaves into Wage Slaves* (forthcoming). The small size of work units on tobacco plantations precluded the operation of sophisticated tasking systems. Hence Chesapeake slaves had less free time and fewer opportunities for earning money than did those in places such as coastal South Carolina (as discussed later in this volume) where a task system prevailed.

81. Register of Abington Parish, Gloucester County, Va., 1677-1761, transcript, Colonial Williamsburg Research Department; Bruton Parish Church Register, microfilm, Colonial Williamsburg Foundation Library. Slave baptisms are regularly noted in the Bruton register between 1746 and 1768; thereafter recordings are sporadic and incomplete.

82. Fairfax Harrison, *Landmarks of Old Prince William: A Study of Origins in Northern Virginia* (Berryville, Va.: Chesapeake Book Co., 1964), chap. 18; Carter Diary, 17 and 21 October 1722; 10 November 1726.

83. Carter Burwell Account Book, f. 34; Stephenson, *Carter's Grove*, 259-64.

84. Burwell Ledger 3, 1764-76; Nathaniel Burwell Day Book, 1773-1779; Nathaniel Burwell Day Book, 1779-86, MSS, Colonial Williamsburg Foundation Library; William Nelson to Samuel Athawes, 19 November, 1771, William Nelson Letterbook, 1766-75, microfilm M-60, Colonial Williamsburg Foundation Library.

85. Burwell Ledger 3; *Virginia Gazette*, Rind, 18 February, 1773. Dismal refers to Jack's origins in or near the Dismal Swamp.

86. Wells, "Kingsmill Plantation," chap. 1; Main, "The One Hundred."

87. York County Project Biographical Files; York County Wills and Inventories, 22, ff. 347-8; 23, ff. 258-9.

88. Stephenson, *Carter's Grove*, chaps. 4-6; James City County Personal Property Tax Lists, microfilm M 1-55, Colonial Williamsburg Foundation Library (summaries are provided in Stephenson, *Carter's Grove*, 311-2.).

89. York County Land Tax Books, 1782-1831, and York County Personal Property Tax Lists for 1782-1809, 1810-32, and 1833-50, originals Virginia State Library, microfilm M 1.46, M 1169.7, M 1169.8, M 1169.9, Colonial Williamsburg Foundation Library.

~

"A RECKONING OF ACCOUNTS"

Patriarchy, Market Relations, and Control on
Henry Laurens's Lowcountry Plantations, 1762-1785

Robert Olwell

In 1785, sixty-one-year-old Henry Laurens penned a portrait of himself as a
slave master. At the time, he held extensive plantations in the South Carolina
and Georgia lowcountry and was the owner of over three hundred slaves. But
such pursuits had come late to Laurens; he was nearly forty when he first became
master of a plantation in 1762. In his younger life he devoted his considerable
energy and abilities to acquiring a fortune as a Charleston merchant. According
to a contemporary, Laurens was "a sober arbitrator . . . in little differences of
accounts and reckonings, . . . skilled in the rate of exchange . . . and in the price
of commodities."[1] Yet, although he was well versed in the vocabulary of the
counting house, Laurens nonetheless chose to portray his relations with his
slaves in quite another language. "My Negroes," he wrote:

> . . . are in more comfortable circumstances than any equal number of Peas-
> antry in Europe, there is not a Beggar among them nor one unprovided with
> food, raiment & good Lodging, they also enjoy property; the Lash is forbidden;
> they all understand this declaration as a Substitute -"If you deserve whipping
> I shall conclude you don't love me & will sell you. . . ."
>
> . . . Yet I believe no man gets more work from his Negroes than I do, at the
> same time they are my Watchmen and my friends; never was an absolute
> Monarch more happy in his Subjects than at the present time I am.[2]

In Laurens's idealized image, his plantations were the equivalent of a little kingdom where he reigned as "an absolute Monarch" and on which the slaves were "his Subjects." He depicted the slaves' provision of labor and his provision of "food, raiment & good Lodging" as part of a reciprocal relationship of obligations and duties. Disobedience and misbehavior, on the other hand, were portrayed by Laurens as evidence that the slaves concerned "don't love me." While claiming to shun "the Lash," he menaced slaves with the prospect of sale and separation from their homes and families. Both by threatening his slaves with harsh punishments and promising to provide for their basic needs, Laurens emphasized his role as patriarch of his plantations.[3]

In another letter, written twenty years before, Laurens cast his relations with his slaves in a different light. In a note written to one of his plantation overseers and accompanied by a shipment of goods sent to the plantation, Laurens wrote:

> . . . I enclose you an Account of sundry articles sent to be dispos'd among the Negroes for their Rice at the prices mark'd to each article which I hope they will take without too much fuss & trouble that I may not be discouraged from being their Factor another Year.
>
> Their several names are set down & your quantity of each ones Rice on the Credit side at 7/6 per Bushel, which is its full value & opposite to that you must make them Debtor for such goods as they take.[4]

In this portrait, Laurens pictured himself not as the "absolute Monarch" of the plantation but instead as his slaves' "Factor." In choosing this term, Laurens harkened back to his earlier career as one of the merchant middlemen that operated between Carolina rice planters and the imperial marketplace. By buying the produce of their gardens and retailing manufactures to them on credit, Laurens now acted to fill the same role for his slaves.

Laurens's two contrasting depictions of himself and his relationship to his slaves, as their "absolute Monarch" and their "Factor," might be seen as yet another example of a familiar story. Like the slave societies of the early modern Atlantic world, of which his plantations were a part, Laurens seemed to speak to his slaves with two mouths. He employed both the language of patriarchy- "Monarch" and "Subject," "love" and "friendship" and that of capitalism- "Prices," "Credit," and "Debt." The contradictions inherent in such a janus-faced world-view have posited fascinating questions for scholars of slavery.[5] The issues raised in the ensuing debate will probably never be resolved. In a recent book review, Lawrence McDonnell provided the "recipe" for scholars interested in imbibing the popular intellectual concoction he termed the "Slaveholders' Dilemma"; "take one part chattel bondage, add one part liberal capitalism and stir endlessly."[6]

For the most part, students of the slaveholders' dilemma have concerned themselves with slave societies' interactions with the greater "world system" of capital and exchange in which they were embedded. While they might disagree strenuously as to whether or not slave masters were capitalist wolves in patriarchal clothing, few scholars have questioned how market relations might have influenced the relations between masters and slaves. Instead, relations between the "great house" and the slave quarters are often portrayed as if they were conducted in a realm where the market could not, or at least did not, intrude.

But Laurens's 1765 letter refutes any simple dichotomy between domestic patriarchy and external capitalism. The letter reveals that Laurens openly and commonly participated in marketplace exchange with his slaves. Nor was he at all unusual in allowing his slaves to engage in independent economic activities. Recent scholarship has detailed the presence of a thriving "domestic economy" within slavery. Throughout the New World slaves commonly enjoyed extensive and widespread access to private property and petty trading.[7] Slaves' participation in the domestic economy of slave societies should not lead us to conclude that they were entirely driven by economic considerations, but it does destroy any notion that slave quarter communities could somehow be kept completely separated from the acquisitive, property-seeking ethos which was the plantation's very reason for being.

The recognition of this domestic economy, and slaves' prominent role in it, has led scholars to consider the impact which slaves' engagement in market relations and their exercise of property "rights" may have had on their families, cultures, and modes of resistance. What did it mean to Laurens's slaves, for example, to be able to buy and sell to their master on credit? Not surprisingly, opinions have differed on these issues. While some scholars have described the provision ground-marketing complex as a mode of resistance against the master class—a "peasant breach in the slave mode of production"—others have argued that it sapped slaves' ability to resist the slave system by giving them a stake in the status quo.[8]

Neither approach is entirely satisfactory. In fact, upon reflection, both views impale themselves on the horns of the slaveholders' dilemma. On the one hand, the power of patriarchal masters is "breached" by the liberating economic initiative of property seeking slaves. On the other, slaveholder capitalists seem to emulate their northern counterparts by deflecting the radicalism of their workers with "lunch-pail" concessions. But while scholars may never resolve the theoretical contradictions between patriarchy and capitalism, in practice slaveholders and slaves must somehow have managed just such a reconciliation.

If the contest between patriarchy and market relations is seen not as a problem to be settled but instead as an ongoing process to be examined, a way around the intoxicating but ultimately unsatisfying slaveholders' dilemma presents itself. When studied in this way, it becomes apparent that the contested ground between the metaphors of patriarchy and market relations was both one of the primary battlegrounds between masters and slaves and one of the principal foundations of the social order. Henry Laurens's relationship with his slave work force in the period between 1762 and 1785, can serve as a window into the day-to-day practice of negotiation and confrontation between masters and slaves and between the metaphors of the great house and those of the counting house. Laurens's plantation accounts shed light on how the language of patriarchy and the market both acted to shape master-slave relations and reveal how their conflicting demands were reconciled with one slave master's need to maintain order and to profit from his plantations and his slaves' desire for property, autonomy, and self-control.[9]

The papers of Henry Laurens contain abundant ammunition for scholars who would see slaveholders as semi-feudal patriarchs reluctantly "slouching toward capitalism."[10] Laurens, for instance, described his slaves on one occasion as "poor Creatures who look up to their Master as their Father, their Guardian, & Protector, & to whom their is a reciprocal obligation upon the Master."[11] In discussing the treatment of a disobedient slave, he wrote of "that humanity which a Man . . . ought to extend to every Creature in Subjection to him."[12] Likewise, upon hearing of the death of a valued worker, Laurens was moved to reply, "I . . . am sorry for Bill but we must both Kings & Slaves submit to the strokes of death."[13] While this last remark raises the notion of death as the great equalizer, it also implies that for the living "Kings & Slaves" were opposite extremes of a hierarchical "chain of being" in which all had a proper place and role.

Alongside these patriarchal allusions, however, a great deal of references also indicate that Laurens's relations with his slaves were also shaped by marketplace calculation. In 1766, for example, Laurens gave instructions to his overseer to "take Account of" a box of "Short pipes" and a barrel of "Yellow Porringers & Muggs" that he had sent to the plantation to be "given to the Negroes," but only after they had been "paid for."[14] On another occasion, he included a selection of "Iron Pots" with a shipment of "Negro Cloth" to one of his plantations and directed the overseer "to sell [the Pots] for what they are worth."[15] It is plain that Laurens customarily and continually acted as "Factor" to his slaves. He not only bought their crops–his account book records the payment of nearly £160 in 1769 to his "Wambaw [plantation] Negroes for their Rice"–but he also retailed manufactured goods to them.[16] Like any successful merchant, Laurens tried to anticipate his customers' desires. In 1765, for example, he delivered to Wambaw "15 very gay Wastcoats which," he hoped, "some of the Negro Men may want at 10 Bushels per Wastcoat." "Unless," he offered the overseer, "you . . . think them worth more or less."[17]

Encounters between Laurens and his slaves could take on a different character when the two parties were engaged in negotiations according to the "law of the market." In market relations there could be no "Monarchs" and "Subjects," but only buyers and sellers. Laurens once instructed an overseer to "purchase of . . . [the] Negroes all [the provisions] that you know Lawfully belongs to themselves at the lowest price they will sell it for."[18] This depiction suggests a process of bargaining in which the master or his representative, the overseer, momentarily faced the slaves as equals at the bargaining table. If the price offered was *too* low, Laurens implied, the slaves, as economic individuals, had the "right" to refuse to sell.

That Laurens simultaneously constructed relations with his slaves in *both* patriarchal and market terms raises the question of how these two seemingly contrary visions of social relations could be reconciled. Must we imagine Laurens as a sort of slaveowning Jekyll and Hyde, alternately seeking deference or profit from his slaves? Did his slaves hesitate to approach their master on any given day until they could discern whether he wore his patriarchal crown or his shopkeeper's visor upon his head? More importantly, if patriarchy and market relations offered two possible discourses within which any given slave-master negotiation could take place, we must consider who, slaves or masters, chose the metaphoric "playing-field" upon which any given encounter would be conducted. Finally, did Laurens and his slaves each have a preferred language of relations, a "home court" so to speak, in which they sought to contain negotiations?

Laurens's letters suggest that his slaves defended and asserted the "law of the market" and of market relations whenever they were able. Slaves strove to convert their claim to the product of their gardens, long since conceded, into a "right" to trade their property in the marketplace and to exchange it for manufactured goods or cash. Some of Laurens's slaves, with regular opportunity to travel between his plantations and the city, even attempted to usurp Laurens's role as his slaves' "Factor" to meet this pent-up demand for trade. Laurens was particularly suspicious of his slave boatmen in this regard and warned his overseer "to give a watchful eye to the behaviour of Abraham [the boat captain] & his gang. I will have no traffick carried on by them & he is very sly & artful [so] that you will find all your skill necessary to counteract him. If he or any one of his people are detected in any trade or trick don't spare them."[19] Laurens feared that "Amos," another slave, had "a great inclination to turn Rum merchant." "This," Laurens instructed his overseer, "I have strictly forbidden

& therefore desire you to search narrowly & if he has more than one bottle to seize it. I suspect he has or may send up some by my flat boat to Mr. Mayrant's Landing."[20]

Laurens and other masters had several reasons to deny their slaves independent access to the market. Slaveholders complained that through such contacts, their slaves would be "debauched," by which they meant that they would develop so strong an appetite for market goods that they would be led "to steal and rob their masters of their corn, poultry, and other provisions" in order to have goods to barter.[21] But more importantly, masters resented the market's ability to provide slaves with a source of self-esteem and material improvement that did not require them to go cap-in-hand to the great house. They rightly perceived the marketplace as a challenge to the patriarchal plantation-centered social order which they defined as the basis of their authority. Thus, although he allowed his slaves to "enjoy property," as he boasted in 1785, Laurens also sought to restrict their access to the marketplace. Slaveholders discovered that efforts to entirely deny their slaves' desire for trade were futile. By way of a compromise, a custom evolved where masters forbade their slaves to go to the market, but instead brought the market to their slaves—via a plantation "store." In effect, slaveholders strove to "domesticate" market relations and contain the market within patriarchal confines. Kept within the boundaries of the plantation, the harmful effects of slaves' marketing on the slaveholders' authority could be minimized, and maximum use could be made of the opportunity it provided for symbolic gestures.

Safe within the plantation, a master could view the exchanges conducted at the plantation store less as a business transaction and more as part of his patriarchal responsibilities. In this restricted context, where the master could still play the central and dominant role, slaves could participate in the market in a way that masked the incongruity of such transactions with the slaveholders' absolute and patriarchal ideal. Moreover, by limiting slaves' purchases to what was offered at the plantation store, slaveholders could restrict their slaves' choice of consumer goods. In this way, Laurens could take some of the most valued commodities "off the shelf" and hold them outside the market where the master's will still reigned supreme.[22] Liquor, for example, was notably absent from any of the plantation purchases of Laurens's slaves. Masters chose to keep a firm control on the rum barrel and distributed its contents sparingly and without charge as a reward for good work or as a treat for holidays or other occasions in the slave quarters.

The cellars of the great house and not the plantation store served as the source of special commodities for extraordinary occasions in the slave quarters. At Christmas, and whenever there was a wedding, a birth, or a death among their slaves, masters provided rum, sugar, and often some of the food, especially meat, that together played a large part in the slaves' festivities.[23] Through these gestures, a slaveholder could play the part of a benevolent patriarch "and contrast the dependent position of the slave with his own status of dominance."[24]

In the short term, the planter's custom of bringing the market to the slaves (but only on the master's terms) may have circumvented the threat which slaves' participation in the slave society's domestic economy posed to the metaphors of patriarchy. In the long term however, masters could not control the process engendered by the intrusion of market relations onto the plantation social order. The practice of growing their own provisions and trading their surplus had the side effect of teaching slaves the commodity value of their labor. By engaging in market relations, even if it were only at the plantation "store," slaves learned that the product of their work had a precise monetary value and could be exchanged for an equivalency of goods. Accustomed to producing for themselves in their gardens for part of every day and aware that through the agency of the market, surplus foodstuffs could be traded for other commodities, slaves may have begun to expect that the products of labor belonged rightly to the laborer.

If slaves primarily sought individual ends—to eat better, to hold wealth as families, and to acquire some few "creature comforts"—and acquired these "privileges" incrementally, the effect of thousands of such personally motivated efforts over a number of years could nonetheless result in wringing significant concessions from slaveholders and transforming the "rules" of the slave society.

An interesting example of such a transformation can be perceived in the long struggle over the product of the garden plots that slaves cultivated at hours when they were not at work in the plantation fields. The customary practice in the first half of the eighteenth century required slaves to use the proceeds from their gardens and free time to supply themselves with their basic food and clothing. In 1742, a visitor to South Carolina noted that "Negroes . . . receive no clothes from their master but must work on Sunday too, and afterwards they turn their crops into money and buy themselves some old rags."[25] As this relieved the slaveholder of the expense of providing his slaves' subsistence, the slaves were, in effect, working for their master on their own time as well as his.

Slaves' ability to produce for themselves in their gardens and to engage in market relations in the evenings and on Sunday stood in stark contrast to the equation of labor with love and duty which governed their work the remainder of the week. According to the metaphors of patriarchy, cash transactions and commodity exchange had no part in the master's claim to the slaves' labor to cultivate his fields. But, as the ideology of the market gained a foothold in the slave quarters, slaves may have found the terms of their labor in the plantation fields increasingly galling. This is not to say that slaves were previously unconscious of their exploitation, but rather to suggest that market relations provided slaves with a language which enabled them to articulate their grievances in terms which their masters would understand and respect.

When interpreted through market metaphors, the masters' unrequited appropriation of the product of slaves' toil was little more than theft. Market relations exposed the extent of slaves' economic exploitation and revealed the hollowness of patriarchy and the arbitrary basis of the masters' authority. For slaves, the realization that they were denied "the just reward of . . . [their] labor," gave moral justification for retribution in the form of theft, sabotage, and flight.[26] At least some worried slaveholders agreed. For example, Thomas Jefferson excused slave theft on the similar grounds that "the slave may . . . justifiably take a little from one who has taken all from him."[27] Ultimately, such interpretations threatened to reduce master-slave relations to little more than a brutal power stuggle in which each side took what it could and recognized no obligations of reciprocity.

While this depiction might indeed have been a closer approximation of social reality than the fictional relations of patriarchy, such a perpetual state of war between masters and slaves could not serve as the foundation to a stable labor regime. If patriarchy could not be restored, the basis for a new "moral economy" between masters and slaves had to be found. The language and metaphors of market relations provided an available discourse of reciprocity and social stability.

Once the "law of the market" had intruded onto the plantations, its logic was difficult for slaveholders to deny. Particularly if it was accompanied by an increase in theft and a decrease in labor discipline and productivity. For profit-minded planters, it was far easier to concede to their slaves' efforts to expand the metaphors of market-relations from their garden plots to the plantation fields than to engage in a long and costly confrontation on the issue. Consequently, by the third quarter of the eighteenth-century, if not before, most masters not only accepted slaves' claim to the product of their gardens but also acknowledged a *de facto* responsibility to make some gesture of compensating slaves for their labor.

By the eve of the Revolution, plantation account books record that the typical slaveholder provided basic clothing allowances and food rations to his slaves as a matter of policy. An observer described the "custom" as it had evolved by 1773. Slaves, he wrote, "do not plant in their fields for subsistence, but for amusement, pleasure, and profit, their masters giving them clothes, and sufficient provisions from their granaries."[28] With the masters' granaries and smokehouses now furnishing their daily subsistence, slaves could feel that their labor in the masters' fields was at least partially compensated for, and a workable plantation equilibrium could be restored.

A rare, because explicit, illustration of how masters and slaves might bargain over the terms of labor is contained in a newspaper advertisement of 1778. A North Carolina correspondent informed Charleston readers of a "negroe fellow" named Tom who had lately turned up on his doorstep. Tom claimed that he had run away from his master in South Carolina seven years previous "that he had lived two years in the woods," and eventually arrived in Wilmington, where "he was taken up by one Nathaniel Williams . . . [and that] Tom agreed to go home with the said Williams and to work for him [in return] for victuals and cloths." However, after working on these terms for five years, Tom decided to try to return to his old master. Tom made this drastic decision the advertiser concluded, "on his being obliged by Williams to pay for his own cloaths out of his Sundays work."[29]

While the slaveholders' desire to play the part of the patriarch could, to some degree, become an end in itself, in the larger world social status was closely related to economic success. To maximize their economic return, slaveholders needed to secure their slaves' labor as regularly and as cheaply as possible, even if that necessitated some encroachments upon the patriarchal ideal. Slavehold-ers' desire to balance these two objectives, that is to play the part of a patriarchal master but to do it profitably, may have influenced them to concede in some measure to their slaves' assertion of a "market-based" metaphor that depicted the masters' provision of necessities as part of a *quid pro quo* exchange.

Laurens, like other slaveholders, still depicted his provision of "food, rai-ment, and good lodging" as the embodiment of his patriarchal responsibilities. Such reassuring reasoning however, served only to mask the fact that through their efforts, slaves had turned a purely symbolic ritual exchange of "protection" for "obedience" into a far more tangible (and, to the slaves, worthwhile) trade of goods for labor. After 1775, if any master sought to deny his slaves this by now "customary right," he would do so only at a cost that was prohibitive in terms of productivity, profitability, and order.

Masters attempted to salvage the guise of patriarchal benevolence by assert-ing that the clothing and foodstuffs they provided were not merely compensa-tion for the slaves' labor *per se* but rather "rewards" for the slaves' good "behavior." In 1771, for example, Laurens instructed one of his overseers to "tell them [his slaves] I intend to send the best cloth next year that ever they wore, together with several additional articles of use to them, for such as shall have behaved well." Three years later, Laurens again wrote:

> Tell the Negroes that I hope to meet them when they are beginning to thrash
> rice, & to find at least as many in number of my cattle, sheep, & Hogs as I
> left, & that I shall be provided with proper rewards for such of them as have
> behaved well.[30]

The ambiguous social meanings attached to the concept of "reward" allowed the term to occupy a middle ground between the condescending gift (and ensuing debt of gratitude) of patriarchy, and the impersonal and transitory cash nexus of market relations. From the master's point of view, a reward was freely given and could not be demanded as a right. For slaves, on the other hand, the significant aspect of the reward was that it was never unrequited. Rewards were something that was "earned." For these reasons, both masters and slaves might therefore have found the concept of "rewards" a useful and acceptable compromise.

The rituals through which the masters provided their slaves with their necessities provides another example of this ongoing interpretive "tug-of-war" between masters and slaves. Food, clothes and other supplies were, of course, necessary to the sustenance of the slaves and thus to the profitable function of the plantation. Yet slaveholders commonly distributed these basics as part of a ceremony where they demanded that their slaves express their gratitude for their master's bounty.

Slaves, as we have seen, perceived the receipt of provisions as part of an exchange of goods for labor in which no ongoing obligation was created or gratitude required. But while they may have seen behind the patriarchal curtain and known only too well that the goods the master so "graciously" provided had been bought with their labor, slaves also knew that to refuse to play their role in the ritual and to humiliate the master publicly moved relations onto a far more confrontational (and dangerous) plain. Therefore, slaves were usually content to take the blankets and the bacon they needed (and had earned) and let the master have the symbolic obeisance that he demanded. In the public ritual at least, slaves bought their sustenance not with their labor, but with their "gratitude." In 1759, for instance, one plantation agent wrote his employer "that your Negroes were all well pleased to receive their cloathes & desired me to thank you for the same."[31]

Another favorite method employed by masters when they provided their slaves with basic necessities was to wait to distribute them until times when a high degree of resistance to the masters' commands could be anticipated. In 1768, for example, Laurens sought to transfer some of his slaves from South Carolina to one of his new plantations in Georgia. He informed his Georgia overseer that to prevent the chosen slaves from running away, "I have been obliged to keep them constantly on board my schooner . . . [and] I have also given a few cloaths amongst the whole to encourage them to go away chearfully as well as because such was necessary to them."[32] According to the planters' patriarchal alchemy, necessities were transformed into gifts which then imposed a debt of gratitude that slaves were then expected to repay with "love" in the form of labor.

Slaveholders hoped that their slaves would internalize a sense of their obligations and dependency and to conduct relations entirely within patriarchal metaphors, but interest and emotion, like economic profit and social reputation, were so closely intertwined in the words and minds of slaveholders themselves that such a slave is hard to imagine. In a letter to one of his overseers, for example, Laurens wrote: "I send old Stepney to s[t]ay three or four Weeks to assist in turning and watching the new Indigo. He is very honest & if you will speak to him he will not allow anybody within his sight to rob you. . . . [G]ive him a dram & a Little Toddy every day but not too much."[33] Apparently, even the obedience of an "honest" slave could not be secured without "speak[ing] to him" to create a personal tie, and some appeal to self-interest by offering a material reward. Accordingly, personal calculations were a fundamental part of the slave system and of a language that equated love with labor and coercion with correction.[34] In practice, most masters regularly appealed to their slaves' self-interest in order to secure their compliance.

Slaveholders played a complicated double game. They were active members of a commercial, market-centered world. Success in this world was the very purpose of their plantation endeavors. At the same time, however, they sought to expropriate labor through a social system whose essence refuted the basic principles of market relations. To maintain their patriarchal dominion on the plantations, slaveholders had to be able to deny, at last resort, the economic independence of their slaves and to interpret their relations in terms of immutable roles, duties, and obligations.

The struggle of slaves to control their own lives and labor and the desire of masters to maximize profit meant that patriarchy could never be perfect. Nonetheless, slaveholders' constant projection of an ideal of patriarchal authority, even if they conceded to the dictates of the market in practice, gave their claims to dominance a degree of coherence that may have induced slaves to negotiate within the dominant metaphor, thereby rendering an overt denial of their servitude more difficult.

When, however, the larger world market demanded that the master class suddenly treat their laborers as commodities, the arbitrary reality of their domination was exposed. The mask of patriarchal authority that masters sought to wear in their relations with their slaves was torn away every time a master sold a slave or broke up a slave family to satisfy creditors or heirs. The slaveholders' accumulative ends and commercial requirements demanded that slaves be readily convertible into "liquid capital" in the form of cash or credit, but such actions destroyed much of their credibility as the patriarchs of their plantations.

In the summer of 1764, the death of Laurens's brother-in-law, John Coming

Ball, compelled a division of a plantation of three thousand acres and nearly eighty slaves in which Laurens himself held a half interest.[35] Before the final settlement of the estate the following spring, Laurens informed the executor of a "design . . . to avoid that inconvenience & I will say inhumanity of separating & tearing assunder my Negroes' several families."[36] Apparently, Laurens wrote that he would agree to purchase the other half of the estate's slaves or "to part with the whole in preference to an act which has always shocked me too much to submit to it."

Despite this offer, Laurens found that in the settlement of the estate "no less than seven or eight families & some of them my best Negroes will be torn to pieces." On a practical level, Laurens worried that a failure "to keep the families together" would "probably cause great disruption amongst the whole" of the slaves and "embarrass my plantation." Privately, the compulsion to deny the patriarchal responsibilities he used to justify his own authority made him uneasy. "I don't know anything," he wrote:

> . . . that could have been contrived to distress me . . . more than this unnecessary division of Fathers, Mothers, Husbands, Wives, & Children who tho slaves are still human Creatures & I cannot be deaf to their cries least a time should come when I should cry & there shall be none to pity me.[37]

Laurens's fear that the break up of the Wambaw families would "cause great disruption" among the remainder of his slaves and "embarrass" his plantation reveals another reason beyond the demands of patriarchy and compassion that moved slaveholders to recognize slaves' family ties. Runaway advertisements indicate what slaveholders who put their slaves on the market could anticipate. For instance, one slave family "Boston, his wife Sue, and child Sib," ran away "immediately" after they were sold at auction in October 1773 and were still at large six months later.[38] Similarly, nine slaves of Thomas Gaillard who "were mortgaged to Mrs. Stoutenburgh, ran off in the spring of 1761 after they heard they were to be "exposed to open and public vendue in order to discharge the said mortgage."[39] An analysis of published runaway notices reveals that recent sale or the threat of it was mentioned as a motivating factor in over forty percent of all advertisements placed between 1740 and 1759.[40]

If such notices provide examples of slaves who sought to preserve their family ties against the pressures of the market, other advertisements report slaves who were motivated to run away through a desire to re-establish family ties that had already been sundered through sale or the division of estates. "Paul, a tall likely black Barbados born fellow, about 40 years of age" became a fugitive in 1752; his master "supposed . . . [he would] be harbored either at Mrs. Bennet's, where he hath a wife, or at Henry Middleton, Esq.'s Savannah plantation, where his mother and sister are."[41] Eight years later, another slaveholder wrote that an escaped slave, whom he had purchased from the estate of Sir Alexander Nisbet, "may be harbored by SOMERSET her father."[42] Likewise, when Richard Wade's slave, Phillis, ran off in 1775, he "supposed [her] to be gone . . . to her husband" at the plantation of "Thomas Adams of Wasmesaw," where Wade had "lately" acquired her.[43] Slaves' engagement in such acts of *petit marronage* in an effort to re-establish family or other affective ties within the slave community seems to have been the rule rather than the exception in New World slave societies.[44] Over seventy percent of South Carolina runaways in the years 1760 to 1790 were thought by their owners to be "'visiting' either friends, acquaintances, or relatives."[45]

While such evidence speaks eloquently of the value slaves placed on maintaining some semblance of familial ties amidst slavery, it also indicates the extent to which the threat of being "torn to pieces" hung over all personal relationships in the slave quarters. If all slave families had been respected according to the dictates of the patriarchal metaphor, slaves would have had no need to run away to visit their loved ones. Slavery possessed a dual and contrary character in a society where slaveholders were both merchant capitalists and plantation patriarchs. As "Subjects," slaves were supposedly under the "protection" of the slaveholder as patriarchal master; as property, they were always threatened with sale at the hands of the slaveholder as a profit-seeking or debt-creating economic individual.

Each individual decision to run away to visit a relative or to prevent being separated from relations through sale was a personal, self-interested act, but it also contributed to a larger "resistance" against the slave society. In "visiting" loved ones, each individual slave was probably responding to private motives. However, when hundreds of such individual acts were compounded, the net effect created a distinct message and had a significant impact. James Scott has noted that when such acts are "rare and isolated they are of little interest; but when they become a persistent pattern (even though uncoordinated, let alone unorganized) we are dealing with resistance." Scott concludes that, although such "forms of resistance will win no set piece battles[,] . . . [they] are admirably adopted to long-run campaigns of attrition."[46]

By running away to visit relations or to protect their families and thereby withdrawing their labor, or by acting in other ways to "embarrass" or disrupt the orderly function of the plantation and thereby reducing productivity, slaves exacted an economic cost upon owners who violated family ties and who reneged upon the promises of patriarchy. If the preservation of patriarchy had its price, slaves ensured that the violation of patriarchy also imposed penalties. In the long run, many slaveholders came to feel that it was incumbent upon a "good" master to preserve the families of his slaves except in case of death or dire economic necessity.

Slaves may have won some gains in the long-term "campaign of attrition" of *petit marronage* through which they asserted their right to a stable family life just as they won the "right" to the produce of their private gardens through a similar imperceptible process of negotiation. Through their individual acts of resistance, slaves gradually altered the "moral economy" of the plantations and won more room for the protection of slave families. Between 1740 and 1775, the number of inventoried estates whose records recognized slave families by listing husbands with their wives or parents with their children increased from under seventeen to over forty-one percent.[47]

While these figures indicate the continued threat to all slave kinship ties, a trend toward a greater respect of slave family life is apparent. The slaves' families were not protected. For the slaveholders to have respected slave families in all situations would have contradicted the economic rationale that saw slaves as commodities as well as persons. Nevertheless, the prospects for slave families would have been far worse if the slaves had done nothing to assert their right to family life. When slaves threatened to withdraw their labor if their kinship ties were violated, they made patriarchy economically prudent for their masters.

If the prospect of a less rebellious and therefore more profitable work force was an important consideration in planters' respect for slave families, the desire of planter to act the part of the patriarchal ideal was another factor. Although in theory irreconcilable, in practice the profit motive and the "patriarchal motive" could be reconciled through the slaveholders' willingness to accept a somewhat reduced economic gain in return for respecting his "duty" to his slaves. In 1768, for instance, an advertisement for the sale of a plantation and its thirty-four slaves included a postscript in which the owner wrote that "if any person inclines to purchase the above settlement and the negroes together, . . . out of compassion to the slaves, I will sell . . . [at] a great bargain, and will give [the buyer] a small flock of cattle, sheep and hogs, and two or three hundred bushels of corn."[48] Presumably the "bargain" was not such that the owner was willing to forego all considerations of profit. Moreover, the advertisement implied that, although the owner preferred to sell "the negroes together," he was willing to sell them individually if no offers for the entire lot were forthcoming. By responding to the dictates of their pocketbooks as well as to those of patriarchy, slaveholders were able to reconcile patriarchy with profit. Laurens's ability to depict himself as an "absolute Monarch" and benevolent patriarch and yet boast that "no man gets more work from his Negroes than I do" exemplifies this conflation. In practice, if not in theory, patriarchy had its price.

Slaves themselves sometimes played an active part in the bargaining process through which patriarchal responsibilities were reduced to cash terms. In 1775, Levinus Clarkson "let . . . his house, [and] sold his furniture" and slaves in Charleston and moved to New York. He "could have got . . . more" for "Dina & [her] Children," he wrote, "But she chose her Master who could give me no more." Clarkson claimed that when, despite "all that I could do or say," Dina persisted in her choice, he consented to accept less for his slave than she was worth "as there we are all pleased."[49]

That slaves chose to negotiate within the metaphors of patriarchy did not mean that they had internalized the metaphor's depiction of master-slave relations. Slaves were capable of seeing the reality of their exploitation behind the curtain of patriarchy. Their ability to interpret actions through a market-based metaphor illustrates that they were aware of alternative points of view. Slaves confronted several possible choices of action in any given situation. The choices they made were shaped by their perception of what was possible and what was most likely to achieve their short-term goals in each instance.

Slaveholders were never free simply to impose their own interpretations of events, that is their metaphoric construction of social reality, upon a passive slave population. Masters contended with their slaves on the meanings to be found in certain social transactions and on the interpretations of the relationships among distinct social actors. In this struggle, neither side completely had its way. Masters tacitly conceded that the provisions and clothes supplied to their slaves were not "gifts" but "rewards." Such recognition gave up the social indebtedness and obligations implied by an unrequited gift. Likewise, although slaves may have thought that these items were theirs by customary "right," or earned through their work in the fields, they still touched their hats and thanked their master when claiming what was their "due."

Ideally, economic motivations and market relations had no place in the patriarchal relationship that was supposed to exist between masters and slaves. In practice however, patriarchal and market metaphors co-existed in the minds of both slaveholders and slaves. The side a particular party took and accorded priority to in a given situation depended upon the issues at stake and the relative strength of the contestants.

In the contest over the slaves' participation in the "domestic economy" and in the masters' provision of food and clothes, slaves usually sought to project a market-based metaphor onto events, and masters generally championed a more patriarchal interpretation. Slaves sought to reject the patriarchal metaphor with its ethos of dependency, deference, and reciprocal obligation and chose to depict the masters' provision of goods as a *quid pro quo* exchange for their labor in the plantation fields in which no lasting dependency was created or implied. In the case of slave families, however, slaves called upon their masters to live up to their patriarchal pretensions and to protect slave families under their "rule" from the threat posed by the market.

Slaveholders continued to hope that their slaves would play the part of dutiful subordinates who recognized the obligations of their station, but in practice master-slave interactions tended to move toward a market-based metaphor in which the exchange was understood as one of goods for labor. Such a development negated, or at least bypassed, the question of the slaves' "natural" dependency.

In 1771, as he set out for England, Laurens described his relationship with his slaves in a mode unlike either of those expressed at the start of this essay:

> . . . Such Negroes as behave well in my absence, I shall remember with gratitude. Those who behave ill, I shall only lose money by. And there's an end of that matter, until they and I come to a reckoning of accounts. And perhaps a consciousness of their error, or some other means may prompt or oblige them to make up all deficiencies.[50]

The vocabulary of the counting house, of "little differences of accounts and reckonings," which Laurens carefully avoided in his idealized depiction of himself in 1785, surfaced here. Yet, the passage is not couched entirely in market metaphors. If patriarchy had no place for a "reckoning of accounts" between master and slaves, neither did market relations allow for the existence of "gratitude" and "obligation." Although in theory the two concepts were implacably opposed, in practice, Laurens—and his slaves—negotiated and reconciled the conflicting demands of patriarchy and the market. If Laurens was motivated by the desire to exercise a profitable control of his plantations, his slaves likewise sought to gain a measure of control over their daily lives.

~

NOTES

1. This description of Laurens is taken from Egerton Leigh, "The Man Unmasked," (Charleston, 1769), printed in Philip M. Hamer, George C. Rogers, and David R. Chesnutt, *et al.*, eds., *The Papers of Henry Laurens*, (12 vols. to date, Columbia, 1968–), [hereafter cited as *PHL*], 6, 457.
2. Laurens to Alexander Hamilton, 19 April 1785, in Harold C. Syrett, *et al*, eds., *The Papers of Alexander Hamilton*, (27 vols.; New York, 1961–87), 3, 605–8.
3. An interesting examination of Laurens as a "patriarch" can be found in Philip D. Morgan, "Three Planters and Their Slaves: Perspectives on Slavery in Virginia, South Carolina, and Jamaica, 1750–1790," in *Race and Family in the Colonial South*,

eds. Winthrop Jordan and Sheila Skemp (Jackson: University Press of Mississippi, 1987), 54–68.

4. Laurens to Abraham Schad, 30 April 1765, *PHL*, 4, 616.

5. See, for example, Elizabeth Fox-Genovese and Eugene D. Genovese, *Fruits of Merchant Capital: Slavery and Bourgeois Property in the Rise and Expansion of Capitalism*, (New York: Oxford University Press, 1983).

6. See McDonnell's review of James Oakes, *Slavery and Freedom: An Interpretation of the Old South*, (New York: A. Knopf, 1990), in the *Journal of Southern History*, 58, (August 1992): 522–3.

7. For a recent overview of this subject see Ira Berlin and Philip D. Morgan, eds., *Cultivation and Culture: Labor and The Shaping of Slave Life in the Americas*, (Charlottesville: University Press of Virginia, 1993). Slaves' property holding is also treated in the essays by John Campbell and Larry E. Hudson Jr., contained in this volume.

8. The phrase "peasant breach in the slave mode of production" is from Tadeusz Lepkowski, *Haiti*, (Havana: CASA, 1968), 59–60. See also Sidney Mintz, *Caribbean Transformations*, (Chicago: Aldine Publishing Co., 1974), 146–56, 180–213. Alternate points of view can be found in Eugene D. Genovese, *Roll, Jordan, Roll: The World the Slaves Made*, (New York: Pantheon, 1976), 535–40; and also Norrece T. Jones Jr., *Born a Child of Freedom, Yet a Slave: Mechanisms of Control and Strategies of Resistance in Ante-Bellum South Carolina*, (Middleton, Conn: Wesleyan University Press, 1990), 104.

9. The argument sketched out in this essay is treated at much greater length in chapters four and five of my dissertation: "Authority and Resistance: Social Order in a Colonial Slave Society, The South Carolina Lowcountry, 1739–1782," (The Johns Hopkins University, 1991).

10. The quote is taken from Peter A. Coclanis, *Shadow of a Dream: Economic Life and Death in the South Carolina Low Country, 1670–1920*, (New York: Oxford University Press, 1989), 60.

11. Laurens to Lachlan McIntosh, 13 March 1773, *PHL*, 8, 618.

12. Laurens to George Appleby, 28 February 1774, *PHL*, 9, 316–7.

13. Laurens to Peter Horlbeck, 15 May 1765, *PHL*, 4, 624.

14. Laurens to John Smith, 29 January 1766, *PHL*, 5, 57.

15. Laurens to Abraham Schad, 31 March 1766, *PHL*, 5, 93.

16. Account book of Henry Laurens, 1766–73, College of Charleston Library, 217.

17. Laurens to Abraham Schad, 7 October 1765, *PHL*, 5, 20.

18. Laurens to Frederick Wiggins, 30 November 1765, *PHL*, 5, 41.

19. Laurens to John Smith, 5 September 1765, *PHL*, 5, 2–3. The struggle between Laurens and his slave boatman Abraham appears in his letters several times throughout this year. On August 15, Laurens wrote, "Abraham made out only 22 cords of wood which he was pleas'd to sell without any orders & therefore I have the greatest reason to suspect him of knavery;" *ibid.*, 4, 661–2. Again on October 1, "You complain of negroes stealing your Potatoes & Corn. Be more careful of the Boat Negroes than usual & if you were to make a search when the Boat was loaded

every now & then it would answer a good purpose. Don't fail to chastize the first one that transgresses & particularly Captain Abraham;" *ibid.*, 4, 11.

20. Laurens to Abraham Schad, 30 April 1765, *PHL*, 4, 616.

21. *South Carolina Gazette*, (Charleston), November 5, 1744.

22. Plantation records are replete with examples of masters' using rum as an emblem of their patriarchal authority. For instance Josiah Smith, a plantation manager, wrote to his employer, George Austin, on July 22, 1774: "Although the grass was very bad in all your fields, none of your people had run from it, they being kept to their work by mere dint of encouragement of a beef & some rum, added to lenient treatment by the overseer," Josiah Smith Jr., Letterbook, Southern Historical Collection, University of North Carolina, Chapel Hill.

23. For examples of slaves being provided with rum and sugar to commemorate births and deaths, see Charles Pinckney Account Book, 1753–57, Pinckney Family Papers, Library of Congress, Washington; and also Plantation Book (1773), William Wragg Papers, South Carolina Historical Society, Charleston. For an example of slaves being given "a hog or two to entertain the company" at a wedding, see James Barclay, *The Voyages and Travels of James Barclay*, (London, 1777), 27.

24. Charles Joyner, *Down by the Riverside: A South Carolina Slave Community*, (Urbana: University of Illinois Press, 1982), 56.

25. George Fenwick Jones, trans., "John Martin Boltzius's Trip to Charleston, October 1742," *South Carolina Historical Magazine*, 8, (April 1981): 104.

26. Frederick Douglass, "The Slaves' Right to Steal," excerpted from *My Bondage, and My Freedom*, in *Frederick Douglass: The Narrative and Selected Writings*, ed. Michael Meyer (New York: Random House, 1984), 137. For an interesting discussion of these issues see Alex Lichtenstein, " 'That Disposition to Theft, With Which They Have Been Branded': Moral Economy, Slave Management, and the Law," *Journal of Social History*, 21, (Spring 1988).

27. Thomas Jefferson, *Notes On the State of Virginia*, William Penden, ed., (Chapel Hill: University of North Carolina Press, 1954), 142.

28. The anonymous author "Scotus Americanus," is quoted in William K. Boyd, ed., "Some North Carolina Tracts of the Eighteenth Century," *North Carolina Historical Review*, 3, (Oct. 1926), 616.

29. *South Carolina and American General Gazette*, 2 April 1778.

30. Laurens to Peter Nephew, 20 December 1771, *PHL*, 8, 111, (first quote). Laurens to John McCullough, 2 February 1774, *PHL*, 9, 262, (second quote).

31. Robert Raper to John Colleton, 6 December 1759, Robert Raper Letterbook, West Sussex County Record Office, Chichester, U.K..

32. Laurens to William Stork, 28 January 1768, *PHL*, 5, 573.

33. Laurens concluded the letter by saying that as "The Old Man Stepney does not seem very willing to be from home . . . you must send him down" as soon as he can be spared; Laurens to John Smith, 15 August 1765, *PHL*, 4, 661–2.

34. In 1765, Laurens instructed a new overseer on how to deal with his slaves:

[U]se gentle means mixed with easy authority first. If that does not succeed make choice of the most stubborn one or two & chastize them severely but properly & with mercy that they may be convinced that the end of correction is to be amendment.

Laurens to John Smith, 30 May 1765, *PHL*, 4, 633.

35. Laurens purchased a half interest in Wambaw plantation in the parish of St. James Santee, northwest of Charleston, from John Coming Ball, in May 1756, for about £400. This was Laurens's first plantation venture. Ball continued to manage the estate until his death in August 1764. In an account book of 1766, Laurens notes that there were seventy nine slaves on Wambaw at that time, *PHL*, 2, 180 and note; 6, 610. For another perspective on this affair, see Cheryll Ann Cody's essay in this volume.

36. Laurens to Elias Ball, 1 April 1765, *PHL*, 4, 595. All the following references to this incident are taken from this letter.

37. The division of John Coming Ball's estate was clouded by an earlier dispute over the estate of Laurens's father-in-law. Laurens felt that his wife was denied her share of the inheritance on that occasion and now believed that he "had a right to expect some little indulgence in the division of the Wambaw Negroes and effects." Thus, Laurens's offer to purchase the other half of the Wambaw slaves may have been pitched at a price somewhat below market value. He may even have argued that he (or his wife) should inherit *all* of the slaves. In any case, the executor of the estate told Laurens that his "proposal concerning the Negroes at Wambaw is not at all liked of by the other part concerned."

It might be argued that Laurens's laments for his slaves' families were "crocodile tears." Had he really wanted to protect his slave families he certainly had the financial wherewithal to do so. This, however, ignores Laurens's other "obligations" to his wife, and to himself as a reputable and independent person, which, he thought, required concessions from his relations. Laurens's dilemma was caused by his inability to reconcile his desire to be a patriarch to his slaves, and to be treated with respect by his peers. Forced to choose, he preferred to shed his slaves rather than his pride.

38. *South Carolina Gazette*, 16 April 1754, in Lathan A. Windley, comp., *Runaway Slave Advertisements: A Documentary History from the 1730s to 1790*, 4 Vols. (Westport, Conn.: Greenwood Press, 1983), 3, 127.

39. *South Carolina Gazette*, 4 July 1761. From their names the runaways appear to have consisted of seven men (or boys) and two women (or girls). One of the men, "Cochoose," was still at large the following October, *South Carolina Gazette*, 24 October 1761.

40. This figure was deduced from an analysis of all runaway advertisements for this period as contained in Windley, ed., *Runaway Slave Advertisements*, 3. The total number of runaways (excluding the 49 described as "new negroes") advertised for between 1740–59 is 778. Of this number 319 (or 41 percent), were described by one of the following terms (with numbers): "formerly belonged to" (172); "for-

merly belonged to . . . deceased" (54); "lately belonged to" (41); "lately belonged to . . . deceased" (16); "formerly belonged to the estate of" (10); "to be sold" (1); or were otherwise described as recently sold or bought (25). I assume that all runaways described by these terms had been recently sold or were faced with imminent sale.

41. *South Carolina Gazette*, August 10, 1752, in, Windley, ed., *Runaway Slave Advertisements.*, 3, 113.

42. *South Carolina Gazette*, February 9, 1760, in *ibid.*, 3, 180.

43. *South Carolina and American General Gazette*, May 12, 1775, in *ibid.*, 3, 471.

44. Richard Price has written, "throughout the Americas, planters seem to have accepted as part of the system the common practice of *petit marronage*–repetitive or periodic truancy with temporary goals such as visiting a relative or lover on a neighboring plantation." Richard Price, ed., *Maroon Societies: Rebel Slave Communities in the Americas*, (Baltimore: Johns Hopkins University Press, 1979), 3.

45. Philip D. Morgan, "Black Society in the Lowcountry, 1760–1810," in *Slavery and Freedom in the Age of the American Revolution*, eds. Ira Berlin and Ronald Hoffman (Charlottesville: University Press of Virginia, 1983), 128–9 and 130 (table 18).

46. James Scott, "Everyday Forms of Peasant Resistance,"*Journal of Peasant Studies*, 13, (Jan. 1986): 26–7.

47. The actual figures are 16.8 and 41.3; Philip D. Morgan, "The Evolution of Slave Culture in 18th-century Plantation America," (Unpublished Ph. D. diss., University of London, 1977), 315, table 4.9. Since these figures include only those inventories which clearly recognized slave families, the percentage above must be treated as indicating only the lowest possible estimate of the true figures. Nonetheless the upward trend is significant.

48. *South Carolina Gazette and Country Journal*, (Charleston), 8 March 1768. Similarly, the *South Carolina Gazette*, 28 April 1767, contained the following advertisement:

> . . . a healthy, likely, Negro wench, born in Charlestown, about 15 years old . . .
> [who was] very unwilling to leave this province being strongly attached to her
> mother and family, the owner would gladly exchange her for a Negro boy, that
> would make no objection to his residence in any other part of the continent; both
> to be valued and the over cash to be paid down on either side.

49. Levinus Clarkson to Anonymous, June 1775, Levinus Clarkson Papers, Library of Congress, Washington, 129–31.

50. Laurens to James Laurens, 5 December 1771, *PHL*, 8, 66–7.

~

"MY CONSTANT COMPANION"
Slaves and their Dogs in the Antebellum South

John Campbell

In 1859, after a decade of numerous editorials, endless discussion, and widespread petitioning to legislative leaders, the South Carolina General Assembly passed a law that would save slaveholders and the state from a growing menace. The target? Not abolitionists, nor cheating Charleston cotton factors, nor even unscrupulous Yankee or British merchants, but dogs, especially those owned by slaves. For during the last fifteen or so years of the slavery era, many slaveowners and their allies waged war against these animals, believing them to be the source of various ills plaguing their lives and state. "Every 'Nigger' must have his 'possum dog," complained "Vive La Moton" in 1855, which makes him a "strolling, pilfering, scamp."[1] "A man should not let his negroes have dogs," argued a slaveholder in 1858; "better [to] give him a gun or sword."[2] Indeed, dogs do "greater injury to the people of South Carolina than all of the abolitionists in the world," concluded one frustrated Carolinian.[3]

While it is tempting to dismiss such a claim as nothing more than good old-fashioned antebellum political rhetoric, we would be remiss in ignoring the underlying concerns that prompted such a comparison in the first place. For despite their colorful, if not comical, rhetoric, slaveowners in South Carolina, as elsewhere, viewed the subject of slaves' dogs with deadly seriousness; during the last years of slavery, these animals were viewed and vilified increasingly for their irksome, often disruptive, and sometimes subversive presence in the rural South. Indeed, as an object of growing slaveowner

53

antipathy, dogs became an important medium through which the ongoing struggles between masters and slaves were enacted, manifested, and perpetuated. Yet despite the many impressive historical studies of slave life and master-slave relations, we know next to nothing about the role of slave dogs in the slave community, let alone the ways they spawned, shaped, and, reflected master-slave conflicts. By examining the role of slave dogs in the lives of both their slave masters and their masters' masters, we shed new light on these conflicts as well as on slaves' ongoing struggles to achieve a modicum of dignity, autonomy, and, control over their lives.[4]

Slaves lived in a world teeming with dogs. No self-respecting farmer or planter went without them, for these creatures served a number of important purposes in the lives of white people. At the bottom rung, serving as a common denominator among most rural white folk, was the common 'coon dog. While these animals were intended first as all-purpose hunting companions, helping their masters track raccoon and other game, they easily filled other roles, such as protecting the family and farmstead, and providing the companionship expected of "man's best friend." Indeed, the eagerness to have such a canine jack-of-all-trades got one man in trouble with his church. In 1804 Big Creek Baptist Church of Anderson District, South Carolina chastised Adam Williamson for bringing home "a stray hound dog" that was clearly not his own.[5]

For wealthier families, the plantation could easily become a veritable kennel, with each animal performing one of the many different functions assigned to dogs. Amongst the many breeds or types one might conceivably find on these larger estates were: multiple braces of hunting dogs, with certain ones trained and used to hunt specific animals, such as raccoon, fox, deer, bear, and gamebirds; dogs deployed in herding livestock, such as sheep and cattle; packs of bloodhounds trained to track and catch runaway slaves; a "bull-dog" or two to protect the white family and its property; and, by the late antebellum years, the pet lap dog, a distinctly non-utilitarian type that provided companionship for plantation ladies much as hunting dogs did for the white men of the family.[6] Not leaving anything to chance, the most canine-conscious of slaveholding families might have possessed a specially trained rat killer, like those which Mr. Walter John Dobbins prominently displayed at the Fourth Annual Fair of the South-Carolina Institute in 1852.[7]

All of these different types, breeds, and purposes insured that the rural South was well stocked with dogs. Indeed, excessively so, thought one critic, who concluded that "a dog mania" was pervading the land.[8] To support such claims, various individuals offered their own estimates of the size of the canine population—state and federal census takers having failed to gather these data. On the low side, some pundits assumed that there was, on average, one dog per family which meant, for example, that there were well over 50,000 dogs roaming the state of South Carolina during the 1850's. Yet the calculations of other observers—who assumed 4 or 5 dogs per family—suggest that the canine population of South Carolina was far higher, as much as 200,000 to 250,000.[9] Whatever the actual number, the central message conveyed by these dog demographers was that South Carolina, like her sister Southern states, was fast becoming a canine menagerie; there were more than enough dogs available to keep the white folks happy, and then some. As long as individual masters allowed their human chattel to have dogs, it would be relatively easy for slaves to acquire them.

Ironically, it was the very abundance of these dogs and their central role in plantation life that may have made slaves less than eager to have their own. In general, slaves abhorred dogs of the master class: they despised the "useless" lap dogs which they (particularly female domestics working in the Big House) had to coddle or pamper in a way more fitting a child-king; they hated the various guard dogs who protected slaveowner and plantation property; and, most importantly, they feared the dreaded bloodhounds who tracked, chased, caught, and often tore apart runaways.[10] So great and profound were their negative experiences with these dogs, that slaves collectively used their "Brer Rabbit" trickster tales to seek fictive vengeance against these odious, ostensibly domesticated animals; as a result, no other creature in the folk tales was treated with the contempt shown the hapless, mockingly-named "Mr."—and not "Brer"—Dog, the character slaves created to represent dogs of the ruling race.[11] In other words, the quotidian, ever-replicating experiences of bondage increased the odds that slaves would become so anti-dog as to abjure possession of their own.

That this did not happen can perhaps be chalked up to slaves' ethnic heritages and the concrete benefits of having dogs. On the one hand, slaves may have valued and desired their own simply because they, as *African* Americans, may have inherited and possessed an alternative model of dog-human interaction which presented these animals in a relatively favorable light. The Beng, a people of West Africa, for example, "resonated . . . strongly" with the dog. Both a mythological being (Dog), who appears prominently in Beng identity myths, and as an "ally" in humans' daily affairs, who offers protection and hunting assistance, the dog played a pivotal, generally positive role in the life and culture of this ethnic group. With this kind of pro-canine cultural heritage, American slave descendants of people such as the Beng would have quite likely desired their own dogs, despite their generally unpleasant experiences with those of the master. Yet even without such a legacy, slaves may have still wanted dogs for much the same reasons that white people did: they offered companionship, protection, and help in hunting.[12]

Whatever the exact mix of motives behind slave desires for their own dogs, there is little doubt that they acquired and made them an integral part of their lives. Having these animals benefitted slaves in three broad ways. With dogs, they were better able: to challenge and partially overcome the ever-present dehumanizing nature and consequences of slavery; to protect themselves from white people and other dangerous creatures; and to augment their meager subsistence allowance, thereby improving the material conditions of their lives. As a result of these capabilities, slaves exercised greater control over their lives, strengthened the slave community, and, ultimately, challenged the interests of slaveowners. In short, the possession of dogs empowered slaves, making it easier for them to endure, if not weaken, the myriad assaults of slavery.

The very fact of having a dog represented a vital assertion and demonstration of slave humanity in defiance of what slaveholder law and daily practice proclaimed to the contrary. Viewed ever in law as a piece of property and only slightly less so in reality, it was impossible, if not illogical, for black slaves to own their own property: for how could chattel own property? how can one object be said to own another? Indeed, it could not; instead, whatever property slaves might appear to own was legally the property of the master.[13] Within the logic of this system, where property ownership was equated with freedom and being completely human, and the lack of property with slavery and being less-than-human chattel, the *de facto* control and acquisition of property became one crucial means by which slaves declared their humanness and insisted that they be treated accordingly. By having a dog, slaves possessed what was–according to the slaveholders' own beliefs, logic, and laws–the very best proof of their being fully human. Through their daily, ongoing control of this property, slaves possessed a firm reminder that–contrary to what slaveowners relentlessly conveyed to them–they were in fact human, and to see themselves thus was perhaps one of the most fundamental acts of resistance that slaves engaged in from day to day.

On a more concrete level, having a dog also helped offset the sharp loneliness and social deracination that many slaves encountered in their daily lives. Unlike white people who enjoyed the companionship of dogs as one of freedom's many quaint, if dispensable, frills, slaves all too often had little choice but to seek their only meaningful companionship in the company of a dog. For as part of the steady diet of dehumanization fed to their chattel, slaveowners split up families or entire slave communities with cruel regularity. Slaves who were thus separated or who otherwise experienced social isolation as part of slavery's horrific logic might find some solace in the friendship of a dog. This was probably the case for the slave Charles Ball; in being sold from South Carolina to Georgia, Ball took his dog, Trueman, with him, thereby alleviating some of the pain of being separated from friends and family.[14]

The importance of a dog's friendship was powerfully rendered by Harriet Wilson in *Our Nig*. In this novel, the first written by an African-American woman, the main character Frado, a nominally free black woman in late antebellum New England, lives as a young domestic amidst a house full of wretched white people. Treated as though she were a slave, Frado can only find solace, support, and love from her dog, Fido. At times "[s]he told him [Fido] her griefs as though he were human; and he sat so still, and listened so attentively, she really believed he knew her sorrows." At one point, her despair and loneliness becoming so great and all consuming, Frado turns plaintively to Fido and asks: "You love me, Fido, don't you?" [15] While certainly no substitute for human beings, a dog like Fido could, as Wilson suggests, certainly help slaves fill the emotional barrenness of their lives, thereby rekindling some sense of their humanity.

For slaves who were fortunate enough not to swallow a daily dosage of social and emotional isolation, the possession of dogs could enhance their sense of self-worth and personal identity amongst their peers. This was especially true for men; as former slaves made clear, it was men, and not women, who hunted with dogs and provided wild game for their families and the slave community. According to the South Carolina slave Peggy Grisby, "the men folks hunted much." Lila Rutherford, also from South Carolina, concurred, recalling that "the young men would hunt lots."[16] Through their hunting with dogs, men derived an element of respect, status, and importance within the slave community. This collective support and recognition in turn made it easier for men to blunt the dehumanizing assaults of slavery and sustain their sense of self worth. For where legal dictum and slaveholder action constantly worked to weaken men's place within the community, most infamously through the frequent separation of husbands and fathers from wives, children, and other kin, the community-sanctioned and -created role of hunting served to shore-up and strengthen men's personal identity and sense of belonging. All the more so when older male slaves instructed younger ones in the arts and mysteries of hunting. Not having this customary, intergenerational experience could be especially painful, as the former slave, John Glover, might attest. Even in the 1930s, when interviewed, the now-elderly Glover still harbored, many decades later, the disappointment of not being tutored by his Uncle Ben, a great 'possum hunter, who had died before John was old enough to start hunting.[17] For Glover and no doubt other male slaves, the process of learning how to hunt under the aegis of a male relative became a rite of passage signalling their arrival into young adulthood and manhood. Where the very existence of this rite–as with the role of hunter itself–was further evidence of the community's interest in claiming and integrating men into its bosom, learning under a male relative's direction heightened the young man's sense of self-identity, investing his knowledge of who he was with a healthy awareness of where he came from.[18]

Hunting with dogs also enriched the lives of male slaves by making living itself more than a painful sentence or something to be endured from day to day. As the bitter and sarcastic Allen Parker recalled, this activity provided some of the very few "pleasures and enjoyments" of his days in slavery.[19] In hunting on their own, as they typically did, without the stultifying presence of a white person, enslaved men enjoyed, if only for a few hours, a precious autonomy and control over their lives. The feeling and duration of independence could be heightened all the more depending on how far through the forests and beyond the plantation the tenacious dogs chased their intended prey.

This sense of independence no doubt helped make the camaraderie of men and dogs as special as it was. "It was grand sport to see five or six hounds in line on a trail and to hear the[ir] sweet music," recalled H. C. Bruce when describing the hunting experience of himself and other male slaves. I. E. Lowery was so enamored of his four-footed hunting companions and their "music" that he could distinguish the different "voices" of the dogs, as though each was "singing the four parts of music . . . soprano, alto, tenor, and bass."[20] Even citified slaves, such as the Charlestonian Sam Aleckson, grew to like certain aspects of the hunting experience. In spending time each summer on a rice plantation, Aleckson often accompanied his two chums, Joe and Hector, and their dog Spot; while he "did not enjoy the sport" of rabbit-hunting, since the "harmless little rabbit [would] not even defend himself when attacked," he very much "enjoy[ed]" the excitement of the "night hunts" for "coon and possum."[21] In short, hunting with a dog gave men, at the very least, a much welcomed break from the grim, predictable grind of the plantation and, more than likely, special joys that made their life as bondsmen somewhat more tolerable, if only for a few hours. With this kind of pleasure, it is understandable that former slaves such as H. C. Bruce viewed their hunting experiences as providing some of the "happiest" moments in their "boyhood days."[22]

Needless to say, slaves possessed a great affection for their dogs. Where utter loneliness no doubt inspired the love of many slaves who mirrored Frado's experience, it was the joy, camaraderie, and independence of the hunting experience that spawned deep affection on the part of slaves such as Allen Parker and H. C. Bruce. Verily, only someone already possessed of great fondness for dogs could have cared to differentiate the "musical" voices of each canine hunting companion, as did I. E. Lowery. Ironically, the depths of slave affection, and the anguish it could spawn, were revealed most poignantly when slaves ran away and left their dogs. In his autobiography, Charles Ball talked movingly and at great length about how difficult it was for him to run away and leave behind his "faithful" hunting dog, Trueman, his "constant companion" for more than four years. He wanted to bring Trueman with him but Ball understood that the success of running away depended on secrecy and silence; lest the dog bark and otherwise make harmful noise or movement, it was thus necessary for him to leave without the dog. Having made this painful decision Ball spent his last night with Trueman and, as a final act of his love, shared his last meal with him.[23]

In addition to helping slaves overcome slavery's dehumanization and taste some of the joys of being human, dogs helped protect slaves, whether at the quarters, in the woods, or even when running away. At nighttime, a growling or barking dog in the cabin might easily warn slaves of the presence of unwanted strangers, such as the nightly patrol searching for a slave out roaming about after dark.[24] Protection against dangerous animals was no less likely. Charles Ball recalled how, one day, while out cutting trees, the growl of his dog alerted him to the presence of a nearby panther, thereby enabling Ball to escape unharmed.[25] H. C. Bruce had a similar experience while living as a slave in Missouri. Once when out gathering hickory nuts, Bruce and his mates were threatened by wild hogs, "the most vicious" animal Bruce met or encountered as a slave. Only because they "heard their [dogs] barking" out a warning, were Bruce and the others able to scamper up trees, thereby avoiding serious injury from the hogs.[26] Most dramatically, a loyal dog could help a master who was running away from slavery. When James Smith, a former slave of Virginia, ran away, he originally tried to discourage his "faithful dog" from going with him but he "couldn't drive him back," and lucky for Smith. At one point, his dog bit two of the pursuing slave catchers; later, when Smith was captured but then escaped, his dog was there to greet him. Eventually, Smith was again confronted by the bloodhounds but this time, his dog engaged them in battle and, by momentarily diverting their attention, enabled Smith to kill two of them with his club. With this kind of vital assistance, Smith was able to make his way north to freedom.[27]

Finally, the possession of a dog helped slaves improve the day-to-day material conditions of their lives in two basic ways. First, despite the ornery, barking dogs used by slaveowners to guard plantation property, slaves' dogs helped their masters filch useful items from *their* master and other white people.[28] Dogs were not an incidental part of the theft, but were indispensable as slaves often planned to steal from the chicken coop or smokehouse only if they had a dog to "stand sentinel."[29] Perhaps more commonly, slaves also acquired food and clothing material when hunting with their dogs. When hunting, slaves took "one or more dogs . . . trained for" the purpose of catching raccoons; these dogs, according to Allen Parker, were "known as 'coon dogs."[30] While slaves sometimes caught squirrels and rabbits by trapping, the odds of acquiring these and other animals, particularly 'coons and 'possum, were much greater if they used dogs. As I. E. Lowery put it, dogs were "[t]he only things necessary to achieve a successful hunt." [31]

Dogs were "necessary" for a number of reasons. First, they set the hunt in motion once they rousted and began to chase the desired quarry. By remaining hot on the trail, the dogs would eventually corner the animal or "run [it] up the trees in the forest," at which point they remained barking uncontrollably, thereby discouraging the treed animal from climbing down, and alerting their masters to where they were. [32] Upon arriving on the scene, the slaves either shook the animal out of the tree or, if that failed, one would climb it and shake the branch where the animal was hiding, forcing it to fall headlong into the jaws and paws of the waiting dogs, who proceeded to kill it. While rabbits and squirrels gave up immediately and opossums played, well, 'possum, hoping their dead act would fool hunters and dogs and enabling them to crawl away, raccoons tested the mettle of even the fiercest dogs. As Isaac Williams put it: "it takes a good dog to kill a coon. It will fall on its back and scratch and bite to the last. No common dog, but a blood-hound has got the knack of catching him right by his breast to master him." [33] In short, much of slave success at hunting hinged critically on the fact that they hunted with dogs (even if "common" ones), who rousted, chased, treed, and killed the prey that slaves would eventually take back to the quarters.[34]

Yet to fully appreciate the significance of this dog-centered hunting strategy, one must compare it to the methods employed by slaveowners. Although white people also used dogs to roust and chase the prey, what made the use of dogs *more* central to slaves—and, thus, made their hunting technique and experience so culturally distinctive—was that slaves generally did not hunt with firearms but, instead, substituted dogs for guns. Where slaves and dogs worked together as a team (slaves coaxing the animal out of the tree, dogs killing it as it fell to the forest floor), white men, by contrast, minimized the messy business of tree climbing and the role of dogs by simply killing the prey with a gun.[35] Where slaves perfected the art of hunting exclusively with dogs, white people became proficient at gun-and-dog hunting. This distinction grew during the course of the nineteenth century as states passed laws discouraging and prohibiting slaves from using—not to mention, owning—guns for hunting.[36] Unlike Charles Ball, a slave during the first quarter of the century, who received "an old gun" from his master, which he then fixed up, slaves living in the 1840s and 1850s "were not allowed to have any" firearms, recalled Allen Parker.[37] Thus, when slaves sang "I wish I had a hundred dog/and half of them was hound/I'd take them into the foddar field/ and run the rabbit down" or "rabbit in de hollow/I ain' got no dog/How can I catch em?" they were not just voicing some kind of universal hunter's lament for a dog. Instead, they were expressing a historically specific, culturally distinctive need for—and appreciation of—dogs as hunting allies.[38] Without the dog to chase, corner, and kill the rabbit or other animal, black folk could only watch it hop, crawl, or scamper away, while whites could always go and gun it down on the spot.

Because of their contributions during the hunt, dogs made it far more possible for slaves to augment the meager food and clothing allowance given to them by the master. For some slaves, such as Thomas Goodwater of South Carolina, the food allowance was so scanty as to only consist of grains, and so hunting was the only way that they acquired meat.[39] For others, such as Solomon Northrup, the meat so obtained supplemented the bland, if regular, allowance of pork.[40] For both groups of slaves, having this animal meat not only improved their diets but offered the small pleasure of variety in what they ate. Although most slaves were no doubt happy to eat any sort of wild game, disagreements existed as to whether opossum or raccoon was the more tasty. For Hagar Brown, a slave of the South Carolina rice coast, raccoon "was better than possum" because it "won't eat everything" that the apparently less discriminating opossum does.[41] Yet Isaac Williams felt otherwise, believing that 'coon was "stringy" where possum was not. Many other slaves also preferred 'possum which was, according to Hector Smith, "sweet eatin'." Peter Clifton concurred, believing that there was "nothing better than possum and yellow sweet potatoes;" and Louisa Davis put it succinctly: "possum was the best meat in slavery."[42] The ever diplomatic Rev. I. E. Lowery, however, thought both were equally "savory and palatable." [43]

Whatever one's druthers, the pleasures of eating were heightened all the more when the food was consumed collectively, as part of a special occasion within the slave community, such as a marriage celebration.[44] Indeed, it was precisely the grand festiveness of these meals that appealed most to some slaves, such as the Charleston native, Sam Aleckson, who cared little for either raccoon—"too fat"— or opossum—"[un]appealing habits"—but very much devoured the "stories told at these feasts!"[45] Finally, once the meat was no longer, slaves still had the fur of the hunted animal to sell or, most likely, use as a supplement to their skimpy cloth or clothing allowances.[46]

All in all, whether helping slaves overcome slavery's all-too-dehumanizing nature, protect their person, or promote their material interests, dogs played a vital, unjustly ignored, role in slave life. For a perhaps fitting example of how central dogs were in the lives of Southern slaves, we need only to turn to the experience of slaves living in Sumter District, South Carolina. Some African Americans in this prosperous cotton region apparently had a habit of taking their dogs to church with them, perhaps because they valued their companion-ship at all times, wanted canine protection during this journey, or hoped to do some impromptu hunting on the way. Regardless of why slaves brought them, white members of the Salem Presbyterian Church of Sumter District grew tired of seeing dogs during Sunday services. So in 1846, they passed a resolution stipulating that "No negro shall fetch a . . . Dog to the Church." [47]

Without minimizing the impact of this prohibition on the subsequent religious experience of these slaves, it is important to realize that the bark of exclusion was far worse than its bite. Rather than condemning on principle the entire practice of slave dog ownership, these upright Presbyterians limited their canine concerns to the narrow sphere of the church; like many other white people at the time, these followers of Calvin implicitly accepted or at least tolerated the custom of slaves having dogs. Indeed, the very presence of these animals on countless plantations implies slaveowner acceptance of them simply because it would have been very difficult, if not impossible, for slaves to keep dogs surreptitiously and without the master's permission. For unlike various types of contraband, such as guns, books, or flasks of liquor, the small size of which made it relatively easy for slaves to have and to hide from the disapprov-ing master, the size and personality of dogs made it pretty much impossible to keep one secretly and without the master's knowledge.

What benefits, if any, slaveowners expected to get by allowing these dogs on their plantations and in their slave quarters is less clear. Some certainly gave their permission as part of a consciously-crafted managerial policy from which they hoped to derive tangible, immediate, and concrete benefits. Among these were those who hoped to reduce the cost of provisioning slaves by encouraging or requiring slaves to use their dogs to hunt, acquire meat, and generally provide for their own food subsistence. Others appreciated less the financial savings on provisions and more the fact that when slaves hunted they uninten-tionally helped clear the masters' fields and bordering forests of raccoons and other scavengers, who might otherwise damage the master's crops.[48] Then there were those, such as W. J. Eve of Beech Island, South Carolina who thought it was "good" that "his negroe[s] . . . keep dogs" because they "chas[e] other dogs even to Augusta, [Georgia] & kill . . . them," thus keeping the plantation free of canine riff-raff.[49] Yet for most slaveowners, allowing slaves to have dogs was probably less a carefully plotted management decision tied to an intended benefit and more an indifferent, lazy acquiescence to social reality: that their slaves had somehow acquired dogs and it was easier and less troublesome to accept this fact of life than it was to banish the animals from the plantation. If they gave it any thought at all, these slaveowners probably tolerated the presence of these yapping, scavenging, biting curs as a small price to pay if it made slaves happier, more tractable, and more obedient workers.

Yet as with so many of the privileges accorded slaves by their masters, the existence and possession of these dogs created no end of trouble for white society. Indeed, so serious and pervasive were the problems that, during the last fifteen or so years of the slavery era, many white people engaged in a widespread and systematic campaign to reduce, if not eliminate altogether, the number of slave dogs in their midst. In combatting this growing canine menace, whites left a rich documentary trail of their efforts, especially in South Carolina, where they succeeded in having an anti-dog law passed in 1859. The litany of complaints and criticisms is so impressive as to suggest that, for slaveholders the slave/slave-dog combination was one of the most disruptive aspects of plantation life. No less an authority than James Henry Hammond, prominent slaveholder and U.S. Senator, clearly believed as much, declaring in 1858, that "a man should not let his negroes have dogs [—] better [to] give him [sic] a gun or Sword."[50]

Perhaps the most widely publicized problem associated with slave dogs were their attacks on sheep. Throughout the nineteenth century, slaveholders in the state of South Carolina, as elsewhere, complained bitterly about the costly attacks on farm livestock. In 1809, the Grand Jury of Abbeville District presented as a grievance, to the Legislature, the fact that sheep were too easily ravaged by dogs, including those of slaves, and requested that "Negroes be prohibited from owning them."[51] A few years later, in the midst of the War of 1812, residents of Sumter District had their minds on seemingly more mundane matters, as they too requested of the Legislature that "no slave or slaves" be allowed to "keep or carry any dog or dogs," believing that "depredations" against livestock were "considerably increased" due to this "ordinary practice."[52] According to "Weoka," "every planter" where he lives "allows the majority of his negroes to feed a crop-eared cur, which helps to kill not only his masters' but his neighbor's sheep and hogs." [53]

Where the killing of any livestock–whether cattle, swine, or sheep–increased the likelihood of slaveowners having to spend money buying meat for plantation consumption, the killing of sheep was viewed as especially grievous by late antebellum planters. For by the last twenty years of slavery, many slaveholders had embraced two key provisions of the agricultural reform movement of those years, plantation diversification and self-sufficiency, and saw sheep raising as one excellent way of achieving these goals. With sheep, slaveowners not only had a valuable meat, which could be fed to slaves or sold on the market, but, more importantly, the sheep's wool offered a valuable marketable commodity that could supplement, if not eventually replace, cotton as a central means for making money.

Yet as attractive as the economics of sheep raising were in the eyes of planters, slave dog depredations were viewed as a central obstacle to raising sheep on a large scale. Individuals in South Carolina were especially quick to blame slave dogs for the stunted sheep industry in that state. In debating "The Necessity of a Dog Law," at their September 1858 meeting, nearly all members of the Beech Island Farmers Club, of Aiken, South Carolina readily concurred with the opinion of Maj. G. B. Mills that "we allow our negroes to have dogs which prevents us from raising sheep." [54] Dozens of residents of Darlington District, South Carolina voiced a similar sentiment to the state legislature, complaining that "we have found it a waste of time to . . . raise sheep, while every Negro in the land owns, in is his own right, one or more dogs . . . "[55] According to citizens of Lancaster District, South Carolina, "as long as dogs are held by negroes, sheep cannot be raised in the county . . . "[56] With the imprimatur of the South Carolina Agricultural Society, O. M. Dantzler argued that only those individuals surrounded by "large plantations, where negroes are not allowed to own dogs," can "prosecute" the sheep-raising "business successfully." [57]

To be sure, it was not only slave dogs that took a fancy to sheep and otherwise hampered the economic fortunes of individual slaveholders, states such as South Carolina, and even the entire South. As some pro-sheep partisans pointed out, the dogs of white people were no less attracted to sheep; according to one equal opportunity critic, they were "so choice in their diet . . . that they seldom take an old [one] when a lamb is to be had."[58] Indeed, from an economic standpoint, a dead sheep was a dead sheep, whether it was killed by a "black" or a "white" dog. Yet rather than dwell on the politically sensitive subject of the culpability of "white" dogs and thus risk alienating elements of the white population, pro-sheep partisans pursued the politically more expedient course of emphasizing the guilt of "black" dogs. In thus "race-baiting"–exaggerating the blameworthiness of slave dogs simply because they were owned by black slaves–sheep crusaders deflected attention away from the guilt of "white" dogs, thereby presumably reassuring white people that any broader societal or governmental action against dogs would be aimed at slaves' and not their own. At the same time, by defining the sheep problem as a race problem it was easier for pro-sheep partisans to muster support; they knew that white Carolinians would instinctively sympathize with any issue or movement that confirmed their deeply-held racist beliefs that black slaves were a permanent source of discord who always needed more, rather than less, white control and domination.

Yet what matters in the present context is not the success or failure of this marketing strategy, but the fact that "race-baiting" transformed the serious economic problem of slave dogs killing sheep into the far more disturbing one of underlying social disorder. For the whole purpose of playing the race card was not to underscore slave dog culpability, but to water and cultivate the fear and suspicion that this canine-inspired havoc merely reflected slaves' unrelenting willfulness and assertion of their own interests over and against those of slaveowners and white society more generally. Indeed, the image of slave unruliness and underlying social disorder is what defined and made the race card worth playing in the first place; as a potentially viable strategy for stoking white racial fears, "race-baiting" presumed, on the one hand, that the normative, and desired role of slaves was to be passive and unthreatening while suggesting, on the other, that black slaves were becoming just the opposite: all too independent, willful, and dangerous to whites. Thus, where the killing of sheep by "white" dogs implied, at most, a certain carelessness on the part of white people, in the "race-baiting" construction of reality, the existence of sheep-killing slave dogs meant, invariably and metonymically, that slaves themselves possessed too much freedom and perpetrated too many disturbing, if not dangerous, acts against white people and the social order.[59]

Where there is smoke, there is usually fire, and the rural South was no exception. The race-baiters' alarmist scenario of social disorder was amply confirmed by the many ways in which slaves used dogs to meet their own needs. As a result, slaveowners were no longer so accepting of these dogs or their association with slaves. The seemingly innocuous practice of hunting with dogs now assumed an ambiguous, if not subversive hue. Slaveholders complained that when slaves hunted with dogs at night they became too tired and ill-fit for work the next day.[60] More troublesome was the sense that hunting itself was becoming a pretext for unsanctioned, potentially disruptive activities, in which slaves took their dogs as they travelled about the rural neighborhood to visit family members or cross-roads shopkeepers who would sell them liquor and other contraband. With or without the pretext of hunting, the presence of dogs enabled slaves "to protect them[selves] from the patrol," which policed the rural neighborhood and sought to catch slaves in their night-time "prowlings."[61]

From the complaints of slaveholders, it appeared that slave dogs were quite successful at helping their masters elude the patrol. "So long as dogs are held by Negroes," noted the Grand Jury of Lancaster (South Carolina) District in its presentment to the State Legislature, "patrol duty cannot be effectively done."[62] With barely controlled indignation, the editor of *The Farmer and Planter* told his readers of a certain instance in which "the dog protected a Negro from a patrol that pursued and overtook him, and enabled the Negro to make his escape."[63] For whites, the idea of slaves eluding the patrol rankled not only because it meant that their chattel could engage in a range of irksome, if not subversive, activities but it also mocked and called into question the entire patrol system which was the primary means by which white society policed slaves outside individual plantations. If slaves, with their dogs, could avoid the patrol with such impunity, what was to keep them, wondered white people, from doing whatever they wanted, whenever they wanted? With such concerns about the safety and stability of their social order, many whites in the 1850s probably now wished for a law, like that requested by citizens of Orangeburg District in 1807, "authorizing the patrols to kill any dog which they may find with Negroes."[64]

No less serious was the fact that slaves shamelessly used their dogs when stealing from slaveowners. While slave theft was so commonplace and widespread as to be genetically-linked to Africans by whites, theft-by-dog was particularly insulting to white society. For here slaves were using a piece of property–presumably allowed them by their master–to help them take the master's property, or that of a neighbor.[65] According to the bloodlessly cold analysis of "Jack Brown," of Kershaw District, dogs were a central part of the slave's strategy. As Brown described:

> [T]he negro inclined to change ownership of property, whether of the chicken roost, the meat house, the corn crib, the potatoe or melon patch, or any other, to him desiderated species of property, will take along with him his faithful dog, which will keep guard whilst the negro is modifying the law of South Carolina by substituting the, to him, more congenial law of Africa. In the meantime, should he be seen or heard by the dogs on the plantation from which he is filching, or by the master or his faithful servants, or peradventure some rare patrol, his faithful Argus gives him the hint–holds a parley with the enemy, intercepts his pursuit, until his master filcher is beyond apprehension.[66]

Now, theft of any sort was understandably distasteful to slaveowners, as it meant, first, an immediate financial loss and second, that they had failed to replace the "congenial law of Africa" with a set of ideas and values much more to their liking. Yet theft-by-dog was especially odious to slaveowners; not only because the dog helped the slave succeed, but also because the very presence and "facilities" of the dog encouraged slaves to steal in the first place. For with the dog's "facilities. . . . Negroes become," observed Brown, "more dishonest and hence a less profitable servant." [67] Presumably, if slaves did not have dogs they would be more honest and "profitable."

Yet, ultimately, dogs' subversive influence went beyond the particular problem of encouraging slaves to steal. For what Brown also seems to be saying is that the "facilities" of dogs made slaves generally more willful, insubordinate, and harder to discipline in all aspects of plantation life; dogs–like the other *bêtes noires* of slaveowner life, meddling abolitionists, disreputable white Southern-ers, and liquor in the hands of slaves–corrupted slaves, making them more inclined to think and act in ways squarely at odds with those desired of them by their masters.[68] However much paternalistic slaveowners tried to transform slave values, attitudes, and behavior, they were doomed to frustration, if not failure, as long as dogs remained an unsavory presence and influence in the slave quarters. If slaves used dogs to perpetrate undesirable acts against the planta-tion and social order, it is no less important to see that dogs, by their very presence and "facilities," helped spawn the willful, independent, and antago-nistic attitude necessary for slaves to commit such aggressive acts in the first place. Dogs, as Brown suggests, made slaves even more unruly and difficult to control.

Given the fact that slaves kept their dogs at the sufferance of their master, it would seem that slaveowners had a very direct method for combatting this Old Testament-like plague: simply prohibiting their slaves from having dogs. After all, this was the solution adopted by none other than President George Washington, who ordered "that all dogs belonging to slaves [on his plantation] be hanged immediately, because they 'aid[ed] them in their night robberies.' "[69] Yet the Washingtonian solution–permanently doing away with slaves' dogs–only worked if all slaveowners in a rural neighborhood adopted it. For if a minority failed to embrace it, those who did would remain vulnerable to the depredations and social ills caused by slaves and dogs living on plantations where dogs were still allowed. Such was the situation faced by anti-canine slaveowners in a state like South Carolina; unwilling to tolerate the continued slave-dog menace or to trust that their slaveowning peers would voluntarily adopt the "Washington solution," anti-canine critics turned to the General Assembly for laws that would force slaveowners to reduce the number of slave dogs in their state.

In this effort, the anti-dog partisans were successful. In December of 1859, the state legislature passed "An Act to Make Owners of Dogs Liable for Sheep Killed by Them."[70] The resulting law reveals the diversity of motivation behind the anti-dog, pro-sheep campaign. On the one hand, it is clear that lawmakers were responding to the economic harm caused by sheep-slaughtering dogs. In the first paragraph, they specified that "The owner of any dog . . . or person upon whose premises any dog may be kept by his or her slave," was liable to pay double the value of any sheep "killed or injured by such dog." By including "the owner of any dog," and not just those kept by slaves, this Act clearly cast a wide net and suggests that protecting sheep from any kind of canine harassment was a central objective of the South Carolina Legislature.

Yet it was perhaps the broader social disturbances and ramifications of dog ownership by slaves that concerned lawmakers most. For in addition to protecting sheep and sheep-raising, the legislature imposed an annual tax of one dollar "upon every dog kept by a slave," with the tax "to be paid by the owner of such slave." Slaveowners who were caught failing to make the annual payment would be subject to a two dollar fine for "every dog so kept and not returned." By placing a tax on dogs kept by slaves, and not on dogs kept by white people, the legislature showed that they accepted what anti-dog partisans had been claiming all along: that slave dogs were such a nuisance, not only to sheep, but to white society in general, that their numbers and impact had to be curtailed. That the social control of African Americans was uppermost in the minds of lawmakers is confirmed further in the final paragraph of the law, which required "any free negro, or other free person of color" to pay a two dollar annual tax for the right to keep their dogs.

In theory, it was conceivable that no slaves would lose their dogs in the aftermath of this law's passage. After all, slaveowners could chose to pay the tax, thereby feeding the financial coffers of the state and preserving the life of these animals. Indeed, on one plantation, the slaves decided whether to keep their dogs or not. Darlington District planter Thomas C. Law basically told his slaves that if they wanted to keep their dogs they would have to pay the tax. At first, one slave named Henry agreed, deciding to give a portion of his cotton earnings to Law who would then make the tax payment; but later, Henry decided not to and, so, as Law eventually recorded, was credited $1.00 "by killing [his] dog." [71] While Law may have been unique in giving his slaves the option of paying the tax and keeping their dogs, he was probably quite typical of his fellow slaveowners in his refusal to underwrite the tax on behalf of his slaves and in his insistence that the dogs be killed when no money was forthcoming. However the decision to eschew the tax and kill the dogs was arrived at, the important point is that dog extermination—whether by hanging or some other means—was now the order of the day in South Carolina. With a diminution in the number of slave dogs, slaveowners would presumably now enjoy and experience more peace and order on the plantation and throughout the rural regions of their realm.

In attacking dogs, the anti-canine campaign in general and the law of 1859 in particular were, in effect, attacking slaves. For while the dogs were the ostensible quarry, it was slaves who, as their owners, became the ultimate target and victims. As a result, the anti-dog movement was but one part of slaveholders' much larger campaign during the last twenty-five or so years of the slavery era to reassert, expand, and intensify their control and domination of their slaves, thereby encroaching upon slave autonomy and truncating, if not eliminating, many of the so-called "customary rights" that slaves had enjoyed during the first three or so decades of the nineteenth century. Just as slaveowners and their allies reduced slave opportunities to sell their small crops or other products to local merchants, to spend their earnings when and where they wanted, to buy what they wanted, or to simply travel off the plantation much as they pleased, so did slaveowners and the State now oversee the undoing of another privilege: having a dog. The cumulative effect of curtailing these and other long-standing customs was to make it much easier for slaveowners to control their slaves and order their society much as they pleased.

The great irony of the entire anti-dog movement was that slaves, if they had been asked, might very well have supported it and a general reduction of dogs. For as much as they valued and cherished their own dogs, they nonetheless despised many of the dogs owned by slaveowners and other members of the ruling race; laws that oversaw the reduction of "white" dogs would have thus served slave interests. Yet, in South Carolina, their interests were ignored, as the State left dogs of slaveoweners untaxed and, hence, unharmed. As a result, slaves were now presented with the worst possible combination: they still had to contend with "white" dogs—whether guard, patrol, or bloodhound—but on their own, without the help of their own. Never a level playing field, the terrain of slave-master struggles in South Carolina would now tilt that much more in favor of the ruling race.

Eradication of slave dogs also left slaves with fewer protections against the unwaveringly dehumanizing potential of slavery. Men were especially harmed by the anti-dog movement and, in South Carolina, state action; for while dogs spent time with the young and old, men and women, it was largely men who hunted and thus spent the most hours with the dogs of the slave quarters, and so it was men who would be most adversely affected by the state-sponsored assault on these animals in South Carolina. Even in the brief time before the Civil War started, male slaves, such as Thomas C. Law's Henry, no doubt suffered considerable pain at losing both their canine hunting companions and the psychic and social rewards that came when contributing to the material needs of the slave community. That the quick onset of the Civil War no doubt interrupted the application of this law should not obscure the fact that, in passing this law, the State of South Carolina was essentially guaranteeing that men would have fewer opportunities to experience a modicum of joy, to contribute to the slave community's well-being, and to sustain a positive sense of self in the face of the impersonal battering-ram of slavery. While it may be an exaggeration to claim that the anti-dog movement and the law of 1859 were intended, from the start, to harm black men, the gendered nature of slaves' dog experiences certainly suggests that it was black men who were most directly affected by the anti-canine actions of white Southerners.

Yet because men shared the fruits of their hunts with other members of the slave community, all slaves ultimately suffered from the attack on dogs. Needless to say, fewer dogs with which to hunt meant that slaves would acquire less meat and fur to supplement their skimpy food and clothing allowances.[72] The resulting decline in their material conditions was made all the worse by the fact that many slaves (at least those living on cotton plantations) were exposed to greater physical hardship as workers. A long-term decline in cotton prices forced planters to intensify the pace of work and production of cotton; during the harvest, for example, slaves experienced greater physical demands as they were now expected, in the 1850s, to pick three times as much as they picked in a day during the early years of the nineteenth century.[73] Overall, the combined effect of harder work, restricted material conditions, and slaveowner encroachments on autonomy and customary privileges was to worsen the conditions of life for slaves during the last decades of the slavery era. In short, the onset of the Civil War should not obscure the fact that the long-term trajectory of slavery was far more bleak for slaves than is sometimes suggested, and to interpret all behavior and experience in light of the fact that the war and emancipation eventually came is to cheapen and trivialize slaves' lived historical experience. For slaves lived each moment without benefit of knowing what was around the bend, and what they knew from their lived, day-to-day moments was not encouraging: each year they experienced foreshortened opportunities and stagnating conditions of life. With the extermination of dogs afoot in 1860, the anti-dog movement and law were understandably seen by slaves such as Law's Henry as only the most recent but certainly not the last assaults on their autonomy and conditions of life.

NOTES

I would like to thank the following for commenting on earlier incarnations of this essay: Colette Hyman, Donna Watson, Conrad Goeringer, Bert Barickman, Kevin Gosner, Leigh Pruneau, Laura Tabili, Larry Hudson, Daniel Littlefield, Stanley Engerman, Charles Joyner, Philip Morgan, Cheryll Ann Cody, Sharon Ann Holt, and participants in the University of Rochester Conference, "African-American Work and Culture in the 18th and 19th Centuries," and the University of Minnesota Colonial History Workshop.

1. Vive la Mouton, "Grass and Sheep" from *The American Cotton Planter* reprinted in *Farmer and Planter* [hereafter *FAP*] 6 (1855): 287; in a similar vein, see Mutton, "Dogs," *FAP* 6 (1855): 228; Mutton, "Taxing Dogs," *FAP* 11 (1860), 247.

2. South Caroliniana Library, University of South Carolina [hereafter SCL], Minutes, Beech Island Farmer's Club, Aiken, S.C., 109–111; see also 46–7, 154. The minutes of the predecessor of this club, The A.B.C. Farmer's Club, are also included in this typescript volume.

3. Mutton, "Dogs," *FAP* 6 (Oct. 1855): 228–9.

4. For the best, albeit quite brief, introduction to the role of dogs in slave life, see Eugene Genovese, *Roll, Jordan, Roll: The World the Slaves Made* (New York: Vintage Books, 1976 {1972}), 488, 651–2. See also Stuart A. Marks, *Southern Hunting in Black and White* (Princeton: Princeton University Press, 1991), chap. 2.

5. Lacy Ford, *Origins of Southern Radicalism: The South Carolina Upcountry, 1800–1860* (New York: Oxford University Press, 1988), 35.

6. Marks, *Southern Hunting*, 18–23, 25; William Elliott, *Carolina Sports by Land & Water* (New York: Arno Press, 1967 [1846]), 93, 102, 110, 125–6, 151, 153,159; *FAP*, (March 1860), 74; Grady McWhiney,*Cracker Culture: Celtic Ways in the Old South* (Tuscaloosa: University of Alabama Press, 1988), 140; Terry G. Jordan, *Trails to Texas: Southern Roots of Western Cattle Ranching* (Lincoln: University of Nebraska Press, 1981), 9–10, 25, 31–3, 36, 38, 50, 73, 118–21, 141, 143–4. On lap dogs, see also "Dogs," reprinted from *The Ohio Farmer* in *FAP* 3 (1852): 185; "About Keeping Dogs," *FAP* 7 (1856): 274; Maj. R. A. Griffin, "Sheep Husbandry–What Protection it Needs, and How Obtained–Report read before the Abbeville District Agricultural Society at its Annual Meeting in October [1860]," reprinted in *FAP* 12 (1861): 195. For a very good study of the changing role and presence of animals (including dogs) in the lives of the English, see: Harriet Ritvo, *The Animal Estate: The English and Other Creatures in the Victorian Age* (Cambridge: Harvard University Press, 1987).

7. *Report of the Directors of the South Carolina Institute* (Charleston, S.C.: Steam Power Press of Walker and James, 1853), 48.

8. "Sheep Husbandry in South Carolina–Col. J.W.Watts' Flock," from *Newberry (S.C.) Sentinel* reprinted in *FAP* 2 (1851): 165.

9. "A" assumed that there were four dogs per family in his plantation belt district of Fairfield, S.C. (or roughly 5,000 dogs), while C. Gage assumed five dogs per family in his South Carolina upcountry district of Union (or 4,845 by his calculation). See: Broomsedge, "A Word or Two About Dogs," *FAP* 3 (1852): 39; A, letter to *FAP* 9 (1858): 198; C. Gage, "On Sheep Husbandry, read before the Union (S.C.) District Agricultural Society," reprinted in *FAP* 9 (1858): 110.

10. George Rawick, ed., *The American Slave: A Composite Autobiography* (Westport, Ct.: Greenwood Press, 1972), vol. 3, part 4, 32; Linda Brent [Harriet Jacobs], *Incidents in the Life of a Slave Girl* (San Diego: Harcourt Brace Jovanovich, 1983 [1861]), 11; Jacob Stroyer, *My Life in the South* (Salem: Salem Observer Book and Job Print, 1885), 71–2. I explore slaves' relationships with dogs of the master class in much greater detail in, "'To Bark and Bite': Dogs and Southern Slaves in the 19th Century," Paper presented to Colonial History Workshop, Department of History, University of Minnesota, March 1994.

11. Joel Chandler Harris, *The Complete Tales of Uncle Remus* (Boston: Houghton-Mifflin Co., 1955), 9, 342, 369, 627; Robert Bone, *Down Home: A History of Afro-American Short Fiction From Its Beginning to the End of the Harlem Renaissance* (New York: Putnam, 1975), 36.

12. Alma Gottlieb, *Under the Kapok Tree: Identity and Difference in Beng Thought* (Bloomington: Indiana University Press, 1992), 98–118. (I would like to thank Professor Nancy Hunt of the Department of History at the University of Arizona, for suggesting this interesting anthropological study). Of course, given the dangers of applying ethnographic data collected in the twentieth century to a much earlier period, it is best to view the present effort as a working hypothesis rather than established conclusion.

13. The law of South Carolina, for example, said explicitly that "a slave may, by the consent of his master, acquire and hold personal property. All, thus acquired, is regarded in law as that of the master . . . A slave cannot contract, and be contracted with"; John Belton O'Neall, ed. *The Negro Law of South Carolina* (Columbia, S.C., 1848), 21–2.

14. Charles Ball, *Fifty Years In Chains* (New York: Dover Publications, 1970 [1837]), 354, 355, 389.

15. Harriet E. Wilson, *Our Nig; or, Sketches from the Life of a Free Black* (New York: Vintage Books, 1983 [1859]), 41–2, 75; see also 37, 42, 49, 61–2.

16. Rawick, *The American Slave*, vol. 2, part 2, 215 (Grisby); vol. 3, part 4, 57 (Rutherford); see also, vol. 2, part 1, 62 (Gordon Bluford); vol. 2, part 1, 152 (C.B. Burton); vol. 2, part 1, 241 (John Davenport); vol. 3, part 3, 56 (Mary Johnson); vol. 3, part 3, 172 (Milton Marshall); vol. 3, part 4, 10 (Ann Rice); vol. 3, part 4, 89 (Morgan Scurry). For a possibly contrary view, suggesting that women also hunted, see vol. 2, part 1, 166 (Granny Cain: "We hunted. . . . ").

17. Rawick, ed., *American Slave* vol. 2, part 2, 138.

18. Where learning how to hunt was also, as Stuart Marks points out, a rite of passage

for young white men at the time, for slave men the social and personal implications and stakes of the rite were far greater, reflecting the far weaker bonds of community that integrated them into the community.

19. H.C. Bruce, *The New Man: Twenty-Nine Years A Slave, Twenty-Nine Years a Free Man* (Miami: Mnemosyne Pub. Co., 1969 [1895]), 24; Allen Parker, *Recollections of Slavery Times* (Worcester, Mass.: Chas. W. Burbank and Co., Printers, 1895), 43.

20. Bruce, *The New Man*, 24; I.E. Lowery, *Life on the Old Plantation* ([probably Columbia, S.C.]: 1910), 55.

21. Sam Aleckson, *Before the War, and After the Union: An Autobiography* (Boston: Gold Mind Pub., 1929), 48–9.

22. Bruce, *The New Man*, 24.

23. Ball, *Fifty Years*, 389–91. For an equally poignant story, see James Smith, in John Blassingame, ed., *Slave Testimony: Two Centuries of Letters, Speeches, Interviews, and Autobiographies* (Baton Rouge: Louisiana State University Press, 1977), 282–3. See also, Rawick, ed., *American Slave* vol. 3, part 3, 172 (Milton Marshall); Margaret Ward, in Charles L. Blockson, ed., *The Underground Railroad* (New York: Prentice Hall, 1987), 101–2.

24. "Sheep, Dogs, etc." *FAP* 5 (July 1854): 177; Griffin, "Sheep Husbandry," 195: "it is well known that the patrol law is ineffectual, as it is impossible to approach a quarter without the alarm being given by these faithful sentinels."

25. Ball, *Fifty Years*, 355–6.

26. Bruce, *The New Man*, 19–20.

27. Blassingame, *Slave Testimony*, 281–3. Although the faithfulness and protectiveness of his dog "endeared him to his master stronger than ever" during the course of his running away, Smith still tried to elude his dog, for no doubt the same reasons that prevented Charles Ball from taking his. Indeed, even after Smith and his dog killed the bloodhounds and made it to the Ohio River, Smith tried to first kill the dog, and when that failed he tried to leave it behind, but this was to no avail as the dog plunged in and crossed the river before the master. Only on Northern soil did Smith become less cautious and more willing to keep his dog, who remained Smith's constant companion for the remaining five years of its life.

28. On dogs used to protect plantation property, see Blockson, ed., *The Underground Railroad*, 24; Rawick, *American Slave*, vol. 3, part 3, 115; William H. Robinson, *From Log Cabin to the Pulpit* (Eau Claire, Wis.: James H. Tifft Pub., 1913), 81.

29. Jack Brown, "Dogs, Sheep, etc.," reprinted from *Camden (S.C.) Journal* in *FAP* 5 (Oct. 1854): 259–60; A, letter to *FAP*, 9 (1858): 198; Mutton, "Taxing Dogs," *FAP* 11 (1860): 247.

30. Parker, *Recollections*. 45. Among the many other former slaves who talked about hunting with a dog, see: Blassingame, *Slave Testimony*, 280–1 (James Smith); Rawick, *American Slave*, vol. 2, part 2, 76 (Aaron Ford, "I take dogs en slip out en de woods en hunt rabbits"); vol. 3, part 3, 272 (Sam Polite: "You kin also ketch 'possum and raccoon wid' your dawg"); vol. 3, part 4, 55 (Joe Rutherford: "We had dogs . . . but our Master didn't like hounds").

31. Lowery, *Life*, 54.

32. Peter Randolph, *Sketches of Slave Life: or, Illustrations of the Peculiar Institution* (Philadelphia: Rhistoric Pub., 1972 [1855]), 30.

33. Isaac Williams, *Sunshine and Shadow of Slave Life* (New York: AMS Press, 1975 [1885]), 71.

34. This strategy is described or implied in B.A. Botkin, *A Treasury of Southern Folklore* (New York: Crown Pub., 1949), 612–5; Parker, *Recollections*, 46–50; Lowery, *Life*, 54–7; Williams, *Sunshine and Shadow*, 71; Aleckson, *Before the War*, 49–50; Randolph, *Sketches of Slave Life*, 30; Rawick, *American Slave*, vol. 2, part 1, 231 (Caleb Curry); vol. 2, part 1, 321–2 (Will Dill); vol. 3, part 3, 186 (Andrew Means); The strategy was also used after slavery; see Rawick, *American Slave*, vol. 2, part 1, 13 (Frank Adamson).

35. For a discussion of hunting in the lives of Southern white men during the antebellum period, see Marks, *Southern Hunting*, chap. 2.

36. In 1831, the North Carolina Legislature, for example, made it unlawful for a slave to possess "or hunt with a gun"; cited in Marks, *Southern Hunting*, 290–1, fn. 52.

37. Ball, *Fifty Years*, 352; Parker, *Recollections*, 53; Solomon Northrup, *Twelve Years a Slave* [1853], reprinted in Gilbert Osofsky, ed., *Puttin' on Old Massa* (New York: Harper and Row, Pub., 1969), 335; Bruce, *The New Man*, 19.

38. Rawick, ed. *American Slave*, vol. 2, part 1, 115–6 and vol. 3, part 4, 105.

39. Rawick, ed., *American Slave*, vol. 2, part 2, 166; see also Northrup, *Twelve Years*, 335; Smith, in Blassingame, *Slave Testimony*, 280–1.

40. Northrup, *Twelve Years*, 335. Of course, Northrup also indicates that there were slaves living on neighboring plantations who "for months at a time, have no other meat than such as is obtained" from hunting.

41. Quoted in Charles Joyner, *Down by the Riverside: A South Carolina Slave Community* (Urbana: University of Illinois Press, 1984), 100.

42. Williams, *Sunshine and Shadow*, 71; Rawick, ed., *American Slave*, vol. 3, part 4, 101 (Hector Smith); vol. 2, part 1, 206 (Peter Clifton); vol. 2, part 1, 301 (Louisa Davis). For other possum partisans, see also vol. 2, part 1, 231 (Caleb Craig); Solomon Northrup, *Twelve Years*, 335.

43. Lowery, *Life*, 53.

44. Robinson, *From Log Cabin*, 152.

45. Aleckson, *Before the War*, 49–50.

46. Parker, *Recollections*, 50: "the skin of the [game] being carefully saved and dried in the sun." According to Botkin, *A Treasury of Southern Folklore*, 615, a "coon [was] hunted for the sake of his hide, and a possum for his meat."

47. SCL, Minutes of the Salem Presbyterian Church, Sumter District, W.P.A. Typescript, 61. To be sure, it was not only black people who brought their dogs to church with them. As part of his broader chiding of white people for their dog obsession, one Southerner complained about "[h]ow pleasant it is to see a troop of dogs following their [white] masters into church on the Sabbath, and then to have them whine and yelp when their toes are trodden on; or to see them mount the pulpit stairs in sermon time, and, to close the scene, to have the sexton chase after them up and down the aisles and expel them with his cane, and thus destroy all

the solemnity and interest of the service." ("About Keeping Dogs," *FAP* 1856, 274). This individual did not specify whether it was Presbyterians or some other denominational group who committed this canine infraction.

48. Parker, *Recollections* 43; Northrup, *Twelve Years*, 335; Moses Grandy, *Narrative of the Life of Moses Grandy* (Boston: O.J. Johnson, 1844), 36; Genovese, *Roll, Jordan, Roll*, 487–8; Smith, in Blassingame, *Slave Testimony*, 280–1.

49. SCL, Minutes, Beech Island Farmer's Club, Aiken, S.C., 1858: 109–11.

50. Ibid.

51. South Carolina Department of Archives and History, Columbia, S.C. [hereafter SCDAH], General Assembly Records [hereafter GAR], #0010–015–1809–1, "Presentment of the Grand Jury, October 1809, of Abbeville." As one of their rights and responsibilities, the nineteenth century grand juries in South Carolina sent "presentments" to the State Legislature, in which they complained about various problems affecting their locale.

52. SCDAH, GAR, #0010–03–1814–00109, "Petition of Sundry Inhabitants of Clarendon Parish, Sumter District, 1814,"; see also #0010–03–1814–00108.

53. Weoka, "Rotation of Crops–Reply to J.M.D.," *The South Carolina Agriculturalist* 1 (1856): 183.

54. SCL, Minutes, Beech Island Farmer's Club, Aiken, S.C., 1858: 109–11.

55. SCDAH, GAR, #0010–003–ND00–04775, "A Memorial of Certain Citizens of Darlington District, Praying for the Protection of Sheep Against Dogs," (undated but internal evidence suggests the late 1850s).

56. SCDAH, GAR, #0010–015–1857–00011, "Presentment of the Grand Jury of Lancaster, Spring Term, 1857."

57. O.M.Dantzler, "On Sheep Husbandry at the South–published by order of the South Carolina Agricultural Society" in *FAP* 12 (1861): 1.

58. "A Fight with a Dog," *FAP* 9 (1858): 236. For other criticisms of the dogs of white people, see: "Profits of Dogs," reprinted from *American Agriculturalist* in *FAP* 1 (1850): 62; Mutton, "Dogs," *FAP* 6 (1855): 228; "About Keeping Dogs," *FAP* 7 (1856): 274; "Sheep and Dogs," *FAP* 9 (1858): 113.

59. One of the underlying assumptions behind the foregoing discussion of "race-baiting" and the presumed rhetorical fanning of flames against slave dogs is that these animals killed sheep without the prodding, connivance, or active participation of their slave owners. Active involvement by slaves would make sheep killing theft, and readily analyzable as that; yet because none of the documentary evidence explicitly said slaves were involved in the killing, I am assuming that the dogs did it on their own. Conversely, any claim that slaves used their dogs in any undesirable fashion could be seen as "race-baiting" and, ultimately, as being a fictitious story that white people made up in order to fan racial fears and hatred. While this conspiratorial view correctly highlights the need, ability, and willingness of the ruling class to lie at will, to adopt it in total is to deny slaves any agency or independence of action, and to make them into passive ciphers, a position I find untenable.

60. Marks, *Southern Hunting*, 28.

61. "Sheep, Dog, etc.," *FAP* 5 (1854): 177.

62. SCDAH, GAR, #0010–015–1857–11, "Presentment of the Grand Jury of Lancaster, Spring Term, 1857."

63. "Sheep, Dog, etc.," *FAP* 5 (1854): 177; see also, Griffin, "Sheep Husbandry," *FAP* 12 (1861): 195.

64. SCDAH, GAR #010–015–1807–8, "Presentment by Grand Jury of Orangeburgh Dist., October Term 1807."

65. A, letter to *FAP* 9 (1858): 198; Mutton, "Taxing Dogs," *FAP* 11 (1860): 247; "Sheep, Dogs, etc.," 177.

66. Brown, "Dogs, Sheep," *FAP* 5 (1854): 259.

67. Brown, "Dogs, Sheep," 259; see also, Mutton, "Taxing Dogs," 247.

68. See John Campbell, "As 'A Kind of Freeman?' Slaves' Market-Related Activities in the South Carolina Up Country, 1800–1860," in *Cultivation and Culture: Labor and the Shaping of Slave Life in the Americas*, eds., Ira Berlin and Philip Morgan (Charlottesville: University of Virginia Press, 1993), 251–2.

69. Gerald Mullin, *Flight and Rebellion: Slave Resistance in Eighteenth-Century Virginia* (New York: Oxford University Press, 1974), 61.

70. Thomas Cooper and David J. McCord, eds., *Statutes at Large of South Carolina* (Columbia, South Carolina: Republican Printing Co., 1874), vol. 12 [acts passed between December 1850 and January 1861], 707-8. The anti-dog movement was also strong in Alabama which passed an anti-dog law: "An act to prevent stock from being killed by dogs," *Acts of the Seventh Biennial Session of the General Assembly of Alabama . . . commencing on the Second Monday of November, 1859*. (Montgomery, Al.: Shorter and Reid, State Printers, 1860), 45–6. Georgia also considered anti-dog legislation; see: Vive Le Mouton, "Sheep vs. Dogs," reprinted from *Alabama Cotton Planter* in *FAP* 5 (1854): 6; "Proposed Dog Law–Preservation of Sheep," *SA* 2 (1854): 23.

71. SCL, T.C. Law Papers, "Slave Accounts." Interestingly, a slave woman on this plantation named Ritta paid the tax, possibly because her dog was the hunting companion of her three teenage sons, Sidney, Sam, and Spencer.

72. The hunting rights and opportunities of African Americans would be threatened as well into the late nineteenth century; see Steven Hahn, "Hunting, Fishing, and Foraging: Common Rights and Class Relations," *Radical History* 26 (1982): 37–64.

73. See Campbell, "As A Kind of Freeman," 270–3. On the increases in daily cotton picking over the course of the nineteenth century, see: John Campbell, "The Gender Division of Labor, Slave Reproduction, and the Slave Family Economy on Southern Cotton Plantations, 1800–1865," Ph.D. Diss., University of Minnesota, 1988, 29–87.

~

"ALL THAT CASH"
Work and Status in the Slave Quarters

Larry E. Hudson Jr.

T he presence of cash money in the slave quarters accelerated the shift from a highly personalized system of traditional exchange based upon a cooperative sharing of goods and services, to one that increasingly incorporated the more depersonalized values of the market place. In the later stages of this process, cash money was sufficiently prominent that it became a primary arbiter of wealth, status, and power. The increased circulation of cash in the slave quarters reflected the slaves' expanding commercial arena, and the internalization of market values.[1]

This essay suggests that the slaves' efforts working for themselves resulted in such property accumulation and wealth that there existed clear social differences among the enslaved, and that a major consequence of their own industry was the creation and expansion of an "internal economy" that extended beyond the confines of the slave quarters into a wider slave community incorporating a growing number of slaves, free Negroes, and white Southerners. This expanded commercial arena weakened the traditional exchange practices that characterized slave quarter communities by depersonalizing commodity exchanges and prioritizing the use of cash money.[2] The wider the area of the slaves' internal economy, the less personalized were the transactions that fueled it, and the more extensive the need for and use of cash money. The growing presence of cash money in the slave community, however, had severe conse-quences for social and structural relations in the slave quarters.[3]

One immediate effect was the blurring of differences between the values of the "public" world of the master—where the masters' rules and practices dominated—and those of the "private" world of the quarters where the institutions of the slaves had ascendancy. Exposed to similar forces, the vast majority of antebellum slaves—quite ordinary and overwhelmingly rural—operated in a market that was rapidly transforming: increasingly organized less around traditional forms of exchange and dominated more by cash money transactions.[4]

Before the end of slavery, large numbers of slaves, having been exposed to the commercial activities of a fairly sophisticated internal economy, were ordering their lives in ways that were influenced, at least in part, by their ability to function in the commercial arena. Even slaves with little or no wealth were obliged to deal with cash money, if they were to participate in certain slave quarter activities. Their familiarity with the use of cash money and with the language of the market place suggests that slaves had internalized values of the market.[5] The growing numbers who engaged in petty market activities accelerated the process of internalization and brought with it a heightened sense of the value of their labor, of goods produced by and for themselves, and even of their extra-legal activities.

The institution of slavery was never such a closed society that there existed no room for slaves to express themselves as human beings. If only in the relative privacy of their quarters, they asserted their individuality, acted upon their personal and religious beliefs, and reacted to the world around them. It was impossible for slaves to distance themselves spatially and culturally from the master's world with its rules and regulations, most of which were designed to inhibit their intellectual and cultural development. The operation of work and garden systems on Southern farms and plantations, however, signals the existence of some spatial distance between the world of the master and that of the slaves. The more complex the labor arrangement, the more marked were the boundaries between the two worlds. In this respect, the task system was the most sophisticated example of work and garden systems familiar to antebellum slaves in South Carolina (on which this essay will focus) as well as slaves throughout the South.

Under the task and garden system, masters encouraged their slaves to work efficiently at a set amount of work; once completed, the slaves were then at liberty to work in their own "gardens," producing crops for their own use.[6] Whenever possible, South Carolina masters allowed their slaves a small piece of land to cultivate for themselves. Seldom smaller than a quarter acre, these plots were sometimes as large as twelve or fifteen acres. The access to some land was common throughout the state, but the labor system under which the slaves worked showed some notable variations.

Although tasking was most prevalent in the Lowcountry area, variations of the system could be found throughout the state. The most widely used system however, often directly based upon the task system, was where masters assigned time for their slaves to work for themselves, usually after the main work of the plantation was done or sufficiently advanced. Saturday afternoons were usually set aside, and on a fairly regular basis, masters allowed their slaves occasional half or whole days to work on their crops. Most slaves had some choice as to how they spent their Sundays; while some were encouraged to work, others were discouraged from engaging in such activity on the Sabbath.[7] The more sophisticated task system made it easier for slaves to exploit their gardening opportunities and so to accumulate property and access cash money, but laboring under any work and garden system allowed slaves, irrespective of their function in the labor force, the chance to produce goods for their own consumption, exchange or sale.[8]

Property ownership among antebellum slaves was not restricted to the older, skilled, talented men, or to the fortunate few who managed to catch the master's eye. Often, young, female, and quite "ordinary" slaves were able to accumulate substantial amounts of property. Beaufort District's Harriet Smith was one such slave. Born in 1826, Harriet had control of some land, two acres of which she planted in corn and "made at least 20 bushels to the acre." She had worked hard and made plenty of provisions and raised hogs and poultry.[9] Pierson Peeples allowed Mooney Sinclair and his other slaves "to work for themselves and to own personal property." James Ruth was another slave not particularly "privileged" or blessed with a special skill, but his mistress, Nath Ruth's widow, allowed him to own personal property and to work for himself in his spare time. James also "worked out among neighbors and made money." A neighbor, Joseph Rozier, recalled that James made money for himself "working for me and my neighbor, Abner Ginn . . . and split rails for us both." Neither a foreman nor a skilled slave, James had little more than hard labor to sell, yet his property included a horse. Thus, without any particular skill or special advantages (except a willingness to work hard) James—as perhaps did many like him—accumulated substantial property.[10]

The work and garden system, and the surplus property that often resulted from it, pulled the slaves into a broader market economy that encouraged the development of more complex relations with their masters. And the distribution of the slaves' accumulated goods to other slaves created an internal economy that spread beyond the confines of individual slave quarters to the wider community, broadening the slaves' world by linking large numbers of quarters in a web of commercial activity.

While attempting to retain an important measure of control, masters

generally felt justified (obliged even) in extending to their slaves the opportunity to increase their commitment to a system essentially at odds with the
slaves' own interests. The apogee of this relationship was summed up neatly by
R. King in 1828: "No Negro with a well stocked poultry house, a small crop
advancing, a canoe partly finished, or a few cubs unsold, all of which he
calculates soon to enjoy, will ever run away."[11] However much this arrangement
served the masters' interests, it also served the slaves'. As one Lowcountry
planter acknowledged in 1858, "by reasonable industry and ordinary provi-
dence, our people [the slaves] all have it in their power to add materially to
their comforts and indulgences. . . ."[12]

The more slaves were able to associate these paternalistic "indulgences" with
their own efforts, the better placed they became to make a life of their own,
largely separate from and somewhat independent of the public world of their
masters. More than any other single factor, it was the development of their
economic activities that facilitated the development of a "social space" between
the public world of the master and the relatively private and autonomous world
of the slave quarters, wherein the slaves planted and nourished the seeds of a
dynamic African-American culture.[13]

Although most masters seem to have encouraged their slaves' extra work
activities, they all displayed more than a little concern for their slaves' acquisition and use of cash money. One Alabama planter, writing in 1853, alerted
his fellow planters to the likely consequences of slaves using their patches to
plant cotton "on their own account." He was convinced that the resulting
surplus would lead to "the possession of too much money," a situation "calculated to generate bad habits and produce disorder." Of course, any increase in
the amount of cash money slaves controlled would allow them additional
market choices and so added to their "power." Masters were not unaware of this
and advised caution. Writing in 1858, another planter warned that allowing
the slaves to accumulate substantial amounts of property would induce the
neighbor's slaves to desire similar opportunities. And, in an attempt to drive
home his point more sharply, he speculated that were slaves generally allowed
to claim a crop of their own "in cotton, or corn, or tobacco" the sum of
twenty-five million dollars "would be a small calculation for the amount of
money handled by slaves as their own, annually." Having allowed this situation
to develop, what this planter feared most were the consequences of efforts made
to curtail the practice of slaves enjoying their wealth. He seems to have clearly
understood what the slaves were just beginning to appreciate fully: "Money is
power."[14]

The responses of individual masters and their representatives in the courts,
and in the state legislature, reveal a determined effort to control an area of slave

life that was both a reflection of the growing economic and cultural autonomy of the slave world, and of public concern regarding the risks such changes presented to white society. Predictably, lawmakers sought to control the slaves' commercial enterprise, particularly when it involved the use of sizable sums of money. Masters were not unaware of the relationship between a high level of commercial activity on the part of their slaves and a work and garden system that "encouraged the trading by slaves among themselves and between whites."[15] Coupled with their fear that enterprising slaves would be tempted to steal goods from their masters and sell them to unscrupulous white traders, was their objection that such ventures could put money into the hands of slaves which could be used for the evil purposes, i.e."buying liquor" and gambling.[16] Commercial and illegal activity, particularly with white men of the "lower orders," could only serve to increase the slave's sense of power and autonomy; it could undermine the structures of a slave society—the foundations of which were based upon the alleged belief in the inherent superiority of the white race. When white Southerners engaged with slaves in intimate economic and social intercourse, they professed their disregard for the dominant values of their society.[17]

Where slaves were able to operate under a work and garden system that both encouraged and facilitated the accumulation of surplus production, they had an opportunity to take control of important areas of their lives. Rather than being dependent slaves relying upon their masters to provide their every need, they could look to themselves, their family, and community members to provide needed goods and services. But in order to exploit these opportunities, slaves had to work hard for their masters and then even harder for themselves. Those who could best provide for themselves, as suggested above, were not neatly divided between house slaves, who reaped the rewards of close proximity to their white masters and mistresses, and the far removed field hands, who labored from sun up to sun down under a life of unremitting toil.

A close look at the slaves in the last generation or two of slavery in South Carolina reveals a different and much more complex picture of work and status in the slave quarters. Inherited rank, such as "born in the house," for example, could actually count against slaves wishing to move toward a respectable level of economic autonomy in the slave quarters. Evidence for John Blassingame's suggestion that slaves reserved the top rung of the social ladder for those [slaves] who performed services for other slaves rather than for whites is substantial.[18] The slaves who worked hardest and produced goods and services for their families and the community set the standard for others. Describing the slaves she had encountered on the Sea Islands, one visitor remarked how the best of them, "have carried their own crops well, and their example is beneficial in stimulating the lazier ones to exertion. There is a good deal of emulation among them, they will not sit quietly and see another earning all the money."[19] And, writing at an earlier time, the much-experienced overseer R. King may have counted upon this very kind of slave quarter sanction when, before listing the benefits that might accrue to masters when slaves accepted the work and garden system, he alluded to "the disgrace attached to idleness."[20] The pressure was on all slaves to work hard, well, and profitably for themselves. Thus, even the most ordinary slaves, with a little luck and a lot of hard work, could expect (and were probably expected) to establish some kind of an economic base from where they could contribute to their own support and eliminate the necessity to rely entirely upon their masters.

The work and garden system made it likely that "cash money" was going to become a significant presence in the slave quarter. In small or large amounts, slaves of all stations demonstrated an easy, if sometimes morally troubling, relationship with "all that cash." The sums of money involved in the trade with masters alone for goods such as cotton, corn, and livestock, were not trivial. James Sparkman who had encouraged his slaves to produce their own crops and to keep livestock, purchased all they had to sell. He even purchased provisions saved from their allowance. Writing in March 1858, Sparkman estimated the value of the goods he had purchased from his slaves during the past year. In cash money, the sum earned was "upwards of $130," he recorded. And in luxuries such as "sugar molasses, flour, coffee, handkerchiefs, aprons, home-spun, and calico, pavilion gause [mosquito nets]," and necessities such as "tin buckets, hats, pocket knives, and sieves," he figured "another $110 could be added." Two men were credited with $27 and $25 each. Both had made the money from selling Sparkman "hogs of their own raising." Whether as individuals or in family groups, slaves could earn quite substantial sums of money. One plantation journal entry shows that Michael Gramling paid out over $200 to sixteen slaves for the year's cotton crop.[21] Such a sum (and this only for the cotton the slaves produced and sold) suggests the productivity of quite "ordinary" slaves, and the amount of cash accumulated by hard-working and enterprising slaves.

To enjoy the rewards of their efforts, slaves could draw upon the master's commissary store for manufactured and other "luxury goods" and have the cost of goods deducted from the balance in their accounts, or they might receive payment for their goods in cash. Masters seem to have preferred slave dependency on their merchandise but probably lacked the necessary self-discipline and effort required to organize the ordering and accounting of a sufficiently large selection of goods.[22] Most masters tended to combine the two methods of settling accounts with their slaves, or else they simply paid their slaves in cash money. For their part, slaves sought as wide an access to goods as they could obtain and, increasingly, only cash money sufficed. However, like Robert, a slave belonging to T. C. Means, most had to abide with a combination of the two methods of payment. With his credit of $25 Robert collected by way of part payment a pair of shoes, valued at $1.50, and "to cash lent to you, $15."[23] Another planter, P. S. Bacot combined both methods of payment. Note an entry in his account book reference to his slave accounts. Dated 15 March, the 1852 account for Gus, a slave, reads:

Order on J.E.G, (local merchant) for	$4.00
Due me on old act.	2.37½ cts
Paid Randall (a slave) for him	1.00
April 21. 1 pair corded pants	3.00
April 22. 1 fine shirt and cravat	2.25
Recd. 50 cts in cash	1.75 cts

A settled account was that of Old Toney:

5 Aug. 1851. Order on J.E.G.	
for 1 yard Drab d/eta [sic]	.50 cts.
10 Sept. Order on J.E.G.	
for 2 galls. molasses c. 37½	.75 cts.
18 Dec. Order on J.E.G.	
for [unclear]	3.25 cts.
18 Dec. By 4 barrels corn	
c. 75 cts. per bus.	<u>4.50</u> cts.
	<u>0.00</u>[24]

And, as an indication as to how the Bacot slaves credited their accounts, in 1860, Bacot paid them $2.50 per 100 pounds of seed cotton. The largest producer was Colon with 488 lbs. for which he was paid $12.20; and the smallest was Daniel who was credited for 8 lbs. earning only 20 cents.[25]

By way of payment for goods and services provided to the masters, and through the slaves' internal economy—a system that facilitated the exchange of goods and services among a widening slave network—money played an increasingly important role in the slave quarters. Cash money and the accumulation of property and wealth created visible social and economic distinctions among the slaves. As Charles Ball pointed out "It may well be supposed, that in our society, although we were all slaves, and all nominally in a condition of the most perfect equality, yet there was in fact a very great difference in the manner of living. . . ."[26]

Antebellum slaves in South Carolina were working toward making a life of their own; they even operated some of the more important institutions of their world. Of course, some did better than others, and the families with greater numbers and more able bodied members usually accumulated more property than those less well-endowed.[27] Indeed, there were such clear economic differences among slaves and slave families that it was possible to identify "rich families" and "poor families," and perhaps even a burgeoning class consciousness. There was a sizable number of slaves whose income would have compared favorably with many free men (black or white) in the South and elsewhere.[28] Such structural differences, based on wealth and earning potential, sometimes proved divisive, as both rich and poor slaves lived side by side in the same quarters, and not always harmoniously. Kerziah Brevard fully understood the financial rewards that could fall to her slaves, particular those who organized themselves into productive family units. She often found the power of certain families too much for her to control; she seems even to have resented the complacent well-being of some of the more well-to-do slaves on the place. On January 23, 1861, she recorded a picture of Jim bringing a cart load of wood for his family. "Perhaps if he were free," she pondered, "he would have to buy this wood . . . maybe have a poor house and a dirty chimney." Instead of this, Jim had "a house . . . brick fire place with three rooms—one to sit in—two bedrooms." For Brevard, the most unruly slaves were members of the largest and most powerful families on the plantation. She struggled to feel any affection for these slaves and wrote that she "didn't wish them very bad luck." She only wished them to "feel like they are no better than other servants." But these slaves were formidable opponents for Brevard, because they were "prop[p]ed up by a large family and presume on it by making others succumb to them." She only wished to have these slaves realize, somewhat ironically (to us), that "power is not always to the strong." She was convinced that if they were all freed, "in a day these very families would enslave the small families."[29]

The use of cash money in the slave quarters could also influence the personal behavior of slaves as well as the community's institutional practices. Consider, for example, the problems parents might have faced in their efforts to control the behavior of their young daughters in a world were cash money was becoming increasingly prevalent and desirable, and where the enjoyment of certain goods and services depended upon one's access to cash. Slave parents probably allowed their daughters a degree of latitude greater than they would have wished, because of the reproduction demands the institution of slavery placed upon slave women of child-bearing age.[30] The intrusion of market values that continually challenged the more traditional values of the quarters was also a factor. The response of young men and women in the quarters may well have paralleled a general movement in the direction of privatizing the decisions of adult life—"in repudiation of community values and parental control"—that was evident in the eighteenth century. Elements in this process, "a decline in age at marriage" and "a surge in premarital pregnancies between 1760 and 1800," by itself, "suggests tellingly the loss of parental and community controls."[31] Gus Feaster, a former slave, provides an example of the emerging value system and what was probably a major source of intergenerational tension: parents' decreasing ability to control or influence their daughters' sexual conduct. Born in 1840, Feaster left a picture of the social interaction between young slaves. "When boys and gals gits up some size," he recounted, "dey feels dey selves." This was about the time that young men went "bird thrashing in de moonlight . . . and sing dis vulgar song. 'I'll give you half-dollar if you come out tonight.' "[32] Expanding market opportunities, and courting rituals with their necessary accoutrements made the possession of cash money imperative. And, the farther the slaves' commercial world extended beyond the quarters, the greater became the prevalence of cash money and the intrusion of market values.

For young adults (males in particular), cash was essential in those crucial areas of courting, sports, and recreation. Not only was money required to purchase the accoutrements necessary to attract the attention of one's heart's desire, their absence could deny a male suitor any kind of access to her society. An incident recalled by a Newberry District former slave, Caroline Farrow, reveals the importance slaves in general, and perhaps those courting, in particular, placed upon clothes and their personal appearances. "Once a nigger boy stole out to see his gal," she related, "all dressed up to kill. De patrollers found him at his gal's house and started to take off his coat so they could whip him, but he said, 'please don't let my gal see under my coat, 'cause I got on a bosom and no shirt.' "[33] Elijah Green of Charleston District exposed what may have been an understandable increase in the level of materialism informing the slaves' courting practices and mate selection. In this case, a concern for material possessions was again manifest in the importance slaves placed on clothes and the way they dressed. Born on Christmas Day, 1842, Green, whose master was George Jones, was the youngest of seven boys and the only one of his family to work in the house. Green would wear his master's cast-off clothing, which he was glad to have. Among the slave's apparel, footwear was of particular importance as it was often a quick and accurate way of assessing status. The pair of shoes Green received from his master was of a very special type and "w'en a slave had one of 'em you could't tell 'em he wasn't dress to death."[34] Therefore, the better dressed the slave, the more he looked the part, and the better would be his chances of winning the object of his desire. In Gus Feaster's world, young men and women placed a great deal of emphasis on their personal appearance.

The slaves' Sunday best was dyed red for the girls, and the boys "made de gals' hoops out'n grape vines." For this favor the girls would give the boys a dime, "if dey had one, for a set of hoops."[35] Obviously, there was a serious problem for young men and women who, unlike Green, could not depend upon their master's or mistress's cast-offs. How could they procure the kind of clothes and pay for the outings necessary to win their desired's affections without cash?

The slaves' courting practices and their concern for their personal appearance made it imperative that they learn to operate in an ever-expanding and increasingly depersonalized slave community in which cash money was becoming the primary means of accessing certain goods and services. As the slaves' commercial world extended beyond the slave quarters, the kind of relationships that operated at home among family, kin, friends, and neighbors were becoming increasingly less appropriate.[36]

A further example of the intrusion of market values into the private world of the slaves is the slave "frolic." Slave dances or parties, commonly referred to as frolics, were popular and frequent. The young gentleman hoping to meet or entertain a young lady at a dance needed to have cash at his disposal. Slave frolics were often the scene of joyous, intense affairs. Usually held on a Saturday night and lasting until the early hours of the morning, slaves used these occasions to rest, to relax, and to meet friends and family living nearby; they danced, sung, and generally had a good time. Evidence suggests that slaves used these dances as a chance to pursue leisure activities such as courting, drinking, and gambling. Coming as they did at the end of a hard working week, such occasions offered slaves a welcome respite from their labors, but the frolics and associated activities required cash money.

For one such slave party held in April, 1838, Jo Thompson's Scipio and a "free boy," Joe Berry, had "employed" Mrs. Mattinson's Austin "to give the supper." As payment for playing host and making his house available, Austin would receive 25 cents per head which would be collected "off the attendants." A fish supper would be included in the admission price of 25 cents. News of the "frolic" was passed among the slaves and given out at church meeting the previous Sunday. Thus, even in this, one of the more private corners of the slave community, social success, in one way or the other, rested upon the acquisition of money; economic success could follow from mastering the skills if not the values of the market place.[37]

Quite ordinary, hard working (and perhaps not so hard working) slaves, then, displayed a level of familiarity with the workings of the market place.[38] When Jason Coachman, a white man, accused Lewis, a slave, of stealing a fiddle after he had seen Lewis with the fiddle, Lewis' explained that the fiddle belonged to another slave by the name of Phil who had asked him to take it to a Mr. Johnson to have it varnished. Phil had purchased the fiddle for $1.75 from Mr. Burroughs's Joe. He had then swapped it to a waggoner for another fiddle and, somewhat ostentatiously, had given the waggoner "a dollar to boot." Not only had cash money been required to engage in a transaction that would eventually lead to the possession of a desired object, the system of purchasing land and slaves (familiar to most white Southerners) was employed in facilitating the transaction. Dave, who was present when Phil contracted with Joe for the fiddle, recalled that Phil was to give Joe a dollar down and 75 cents "on a credit."[39] The market place, its values, and its language, was a familiar part of the world these slaves made. That waggonners, free Negroes, and white Southerners interacted with slaves in these kinds of transactions attests both to the widening reach of the slaves' internal economy and the challenge to the more traditional means of exchanging goods and services and the associated values.

Evidence from the wider slave community reveals a growing appreciation for the worth and use of cash money, and the close relationship between the slaves' own productivity and financial reward. The petty enterprise of two "inter-state" businessmen, Elijah and Jerry, the former living in Georgia, the other in South Carolina, provides a useful example. Elijah would come over the river from the Georgia side and set a keg containing liquor in the house where Jerry lived. A white man, Thomas Beaty, sold the whisky for which Elijah received one dollar. The arrangement that had existed between Elijah and Jerry was that the latter would send chickens to Augusta, where Elijah would then sell them and purchase whisky with the proceeds. The whisky would then be resold by Beaty. Thus, the opportunity for Jerry to keep and raise chickens had provided the means by which he could engage in the slaves' internal economy. Armed with a small stake, Jerry took a dangerous step into what was probably the more risky and more lucrative (but illegal) side of the internal economy.[40]

Exchanges such as those between Elijah and Jerry begs the question—were slaves subordinating more traditional and perhaps morally superior means of commodity exchange for what appears to be those based on the dictates of the market forces? The former slaves who testified before the Southern Claims Commission [SCC] had all acquired fairly sizable amounts of property under slavery, and Henry Newton, formerly a slave in Beaufort District, provides a glimpse into the their financial dealings. Allowed to farm for himself "long before the war," by working in his spare time, Newton was able to purchase a horse in the spring of 1864. By this time he was in a position to pay the $500 "rebel money" as well as some "state money."[41] Before he finally became the owner of the horse, he had to throw in the $30 in silver and gold that he had been "saving for years."[42]

Working hard to scrape together small surpluses that could then be turned into cash money made it hard for most slaves to aspire beyond concern for the present. As Wilma King points out, what most slave parents concerned themselves with, was the transmission of social skills–defensive in their nature–that might help children to learn how to survive under slavery. Parents could also provide their offspring with marketable skills such as hunting, sewing, cooking, and survival skills which could also be "exchanged" or "sold" in the slaves' economy.[43] When Daniel and Abram, both belonging to Robert Lipscomb, were tried for stealing two bushels of wheat from the Reverend Thomas Curtin, and two more from their master, Sally, a slave, told the Court that the defendants brought the wheat to her house, and that Daniel "sold her a part of it for sewing."[44] The value placed upon what was traditionally female skills is in evidence. Daniel may have had to steal the wheat in order to "pay" Sally for her skills. The exchange, moreover, here as elsewhere, is a direct one, a commercial transaction: Daniel "sold" her a part of the stolen wheat "for sewing." The language is exact and to the point, capturing perfectly the impersonal nature of the exchange.

If slaves were going to provide a financial cushion for themselves and their families, they had to go beyond mere exploitation of their gardens for the seasonal produce that might result; they had to look to a more distant future. While most slaves could not have aimed for much more than the provision of much needed extras, there were clearly others who aspired toward a level of self-sufficiency and much more: Pompey Smith was such a slave. Smith, a Beaufort slave, had planted some land and raised a crop which he worked "in all the spare time I had." He testified that the property he had lost to Union troops had been acquired by "hard work" from which he had "made money and bought it." The horse, included in his claim before the SCC., had been purchased from a K. S. Smith at a cost of $200. His former master's son testified that Pompey had "always planted ten to fifteen acres," which had been worked with the help of Pompey's horse. Smith had not only saved and used his money well, he had accumulated sufficient money that he was able to loan money at interest.[45]

Because much of the individual's ability to acquire cash money was dependent upon the family's aggressive exploitation of available opportunities, it is especially noteworthy that some slaves looked beyond their own life span and made provisions for their loved ones. Edward Brown, a young man under slavery, had been left a mule by his grandfather and had "used the mule as his own property for two or three years before he left to join the Union Army." A fellow slave on William Middleton's Beaufort plantation was William Drayton who explained that his father had died and "left me the means with which I bought the Jenny mule." Drayton's father had left "the means and property he left for his children" with his oldest brother, and Drayton had purchased the mule on the advice of his uncle, the payment for which had been made in three installments. The first was $100 in gold and silver, then a second payment of $50 "all in silver," and a final payment of $100 in "state bank bills."[46] That some slaves managed to make provisions for their children's economic future is evidenced in the story of the Draytons. The sums involved may well have been outside the range of most slaves, but the practice of passing on goods from generation to generation was probably not uncommon. The behavior of slaves like the Browns and Draytons would have disturbed slaveholders who agreed with the observation of a Georgia planter who, writing in 1860, claimed that "The negro . . . never looks ahead," and that money will only "lead him into temptation."[47] It would seem that he was both wrong and right.

Slaves worked hard because they had to if they were to survive slavery, but some endeavored to go beyond the immediate demands made upon them. There were also those who used their non-work time to rest, recuperate, or to "frolic." But, as we have seen—given the apparent penetration of cash money into the private world of the slave—some forms of rest and recuperation had a price tag. Slaves who could not, or would not, invest the time or energy in working their gardens to produce surplus crops, were obliged, nonetheless, to compete with those who succeeded in these endeavors: those who worked in family groups, pooled their earnings, and drew economic, political, and social strength from the results of such arrangements. Less productive slaves, on the other hand, may well have engaged in extra-legal means in order to compete with those "richer" than themselves.

In some ways cash money in the slave quarters rendered the slaves' world less private, more like, and increasingly reliant upon the public world of the master to satisfy a growing demand for goods (and clients) with which to trade. But a strong internal economy provided the slaves with alternative means of dispensing with their surplus produce and obtaining desirable goods and services. The price to pay (if such it was) was the intrusion of market forces into the slave quarters. Accompanying this intrusion were market values that altered the more traditional commodity exchange practices and strained the value system of the slave quarters.

Antebellum slaves demonstrated and acted upon what was an increasingly sophisticated understanding of the operation of the market forces. The process, however, would be fraught with tension as slaves were seldom able to fully develop their entrepreneurial talents or completely break away from the more persistent communal values of the slave quarters.

∾
NOTES

1. Traditional exchange and non-market values are here associated with systems that values mutuality, reciprocity, and care for others. Cash money, by its very nature, threatens these relationships. As Christopher Clark writes, "Cash payment connotes a certain immediacy and a certain anonymity between dealers. Once a debt is paid off, obligation ceases. A debt paid off in cash implies abstraction–a social distance between buyer and seller–because the form of payment can be turned to any use." *The Roots of Capitalism: Western Massachusetts, 1780–1860* (Ithaca: Cornell University Press, 1990), 33.

2. One example of the what might be considered "traditional exchange practices" is provided by the slave, Charles Ball. While enslaved on a plantation in South Carolina in the early years of the nineteenth century, Ball recalled, that the slaves were "supplied with an abundance of bread, for a peck is as much as a man can consume in a week, if he has other vegetables with it;" but this was not always the case as "we were obliged to provide ourselves with other articles, necessary for our subsistence." It seems that for the slaves with whom Ball lived subsistence was achieved through sharing. "Nero had corn in his patch," Ball wrote, "which was now hard enough to be fit for boiling, and my friend Lydia had beans in her garden." At this earlier time, perhaps, the solution appeared more simple–"We exchanged corn for beans, and had a good supply of both. . . . " See *Fifty Years in Chains* (New York: Dover Publications, 1970) 194 (originally published in 1837).

3. Non-cash payment and extended indebtedness entailed a different kind of relationship. "Forms of payment had always to be negotiated, with due recognition of particular household needs and abilities. . . . Local exchange created networks of obligation alongside those already created by kinship or neighborhood. These obligations . . . were real, and they embodied the distinctive moral demands made by rural people on each other when they exchanged goods, labor, and other services." Clark, *The Roots of Capitalism*, 33.

4. For a discussion of traditional social divisions among slaves. See John Blassingame, "Status and Social Structure in the Slave Community: Evidence from New Sources," in *Perspectives and Irony in American Slavery*, ed. Harry P. Owens (Jackson: University of Mississippi Press, 1976), 137–51.

5. Rural slaves, by and large, had fewer opportunities to accumulate large amounts of property and money with which to purchase their way out of slavery, but the accumulation of smaller sums of money and property could have a significant impact on the quality of life a slave might expect, and affect his or her place in the slaves' social hierarchy. See Mary Beth Corrigan, in this volume; Loren Schwenin-

ger, *Black Property Owners in the South, 1790–1915* (Urbana: University of Illinois Press, 1990), chap. 2.

6. See Philip D. Morgan, "Work and Culture: The Task System and the World of Low Country Blacks, 1700 to 1860," *The William and Mary Quarterly* 39, (October 1982): 563–99.

7. Mary Scott of Florence District told her interviewer of her uncle who "when white people come by going to church [and] he hoeing his rice. Dey didn't want him work on Sunday." Their mistress, Elizabeth Gamble, "tell dem he gwine to chop his rice on Sunday." Mary Scott in George P. Rawick, ed., *The American Slave: A Composite Autobiography, South Carolina Narratives* (Westport, Conn.: Greenwood Publishing Company, 1972), vol 3, part 4, 117. [hereafter noted as *The American Slave*].

8. The slaves' system for producing goods for exchange was akin to the "subsistence-surplus" one described by Christopher Clark: "that is, most of the products exported [sold] . . . were necessities extra to the requirements of local households or by-products of their production." See *The Roots of Capitalism*, 28.

9. Set up in 1871, the Southern Claims Commission "was a sincere, well-meaning attempt to reimburse claimants throughout the former Confederacy whose property had been seized for the use of the United States Army during the Civil War." See John Hammond Moore, "Getting Uncle Sam's Dollars: South Carolinians and the Southern Claims Commission, 1871–1880," *South Carolina Historical Magazine* 82, no. 3 (July 1981): 248. See also Moore's unpublished manuscript, "South Carolina and the Southern Claims Commission, 1871–1880," in the State Archives, Columbia, South Carolina [hereafter, the Commission will be noted as SCC.]. Testimony of Harriet Smith before the SCC.

10. Testimony of Jane Ruth, Joseph Rozier, and Adam Ruth before the SCC.

11. R. King Jr. in Breeden, *Advice Among Masters: The Ideal in Slave Management in the Old South*, (Westport, Conn.: Greenwood Publishing Company, 1980), 266–7.

12. Sparkman to Benjamin Allston, March 10, 1858, in J. H. Easterby, *The South Carolina Rice Planter* (Chicago: University of Chicago Press, 1945), 350.

13. See Eugene Genovese on the slaves' use of religion in *Roll, Jordan, Roll: The World the Slaves Made* (New York: Pantheon, 1972) especially book 2; also his *From Rebellion to Revolution: Afro-American Slave Revolts in the Making of the New World* (New York: Vintage Books, 1979), chap. 1. On the developing African-American culture under slavery, see Sterling Stuckey, *Slave Culture: Nationalist Theory and The Foundations of Black America* (New York: Oxford University Press, 1987), chap. 1; and Lawrence W. Levine, *Black Culture and Black Consciousness: Afro-American Folk Thought From Slavery to Freedom* (New York: Oxford University Press, 1977).

14. James O. Breeden ed., *Advice Among Masters*, 274.

15. H.M. Henry, *Police Control of the Slave in South Carolina* (New York: Negro University Press, 1968), 85.

16. Henry, *Police Control*, 86; For an extended discussion of additional implications particularly for slaves trading with their masters, and what was probably an

additional motivation for slaves to move from commodity exchange to the more "liberating" use of "cash money," see Lawrence T. McDonnell, "Money Knows no Master: Market Relations and the American Slave Community" in *Developing Dixie: Modernization in a Traditional Society*, eds. Winfred B. Moore, Jr., Joseph F. Tripp, and Lyon G. Tyler, Jr. (Westport, Conn.: Greenwood Publishing Company, 1988), 31–44.

17. As David M. Potter wrote, "A slave system, since it means the involuntary subordination of a significant proportion of the population, requires a social apparatus distinctively adapted in all its parts to imposing and to maintaining such subordination . . . this subordination was also racial, involving not only the control of slaves by their masters but also the control of a population of 4 million blacks by 8 million whites." (452) In the South, the "determination to keep blacks in subordination took priority over other goals of southern society, the entire socio-economic system had to be conducted in a way that would maximize the effectiveness of racial control." (455) *The Impending Crisis, 1848–1861* (New York: Harper, 1976).

18. See Blassingame, "Status and Social Structure," 142.

19. See Genovese, *Roll, Jordan, Roll*, 537; Letter from C.P.W., November 16, 1862, in Elizabeth Ware Pearson, *Letters From Port Royal: Written at the Time of the Civil War* (Boston: W.P. Clarke Co., 1906), 112.

20. R. King quoted in Breeden, *Advice Among Masters*, 266.

21. Although not dated, the list coincides with another dated 12 January, 1854. See Gramling Journal. in the South Caroliniana Library, University of South Carolina, Columbia, South Carolina [hereafter SCL.].

22. Some circumvented these demands upon their time and contracted out such services to local merchants. For a fuller discussion of this practice see John Campbell "As 'A Kind of Freeman'?: Slaves' Market-Related Activities in the South Carolina Upcountry, 1800–1860," in *The Slaves' Economy: Independent Production by Slaves in the Americas*, eds. Ira Berlin and Philip D. Morgan (London: Frank Cass, 1991), 147–8.

23. T. C. Means Cotton Book for 1858 in the SCL.

24. P. S. Bacot Account Book, 1852–7 in the SCL.

25. Bacot Account Book, 1860.

26. Ball, *Fifty Years in Chains*, 275.

27. Larry E. Hudson Jr., "Work and Slavery: The Slave Family in South Carolina, 1820–1860" [forthcoming].

28. This was not peculiar to South Carolina. See Schweninger, *Black Property Owners*, 30–36.

29. Brevard Diary March 10 and Jan. 26, 1861 in the SCL.

30. See Herbert G. Gutman, *The Black Family in Slavery and Freedom, 1750–1925*, (New York: Vintage Books, 1976), chap 2, particularly 64–6 and 76.

31. See Winifred Barr Rothenberg, *From Market-Places to a Market Economy: The Transformation of Rural Massachusetts, 1750–1850*, (Chicago: University of Chicago Press, 1992), 38.

32. Gus Feaster in *The American Slave*, vol. 2, part 2, 51.
33. Caroline Farrow in *The American Slave*, vol.2, part 2, 39. Shirt Bosom: The practice was to wear a stiff white shirt bosom over the shirt and held up around the neck. When no shirt was worn the bosom, worn alone, gave the appearance of a shirt and bosom.
34. Elijah Green in *The American Slave*, vol. 2, part 2, 83.
35. Gus Feaster in *The American Slave*, part 2, 47.
36. As Bruce Mann argues, market relations will intrude when the "local" market extends so far that it goes beyond the usual borders "to include strangers as well as neighbors." If nothing else, it "allows people to treat their neighbors as they did strangers." See *Neighbors and Strangers: Law and Community in Early Connecticut* (Chapel Hill: University of North Carolina Press, 1987) 166–8.
37. Fairfield Magistrates and Freeholders Court, Case 26 Aug. 8, 1851; for the operation and organization of the Court, see William C. Henderson, "Spartan Slaves: A Documentary Account of Blacks on Trial in Spartanburg, South Carolina," Northwestern University, unpublished Ph.D. Thesis, 1978, 141–61; Philip Racine, "The Spartanburg District Magistrates and Freeholders Court, 1824–1865," *South Carolina Historical Magazine* (October 1986): 197–212. Records housed in the State Archives, Columbia, South Carolina [hereafter MFC].
38. The expansion and increasing sophistication of the internal economy made it possible for slaves inclined not to labor in their gardens to earn extra income from legal and quasi-legal commercial activites.
39. MFC., Anderson Case 94, 21 July, 1838.
40. MFC., Anderson, Case 176, 30 December, 1845. As discussed above, masters were fearful that their slaves would use money to purchase alcohol. As late as 1860, one Newberry District slaveholder, determined to halt the illegal trading between slaves and white men, offered a reward of $500 "for proof to convict for any one buying pork, corn, fodder, or any other produce from my negroes without a special order from me." See Henry, *Police Control of the Slave*, 83.
41. Regarding the testimony of Henry Newton, "rebel money" probably refers to paper money drawn upon the Confederate Bank, and "state" money—paper currency drawn upon a state bank. Testimony of Henry Newton and his master, James B. Smith before the SCC. No. 9586.
42. A. Jackson, claim SCC. No. 11199.
43. See Wilma King's essay in this volume. Teachers were highly esteemed in the quarters. Old men and women with great stores of riddles, proverbs, and folktales played a crucial role in teaching morality and training the youth to solve problems and to develop their memories. See also Blassingame, "Status and Social Structure," 148.
44. Testimony before the SCC. No. 8018.
45. MFC., Spartanburg, Case 102, 3 September, 1849.
46. See Ira Berlin et al., *Freedom: A Documentary History of Emancipation, 1861–1867*, Series 1, vol. 1, The Destruction of Slavery, (Cambridge: Cambridge University

Press, 1985), 140–1; Bryan Edwards, *The History, Civil and Commercial, of the British West Indies*, 5 vols. (New York: AMS Press, 1966), vol. 2, 163, (originally published in 1819); see also Sidney Mintz, *Caribbean Transformations*, (Chicago: Aldine Publishing Co., 1974), 207. Testimony of William Izzard before the SCC., claim No.10096, and that of E. Brown, claim No. 21768.

47. James O. Breeden, *Advice among Masters*, 331 or 309.

~

MATERIAL CULTURE & COMMUNITY STRUCTURE
The Slave And Tenant Community At Levi Jordan's Plantation, 1848-1892

Kenneth L. Brown

T he cultural evolution which occurred in rural areas of the South after slavery resulted in what may be effectively conceived of as a continuum of development in many respects of African-American culture. Slavery may have legally ended, but "Freedom" did not pay the rent or buy the food. Freedom meant that new behavioral adaptations were required for the survival of the former slaves. After emancipation, African Americans who remained within the plantation system faced a new set of adaptive forces. To some extent, they may have negotiated some successes in their labor relations with their masters during the long period of slavery, but with emancipation those rules, and the economic and social basis for them, were suddenly and irrevocably altered. Former slaves and masters had to begin the negotiation process from a radically different point. As before, this process had to involve both the conditions of each plantation community as well as the historical processes into which (and from which) the "players" were embedded.

Indeed, it has been suggested that in many respects the postbellum period may have been materially worse for African Americans than was slavery.[1] If true, this would mean that freedmen had to adapt to new conditions of life that may have been more severe in some aspects than slavery. The depressed post war economic condition of the South was a major factor in formation of the environment that former slaves and slave owners were forced to confront during the new period of negotiation. Both of the primary plantation classes had to face reduced material conditions, as well as abrupt changes in the dependant relationship between the classes. The plantation owners continued to control the means of production, including both the land and a majority of the tools; and the former slaves continued to provide the primary source of labor. Wages and/or money earned through "shares" became the primary mechanisms for providing for the material needs of the labor force. The "legitimate" needs of each group had to be met through a process of negotiation with the other. Thus, these new conditions of life forced additional change and adaptation. However, as a result of the earlier period of adaptation and cultural development under the conditions of slavery, the cultural matrix for African Americans of 1865 was substantially different from the culture of the earlier, enslaved arrivals.

Within the past decade elements of this discussion in southern historiography have begun to filter into historical archaeology.[2] Traditional archaeological concerns with artifact classification, temporal distinctions, and the definition of ethnicity have begun to give way to other types of questions concerning the lifeways of the plantation's inhabitants.[3] In part, this change has developed as a result of the realization that historical archaeology controls data that is at once the product of historically defined processes and individual/group beliefs and behaviors of the European Americans and the African Americans. Archaeologists have the potential to deal with the end products (the artifacts and artifact associations) of the actual lifeways and beliefs of African Americans.[4] Instead of looking for the presence of "ethnic identifiers" and/or "African retentions," historical archaeologists have begun to investigate why these end products came about and were perpetuated through slavery and freedom.[5] The focus is shifting toward the investigation of cause and meaning to those who produced, utilized, and deposited the recovered artifacts and artifact contexts.[6]

Material remains (both artifacts and their contexts) recovered from the slave and tenant quarters areas of the Levi Jordan Plantation, Brazoria County, Texas will be employed to investigate a number of issues related to the evolution of African-American culture from slavery into tenancy. As Randolph Campbell has stated: "Once defeat destroyed slavery and emancipated approximately 250,000 blacks, most white Texans for generation after generation regarded them and their descendants as more of a problem than an asset."[7] This paper will emphasize the role(s) served by certain artifacts and/or artifact contexts identified in the slave and tenant cabins in the survival and community adaptation to ante- and postbellum conditions that existed on the plantation and in the surrounding area. Of particular concern here will be interpretations of economic, political, and ritual life and adaptation within this community from 1848 to 1892. This should provide an example of the interpretive power of archaeological research in the study of the evolution of African-American culture within the United States.

Levi Jordan and twelve slaves arrived in Texas in 1848 from Union County, Arkansas, determined to establish a new plantation. Jordan purchased 2,222 acres (at $4.00/acre) in Brazoria County, from Samuel M. Williams.[8] The plantation is located approximately sixty miles south of the modern city of Houston, Texas, and fifteen miles inland from the Gulf of Mexico. Throughout the ante-bellum development of the plantation, the primary cash crops produced were sugar and cotton. Historical documentation suggests that Jordan raised as well as imported slaves for sale to other planters . Also adding to the profitability of the plantation, Jordan built the largest sugar mill in the county to process the cane raised by himself and several of the surrounding planters. After 1865 sugar was produced in decreasing quantities, while cotton production increased in importance. By 1870, cotton had become the dominant crop raised for external sale.[9]

After Jordan's death in 1873, the plantation was divided among his heirs. The northern half, which includes the main house and the slave/tenant quarters, was inherited by William Archibald Campbell McNeill, one of Jordan's grandsons, who was a minor at the time of Jordan's death. As a result of a number of events, the operation of this portion of the plantation between 1873 and 1892 was primarily left to a series of managers hired by Jordan's grandsons. The operation of the plantation during this time was organized by a system that included wage laborers along with tenants/sharecroppers. Plantation ledger books indicate the lease of land and equipment, the sale of seed, and the payment of wages to a number of individuals residing on the plantation. Non-plantation residents appear only in the wage payment portion of the ledgers, suggesting that at least some of this labor was secured from people not otherwise farming the plantation's lands. Nearly all of the wages reportedly paid by these ledger books was paid during the months of November through February—the prime months for sugar production. Thus, while not directly stated within the ledgers, a majority of the wages paid was for work in the sugar mill. With the primary exception of the foreman, the wage laborers during any year, were not the most productive sharecroppers for that year, although members of the same nuclear family might fall into both categories. Individual families could, therefore, operate within both of these systems, although individuals might not. Finally, the data strongly suggests that a majority of the families sharecropping on the plantation did not raise cotton in every year. All of the families do appear to have produced food crops. However, only a few families each year attempted to produce cotton for the external market.

This system ended in 1892, when four of Jordan's great-grandsons (the

Martins) took sole possession of the northern portion of the plantation, divided it among themselves, and evicted the tenant/sharecropper families from their quarters. This eviction appears to have been the result of a court case which involved the McNeills and the Martins. During this case, two of the tenant/sharecroppers (both of whom had been slaves on the plantation) testified against the Martins. Once the case was settled in favor of the Martins, they appear to have exacted a tremendous price for this testimony. The eviction took the form of removing all members of the tenant/sharecropper community without their being permitted to take any of their possessions with them.

One critical aspect of this research into the evolution of the African-American community has been to demonstrate a high level of continuity between the pre- and post-emancipation population on the plantation. Archaeological research demonstrates that the same residential buildings were being employed during both of these time periods. Any investigation of cultural evolution, however, depends upon the ability to demonstrate a high level of residential continuity (from slavery to tenancy) and community involvement among the settler generation and their decendants. Otherwise, the cultural change noted may have been the result of people moving into the community, rather than the adaptive change of individuals within the community.

At least twelve families and/or heads of households can be shown to have been tenants/sharecroppers, who were working for wages, and/or practicing some other economic activity, on the plantation through the 1870s and 1880s. Additionally, five male children listed in 1870 are identified as heads of households on the plantation in 1880. Further, two females listed as wives in 1870 are identified as heads of households/widows in 1880, still continuing to live on the plantation. Finally, it is possible that two females listed as children in the 1870 census each married two of the male children noted above, and were still living on the plantation in 1880. Thus, of the twenty-nine families that can be identified as living on the plantation in 1870, a minimum of fourteen of them continued to have members living on the plantation in 1880. This group actually comprises nineteen of the twenty-three families living on the plantation in 1880. As noted above, two of the adult males from these families testified in the 1889–92 court case and appear to have been residing on the plantation at the time of their testimony. They were related through marriage to at least five of the other tenant families.

Further, the demographic structure of the African-American population residing on the plantation, based upon the 1850–80 Federal Census records help to demonstrate this continuity in population as well. Continuity can be observed in terms of the structure of the adult male population. Over time, the ratio of the cohort of adult males within the age categories from 20 to 50 years old remains approximately the same (Figure 1). This would suggest that this group of males is aging, rather than being replaced by a variety of individuals from outside of the original population. A number of the "replacements" are actually sons and grandsons of the original slave residents.

As noted above, the people residing in the plantation's slave and tenant communities did so in the same cabins. These cabins have been identified through both archaeological and historical evidence. This evidence indicates that the main house, the original plantation hospital, the house slave/domestic servant quarters, and a few of the smaller outbuildings around the house were made of wood. However, the bulk of the buildings concerned with production on the plantation, including the slave/tenant quarters, were constructed of brick. The main set of slave and tenant quarters are located approximately 400 feet northwest of the main house (Figure 2). The quarters area was occupied from 1848 until the forced abandonment in 1892. The actual buildings that served as the bulk of the slave and tenant quarters consisted of eight long, almost barracks-like structures built in units of two. Each of the units of cabins shared a central "hallway" and may have had a single continuous roof. Archae-

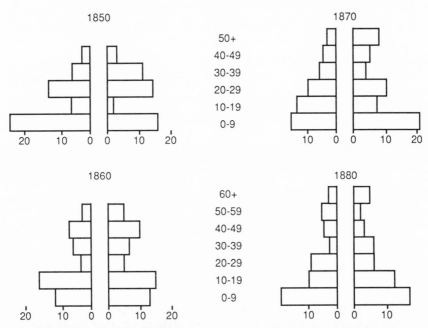

FIGURE 1. DEMOGRAPHIC PROFILES OF THE PLANTATION'S SLAVE OR TENANT POPULATIONS RECORDED IN THE 1850–1880 FEDERAL CENSUSES. PERCENTAGES ARE GIVEN FOR EACH OF THE AGE GROUPS, WITH FEMALES SHOWN ON THE LEFT AND MALES ON THE RIGHT.

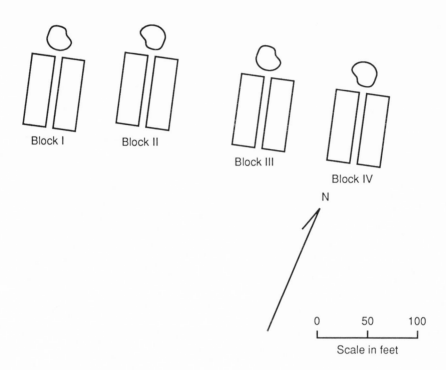

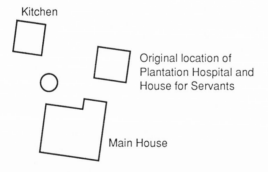

FIGURE 2. DIAGRAM SHOWING THE LOCATION OF THE MAIN HOUSE AND NEARBY OUTBUILDINGS AND THE FOUR BLOCKS OF SLAVE AND, LATER, TENANT CABINS.

ological evidence further demonstrates that each of the long buildings consisted of three to four individual cabins. That is, in blocks I, III, and IV, there were a total of six cabins (three in each of the long buildings), while in block II there were eight cabins (Figure 3).

The 1860 Federal Census lists a total of twenty-nine slave cabins on the plantation. The archaeologically defined configuration of four blocks would

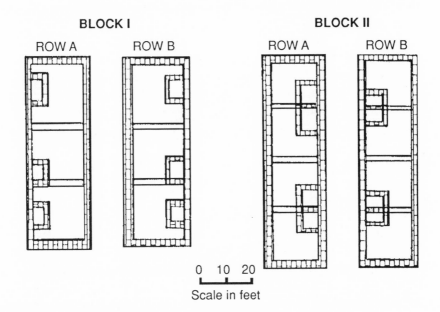

Cabin I-A-2: Political Leader
Cabin I-B-3: Shell/Bone Carver (tenant)
Cabin II-A-3: Shell/Bone Carver (slave)
Cabin II-B-I: Curer
Cabin II-B-2: Munitions Maker/Metal Worker
Cabin II-B-3: Seamstress
Cabin II-A-I: "Quilter"
Cabin II-A-4: "Hunter" (slave)

FIGURE 3. DIAGRAM OF BLOCKS I AND II WITH INDIVIDUAL CABINS DE-FINED WITHIN THEM. OCCUPATIONAL DESIGNATIONS HAVE BEEN BASED UPON ARTIFACTUAL DIFFERENCES NOTED IN THE COLLECTION OF ARTIFACTS FROM EACH OF THE CABINS. THE ARCHITECTURE OF BLOCKS III AND IV IS IDENTICAL TO THAT OF BLOCK I.

only have accommodated twenty-six cabins. An undated photograph of the main house, a diary written by one of Jordan's granddaughters, and excavation indicate that the remaining houses were wooden frame structures built near the main house. These buildings housed the domestic slaves/servants and provided space for other plantation functions (e.g., the hospital and weaving/sewing house).

An extremely large percentage of the artifacts and artifact contexts thus far recovered represent the preserved remains of possessions abandoned by the tenants as they were forced to leave in 1892. The result of this forced abandonment, the locking of the quarters for nearly twenty-five years prior to their systematic demolition, and flooding which resulted in the deposition of soil over the site has provided an important set of materials representing items hastily abandoned by their owners. Further, the materials have been recovered in a position relatively close to that in which they were left by their owners. (At least, that is, in terms of their general position relative to other materials within each of the cabins.) It is from these abandonment deposits that evidence of occupational specialization, political status, economic status, African behavioral and belief systems, and cultural evolution has been recovered. Given the large number of native Africans listed in the 1870 Federal Census for Brazoria County, Texas (123), this evolution was likely the result of several processes, including acculturation, the direct "importation" of African behaviors/beliefs, and changes brought about by emancipation.

To date, excavations have been conducted into fourteen individual slave/tenant cabins within the community. This figure includes excavation into all eight of the original cabins in block II, three cabins in block I, two cabins in block IV, and one cabin in block III. The data is being employed to demonstrate a variety of aspects concerning the lifeways of the members of these temporal communities. These aspects include evidence of the presence of a political hierarchy, ritual activities, and economic differences among the members of the communities. When this archaeological data is combined with the historical research, there is, again, the strong suggestion of continuity, although certain aspects (particularly ritual ones) may become more pronounced over time. The major behavioral changes noted within the archaeological record appear in occupation, diet, access to "store bought" items, location of ritual activities, settlement patterning of the community, and other aspects of behavior.

However, some of the apparent changes might be the result of differences between two of the archaeologically defined deposits in the cabins (e.g., the "abandonment deposit," and the "sub-floor" deposit), rather than the reflection of actual changes in the behavior and/or beliefs of members of the communities. That is, the so-called abandonment deposit is larger and more complete, because it represents the remains hastily left by the cabins' occupants. This deposit is defined by the observation that many of the items are complete (thus, usable at the time they became part of the archaeological deposit) and normally curated (removed when people leave one location for another). The sub-floor deposit was built up during the use of the cabins. Therefore, the sub-floor deposit would represent only those items which were lost, intentionally discarded, or merely deposited as a result of cleaning activities in the cabin—they fell through cracks in the floor boards. Items placed below the floor boards for safe keeping can be distinguished from either of the above deposits as a result of their having been placed into holes dug into the soil below the floor boards.

The problem with any direct comparison of these two deposits is that items infrequently utilized, heavily curated, or not likely to have been accidentally lost within the cabin, would not be well represented within the sub-floor deposits. This would make it difficult to interpret the exact types of behaviors connected with the use of such artifacts, or of their having occurred at anytime earlier than the abandonment of the cabin. Indeed, the abandonment event is likely the primary reason that these deposits have been the first to yield archaeological evidence of African ritual activities/beliefs within a tenant community in the South. There is limited evidence for ritual activities within the sub-floor deposit of the cabins. Despite this problem, however, the data suggests that there may have been an increase in the intensity of these types of activities during the period from slavery through tenancy.

Finally, it should be pointed out that not all of the cabins thus far tested have revealed evidence of the sudden, forced abandonment. It appears likely that only nine of the fourteen archaeologically tested and defined cabins were occupied at the time of this "eviction." The other five cabins appear to have served as residences during the post-emancipation period, but were apparently not occupied when the Martins forced an end to the community. The occupants of these cabins appear to have moved, taking many, if not all, of their possessions with them. At present it is not possible to determine when these earlier moves occurred. However, historical records do indicate that a number of the families known to have been residing on the plantation in 1880 moved out prior to 1892.

Two aspects of the archaeological and historic data relative to the slave and tenant community will be addressed in the remainder of this paper: the economic activities defined within these temporal communities and the structure of the communities. Both of these aspects aid in addressing the question of the role of the community in the survival and adaptation of slaves and tenants in the rural South during the latter half of the nineteenth century. While the issue of the "typicality" of the Jordan Plantation communities can be debated, it is within the context of this larger question that the data and interpretations derived from this excavation may prove to be most important.

As with any community of people that is not completely self-sufficient and self-contained, the slave and tenant communities of the Jordan Plantation functioned, in an economic sense, at several levels. At their most general, these levels could be labeled as the "internal economy" and as the "external economy." The internal economy would consist of those relationships and behaviors whose primary functions were to maintain the plantation as a community. These would include the economic activities of individuals, as well as families, within the slave/tenant communities and the relationships among members of these communities and the European-American power structure on the plantation (owner, overseer, and manager). The external economy would consist of those activities and relationships whose primary functions were to connect the plantation communities to the outside world. While these are not mutually exclusive sets of relationships and behaviors, the economic viability of any individual or family requires success in both of the arenas. However, what is not necessarily obvious, is that within the levels, very different relationships and behaviors were emphasized.

The economic structures of the Jordan Plantation's slave and tenant communities are being investigated through the study of a number of artifacts and their distribution within the archaeological deposits. For example, diet (particularly the use of animal proteins), occupation, the distribution of "non-utilitarian" and/or "expensive" items (e.g., jewelry and other personal items, porcelain and less expensive ceramics, and silverware and other utensils) are currently being studied. The question here is: are there artifacts and/or artifact contexts that demonstrate the relative economic status of a cabin's inhabitants within the slave and/or tenant communities? If such artifacts and contexts exist, are there changes over time?

Clearly, there are some major problems with the interpretation of an economic hierarchy based solely on archaeological data. Materials employed as economic indicators may have entered the households in a number of ways (e.g., as purchases, gifts, or through theft). In an archaeological setting it is obviously not absolutely possible to determine the mechanism(s) by which the items entered the various households. Further, it is not possible to completely establish the number of individuals within these households who could have obtained the items. However, these and other problems notwithstanding, the economic structure may be investigated through questioning the type, amount, and continuity of artifacts within the archaeological context of the tested cabins. Historical records can be employed to demonstrate that certain types of artifacts were more expensive than others. Some households have more of these items, and they have a history of having more of them.

From the data, it is possible to define a number of aspects of the economic structure of the slave and tenant communities. There appears to be patterned variability in the artifacts/artifact types represented within this data. Both the patterns of variability and the large number of some of these items argue against the hypothesis that theft was a primary, or even major, mechanism for obtaining the items. Archaeological evidence clearly demonstrates that some of the community's households invested a larger amount of capital in obtaining "expensive" personal items, while other households did not. A possible reason for these decisions was the difference in expendable income between households in the communities. Further, differences in consumer choice might help to explain why households vary in the items on which capital was expended.

The data on sharecropping demonstrates that only a few of the plantation's residents cropped cotton for shares. Even among this group, the amount of cotton produced varied from person to person and year to year. For example, Table 1 shows that the range of production was from three to seven approximately 500 pound bales, or $150.00 to $350.00. This would amount to from $75.00 to $175.00 after the McNeills removed their one-half share. In 1875, the range was from one to five bales, or from $40.92 to $240.30. Again, this would have produced from $20.46 to $120.15 after the owner's share was removed. However, only six of the eleven individuals who sharecropped cotton

TABLE 1. Table of Sharecroppers and Wage Earners who Lived in the community for the period covered by the most complete of the jordan plantation ledger books.

Name of sharecropper/ Tenant	1874 cotton produced	1875 wages (Jan-July)	1875 cotton produced	1876 wages (Feb-May)	Total Recorded Income
John McNeill		$103.25	$120.15	$100.50	$323.90
Promise McNeill	$150.00	$18.00	$38.27		$206.27
Claiborn Holmes	$150.00	$10.00	$104.89	$4.75	$269.64
Issac Holmes	$100.00	$1.25		$16.00	$117.25
George Holmes	$125.00	$3.00	$20.46		$148.92
Daniel Boxton	$100.00	$5.25	$96.35		$201.60
Henry Sibley	$ 75.00	$3.25			$78.25
Ely Lemmons		$4.00	$92.18		$96.18
Doc Hendricks	$175.00		$21.50		$196.50
John Greenwood	$125.00	$9.25		$5.00	$139.25
Manuel McPherson	$150.00	$4.00	$39.82	$8.59	$202.41
George Green			$28.87		$28.87
Holland Sherman	$125.00				$125.00
Walter Brown	$150.00	$1.25			$151.25

in 1874 did so in 1875. Table 1 also demonstrates that for these two years at least, the amount of money paid as wages was extremely low, with the exception of the "foreman," John McNeill. The ledger books also indicate that individuals who did not sharecrop cotton, did lease land and tools from the McNeill's. As they are credited with having paid their rents in cash, it is likely that they used the land to raise basic food crops which were then sold.

This production of a cash crop for the international market likely brought in much of the expendable income for the purchase of the items noted above, along with the rent for land and draft animals. Access to the plantation's fields for production of this cash crop was controlled by the McNeills (Jordan's primary heirs) and/or the various farm managers. However, the individual tenants also had some input into this production system, as they could choose to sharecrop. Therefore, the members of the tenant community appear not to have been a homogeneous group in terms of expendable capital. Further, the archaeological evidence demonstrates that a similar pattern of purchase of "wealth indicators" existed within a number of cabins during both the slave and tenant periods of occupation. Thus, slaves did have income which could be expended by them according to their own "desires." These patterns of consumption carried over into the tenancy period; similar items were purchased in many cases.

The research has also developed evidence concerning occupational differences among the residents of the community. These occupations relate to both the internal and external economies of the plantation. Identified occupations that can be related to the external economy include: carpenter (two slave, three tenant), blacksmith (one slave, two tenant), and seamstress (three slave, two tenant). Clearly, the emphasis on the external economy here is that these crafts were necessary to keep the plantation functioning, they could be "hired out," or they required items that came from outside of the plantation. Not well represented within the archaeological record are the agricultural workers (both field hands and/or sugar mill workers), especially for the slave period community. This is most likely the result of the nature of agricultural tools, the separate location for tool storage, and the separate location for the use of such tools. For the tenant period, these tools are better represented within the archaeological record in the form of metal parts of bridles and harnesses (bits, buckles, rings, and rivets) for mule teams: items that the tenants are known to have purchased and for which no secure, individual storage facilities are known. While a number of hoe blade fragments have been recovered from the cabin deposits, there is no way to accurately date their deposition.

Limited documentary evidence suggests that the house slaves/servants occupied dwellings away from the slave/tenant cabin area and closer to the main house. If this was indeed the case, then the economic hierarchy appears to be based solely on the non-domestic service occupations. When this economic scale is combined with the data related to occupation, and occupational change, of a cabin's residents, the results are revealing. Some of the "wealthiest" members of the slave and tenant community do not appear to have had specialized craft occupations within the external economy of the plantation. That is, during the tenancy period the blacksmith and the seamstress cabins rank lower than at least three cabins whose occupants have no obvious specialties in the external economy. However, the specialized occupations represented in these three cabins were extremely important within the internal economy.

In this context, it is important to note a difference between the slavery and tenancy periods with regard to this economic hierarchy. Historic and archaeological evidence indicates that the plantation's blacksmith and his family were able to move off the plantation by 1872. While this family was not the first to leave the plantation, it was the first to leave after purchasing land–360 acres (later reduced to 120 acres through non-payment of the loan).[10] The second family to purchase land, though not move off the plantation was the carpenter and his wife, a seamstress. The seamstress moved into the town of Brazoria and opened a small shop, while the carpenter remained on the plantation, ultimately becoming the farm foreman.[11] He lived on the plantation until the 1892 forced abandonment. His was one of the two African Americans to testify against the Martins. The house slave/domestic servant family, and descendants, did not move off the plantation, or purchase land, until the forced abandonment in 1892.[12] Thus, prior to 1865, a specialized occupation that could be hired out may have provided the initial capital necessary to purchase land–a significant "wealth indicator"–within a few years of emancipation. Further, it is interesting to note that the "most prestigious" of the slave occupations on the plantation did not produce the wealth needed to purchase land after 1865.

To date, a number of crafts/occupations have been defined within the archaeological record that fall under the heading of the internal economy. These crafts/occupations include: quilter, munitions maker, hunter, bone and shell carver, the seamstresses, political leader, and the magician/curer. While all of these require some externally produced and, therefore, purchased items, the consumption of the end product was within the slave/tenant community, or for the control and survival of these communities. Indeed, it is possible that consumption was limited solely to the immediate community, although their use may have extended into several of the surrounding plantations' tenant communities.

At least two of these internal occupations (and the political leader) clearly functioned to maintain and reinforce community identity and social control through the use of African and African-American cultural beliefs and practices. The bone and shell carver produced a variety of items that form a majority of the "ethnic identifiers" discovered within the deposits of the slave/tenant cabins. That is, recovered within the deposits of this cabin (slave: II-A-3; tenant: I-B-3) are tools for the manufacture of carved shell and bone objects along with a number of unfinished carved objects. Included here is a flat sandstone cobble, shell "blanks" for carving (including both fresh and salt water species), several knives, files, a metal punch, two small drills, a small saw blade, and grinding and shaping tools made of bone. While a number of the shells appear to have been employed in the production of buttons, many are not of the type generally employed for this purpose. Culturally modified coquina, whelk, snail, clam, and cockle shells are found in fairly large quantities throughout the archae-ological deposits, although they are not evenly distributed and their function is currently under investigation. Further, at least one of the "store bought" shell buttons recovered had a six-pointed star carved on one side at some time after it arrived on the plantation (Figure 4). Examination of the button demonstrates that the star was worn facing to the inside. That is, the pentacle was not visible while the button was being worn.

A total of twelve pieces of carved bone and one elaborately carved shell "cameo" have been recovered—all from the abandonment levels within their respective cabins. Four of these pieces are fairly simply carved and have been found in a context that suggests they may have served as "oracle bones." Three are flat, carved pieces that may have functioned as hair pins. One is a pendant made from the spur of a fighting cock. The other four pieces are intricately carved and appear to have functioned as a single object—probably a fly whisk (Figure 5). The spur pendant necklace and the fly whisk were found within the so-called political leader's cabin. The "oracle bones" were discovered within the magician/curer's cabin. The hair pins were excavated from a seamstress' cabin (2) and the munitions maker's cabin (1). Finally, the cameo (Figure 6) was unfinished and found within the abandonment deposit of the shell carver's cabin.

The community-wide function of one of the other "high-ranking cabin" occupants appears to have been that of a magician/curer.[13] A majority of the artifacts that formed part of the ritual paraphernalia for the magician/curer date to the rapid abandonment episode, suggesting some time depth for this activity within the cabin. However, a number of identical artifacts were found within the sub-floor deposits of the cabin. This ritual kit was recovered from a small area of the floor of the cabin, near the southeast corner of the room. It consists of several cast iron kettle bases; cubes of white chalk; bird skulls; an animal's

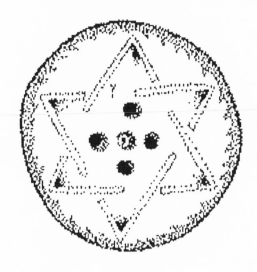

Scale in centimeters

**FIGURE 4. SMALL SHELL BUTTON WITH A PENTAGRAM CARVED ON ONE
SURFACE. THE CARVING WAS PLACED ON THE INWARD FACING SIDE OF
THE BUTTON, AND, THEREFORE, COULD NOT HAVE BEEN SEEN WHILE
THE BUTTON WAS IN USE.**

paw; two sealed tubes made of bullet casings; ocean shells; small dolls; an
extraordinarily high (for this site) number of nails, spikes, knife blades, and
"fake" knife blades; small water rolled pebbles, two chipped stone scrapping
tools; several patent medicine bottles; and a thermometer. While all of these
artifacts could have, and likely did, function in other activities during their
use-lives, taken together in their depositional context, they suggest a functional
group only partly related to the dominant European-American culture. Ethnographic analogies drawn from the West African, Afro-Caribbean, and Creole

0 1 2

Scale in centimeters

**FIGURE 5. DRAWING OF THE CARVED BONE PIECES OF THE FLY WISK
RECOVERED FROM EXCAVATIONS OF THE SLAVE/TENANT QUARTERS
OF THE LEVI JORDAN PLANTATION. LONG HAIRS WERE ORIGINALLY
PLACED INTO A HOLE PLACED IN THE UPPER (WIDE) END OF THE
WISK, AND HELD IN PLACE BY A METAL SCREW THAT EXTENDED
INTO THE UPPER PORTION OF THE HANDLE.**

curing rituals support this functional group as a magician/curer's or conjurer's kit. For example, Thompson records the following description of the beginning of a charm ritual: "On the island of Cuba, when Kongo ritual leaders wish to make important Zarabanda charm . . . , they begin by tracing, in *white chalk*, a cruciform pattern on the bottom of an *iron kettle*"[14] (emphasis mine). Such a pattern was found on a brick placed into the wall of the political leader's cabin (Figure 7).

The cross, with its encircling line, is identical to what Thompson refers to as the "Kongo Cosmogram." Archaeologist Leland Ferguson[15] has discovered several slave-made colonoware vessels/vessel fragments with this design on them. Each was found in or very near a body of water, and Ferguson believes these vessels were important in rituals connected with water and possibly with death. The placement of the cosmogram on a brick within the wall of a cabin suggests that the symbol, as employed with the Americas, has a broader meaning than Ferguson suggests, or that the meaning changed over time to a certain degree. Both ethnographic and archaeological evidence would suggest a broader meaning than that proposed by Ferguson.

0   1

Scale in centimeters

FIGURE 6. AN INCOMPLETE CARVED SHELL "CAMEO" FOUND WITHIN THE ABANDONMENT LEVEL OF THE SHELL AND BONE CARVER'S CABIN AT THE LEVI JORDAN PLANTATION. THIS PIECE WAS CARVED OUT OF OYSTER SHELL.

The broader meaning of the symbol may be interpreted from excavated contexts within the curer/magician's cabin. Figure 8 represents a schematic drawing of this cabin. Placed into the "subfloor" strata of the cabin were four deposits of artifacts which appear to have functioned within a single context—that of a large cosmogram, and the resulting definition of ritual space. The first of these deposits discovered was the curer/magician's kit, found in the south-

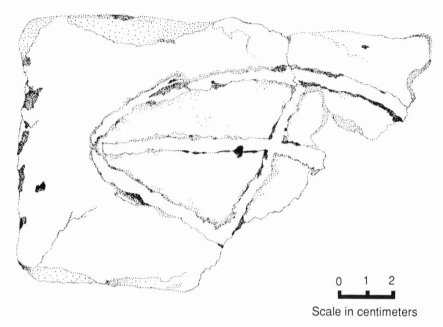

0 1 2

Scale in centimeters

FIGURE 7. TWO FRAGMENTS OF BRICK WITH A "COSMOGRAM" CARVED INTO ONE OF ITS SURFACES. THE ENCLOSED CROSS SYSMBOL WAS RAISED ON THE BRICK'S SURFACE AFTER THE BRICK WAS FIRED.

eastern corner of the cabin. Immediately adjacent to this kit, but likely placed below the floorboards of the cabin, we discovered an extremely large quantity of nails, spikes, real and "fake" knife blades, and small porcelain dolls, which appear to be all that remains in the archaeological record of a wooden Nkisi.[16] This Nkisi likely functioned along with the magician/curer's kit, patent medicine bottles and the thermometer within the ritual activities conducted. They represent a major portion of the tools utilized in the manipulation of the supernatural world for the benefit and life of members of the community.

The second deposit discovered contained seven coins. This set of coins consisted of four quarters, two dimes, and a half-dime. Thus, all the coins were made of silver. The coins had been tightly wrapped together inside a coarsely woven cloth object. With the exception of a small amount of this cloth actually touching the coins, nearly all of it had decomposed prior to excavation, and therefore it is not possible to determine the size of the original cloth or the type of fiber used to make it. However, the coins had been arranged within the cloth before being placed in a small hole dug into the dirt below the floor. The coins were placed so that they were "standing" in a nearly vertical fashion on their

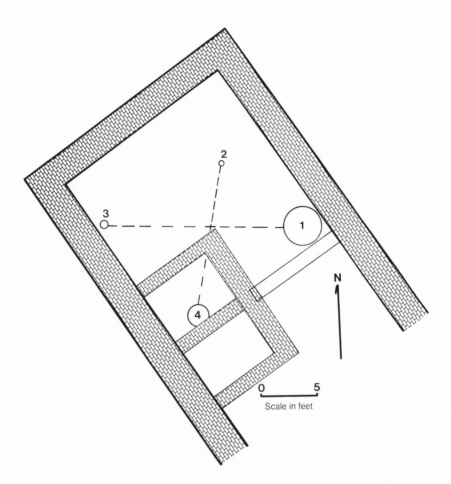

**FIGURE 8. DIAGRAM OF THE CURER'S CABIN (II-B-1) WITH THE LOCA-
TIONS OF THE FOUR RITUAL FEATURES AND THE LINES (DOTTED) FOR
THE CONSMOGRAM: 1 REPRESENTS THE LOCATION OF THE CURER'S KIT
AND NKISI; 2 THE SET OF COINS; 3 THE NKISI BELOW THE ENTRYWAY
TO THE CABIN: AND 4 THE ASH, METAL AND SHELL FEATURE PLACED
INTO THE HEARTH WITHIN THE CABIN. CURING/CONJURING RITUALS
LIKELY TOOK PLACE AT THE INTERSECTION OF THE NORTH-SOUTH AND
EAST-WEST LINES DEFINED BY THESE FEATUERS.**

sides. They faced north-south. The coins were also carefully arranged such that
the perforated half-dime was on the outside facing south, then came two of the
quarters (both dated 1853) then an 1853 dime, and then the other two quarters
(both dated 1858).

The third deposit discovered consisted of a wide variety of objects within and surrounding two complete cast iron kettles. The kettles had been placed below the floorboards immediately inside the cabin's door. The kettles had been positioned one inside the other with a few small metal, ocean shell, glass, and bone fragments placed inside the upper kettle. Approximately three inches of ash was also placed within the kettle. Soil was either placed on top of this ash, or filled the kettle in the years after it was deposited. Finally, a smaller cast iron kettle was broken up and placed over the top of these two. This broken kettle's base was not placed with the five fragments of its sides over this feature. However, one of the kettle bases from the curer's kit does match the size of this broken kettle. A number of objects were then placed around, or in two lines radiating out from these kettles. Toward the northeast were two small Confederate military buttons, several large bones, metal chain links, and a bayonet. Toward the southeast were several more lengths of metal chain, numerous large metal objects (including a hinge, spike, bolt, and a piece of a plow), several ocean shells, a quartz crystal, glass fragments, and two additional Confederate military buttons. This set of artifacts likely formed a Nkisi that aided in securing the protection of the cabin and its occupants from harm caused by powerful elements from the outside world.[17]

The fourth deposit discovered was found placed into a hearth of the cabin. Sometime after the construction of the hearth, the bricks at the back of the hearth, below the chimney, were removed and a hole was excavated into the fill and dirt below this portion of the hearth. A clay plaster surface was put over the bottom of the hole, which was then covered with ash, broken up and heavily burned ocean shell (especially oyster and whelk shell), and a few small nails. The hole was then refilled with soil and brick fragments to its original height. The floor of the hearth was then likely replaced, and the hearth continued to function for cooking and heating of the cabin.

Each of these four sets of artifacts within a single cabin support the interpretation of an African and African-American behavioral/belief system— one that serves to control the outside world through the manipulation of the supernatural world. The full set of artifacts suggest the many of the basic ideas/rituals are of African origins. The patent medicine bottles and the thermometer demonstrate some adaptation on non-African ideas. Specifically, all of these elements support the hypothesis that the curer had sanctified the floor space of the cabin for its use within the ritual performance of curing and/or conjuring. As Thompson notes, such rituals take place within space marked out with a cross oriented to the compass directions. Such a cross with compass orientation can be drawn employing the four deposits as the ends of the lines (Figure 9). The meanings noted by Thompson for each of the four end points of the cross within an "African" cosmogram,[18] are perfectly represented by the types of artifacts found within each of the features. Thus, the intersection of these lines would have defined the center from which curing and conjuring was accomplished.

Finally, the political leader functioned within the community as both an element for social control and as a mediator with the outside world. This individual has been defined within the archaeological record of the community through the fly whisk, a necklace comprised of glass beads and the fighting cock spur, several ebony rings, an elaborately decorated metal ring, and a large number of amber beads. The necklace has a central element that resembles the animal claw necklaces worn by West African nobility. Sub-floor deposits contained an additional cock spur pendant. The most intriguing aspects of the archaeological data from this cabin aiding in the identification of the occupant, however, is the recovery of a number of carpenter's tools, along with numerous items associated with sewing. Historical records demonstrate that the supervisor of the farm laborers on the plantation was an ex-slave who had been a carpenter and whose wife was a seamstress. These same records indicate that this individual was never paid for doing carpentry work, although others were hired during this time.

Thus, in terms of the economic structure of the tenant community, the wealthiest cabin occupants are those who appear to have been important within the internal economy. The archaeological record of the political leader's cabin, the magician/curer, and the shell/bone carver, either failed to yield evidence of specialized occupations within the external economy, or the evidence was limited. The fourth ranked cabin, that of the munitions maker, on the other hand, does appear to have had a specialized occupation–the blacksmith. The seamstresses' cabin and that of the quilter rank approximately equal to one another and just below the munitions maker and blacksmith. No evidence has been excavated that demonstrates an economic activity other than that for the internal economy. All of these cabins yielded some evidence that agricultural activities were practiced by the occupants. Thus, the "wealth" may have been the result of their internal economic activities, rather than those of the external economy. Certainly, the blacksmith had the opportunity for wealth accumulation beyond that from the external economy. The occupants of this cabin, however, appear to rank below the occupants of at least three other cabins.

In summary, the data from the archaeological and historic investigation of the Jordan Plantation suggests the presence of change in the economic and political structure of the slave and tenant communities. The evidence generated can be employed to support the concept of "capital generation and expenditure" by slaves and tenants. This capital was generated through the practice of wide variety of specialized occupations. During the period of slavery, those occupations which could be hired out appear to have provided the ability to accumulate more capital. After 1865 there was the opportunity for this capital to be converted into land as well as other types of so-called wealth indicators, and several members of the community did purchase portions of the Jordan Plantation. For this community, however, the purchase of land meant the movement of the individuals off the plantation and, therefore, out of the physical community. After 1865, capital generation and expenditure appears to have been greatest for those occupations that were most important within the internal plantation economy.

While agriculture formed the basis of the community's economy throughout both of these periods; from 1865 until the forced abandonment, the highest ranking cabins were those occupied by the political leader, the magician/curer, and the shell and bone carver. With the exception of the political leader, all of these were specializations for the internal economy of the plantation. The political leader would obviously have had an important function in the relationship between the community and the outside world. In this case, the leader was a carpenter and his wife a seamstress. The magician/curer would, on the other hand, have led the members of the community in shaping their relationship to and manipulating their way through the outside worlds–both human produced and supernatural. The blacksmith/munitions maker represents the fourth ranked cabin, and it was occupied by an individual who operated in both levels of the economy, but whose status within the internal economy is below that of the others.

In conclusion, this data and its interpretation are important because of the insight they provide into the evolution of African-American culture after 1865. That is, the data appear to indicate that certain activities, many ultimately of African origin and directed toward the internal functioning of this community, played a critical and increasingly important role in the community's survival. If this is correct, it would provide archaeological support for Fogel and Engerman's observation on the post-1865 attack on the material conditions of life for African Americans in the rural South. This process appears to have fostered the intensive re-organization of the community toward mechanisms of internal control and self-sufficiency. Behaviors and beliefs that fostered a sense of belonging were increasingly integrated within this community. Such behaviors and beliefs were increasingly important for the survival of a potentially more stable community. The internal management of affairs, both political and supernatural, functioned to help keep the increasingly oppressive outside world from negatively impacting this community.

~
NOTES

1. Robert W. Fogel and Stanley L. Engerman, *Time On The Cross: The Economics of American Negro Slavery* (Boston: Little, Brown, and Company, 1974).

2. Charles E. Orser, Jr., *The Material Basis Of The Postbellum Tenant Plantation: Historical Archaeology In The South Carolina Piedmont* (Athens and London: The University of Georgia Press, 1988). C. E. Orser Jr., "Historical Archaeology on Southern Plantations and Farms: Introduction," *Historical Archaeology* 1990, 24 (4):1–6. Leland Ferguson, *Uncommon Ground: Archaeology And Early African America, 1650–1800* (Washington, D.C.: Smithsonian Institution Press, 1992).

3. Theresa A. Singleton, *The Archaeology Of Slavery And Plantation Life* (Orlando, Fla.: Academic Press, 1985). Singleton, "An Archaeological Framework for Slavery and Emancipation," in *The Recovery Of Meaning: Historical Archaeology In The Eastern United States*, eds. Mark P. Leone and Parker B. Potter, Jr. (Washington, D.C.: Smithsonian Institution Press, 1988), 345–70. Jean E. Howson, "Social Relations and Material Culture: A Critique of the Archaeology of Plantation Slavery," *Historical Archaeology* 1990 24 (4): 78–91. For earlier views on this basic issue in historical archaeology, see Ivor Noel Hume, *Historical Archaeology* (New York: Alfred A. Knopf, 1969).

4. Stanley South, *Method And Theory In Historical Archaeology* (New York: Academic Press, 1977). Robert L. Schuyler, ed. *Historical Archaeology: A Guide To Substantive And Theoretical Contributions* (Farmingdale, N.Y.: Baywood Publishing, 1979). Charles E. Orser, Jr., "On Plantations and Patterns," in *Historical Archaeology*, 1989, 23 (2): 28–40.

5. Robert L. Schuyler, ed. *Archaeological perspectives On Ethnicity In America: Afro-American and Asian American Culture History* (Farmingdale, N.Y.: Baywood Publishing, 1988). John S. Otto, *Cannon's Point Plantation, 1794–1860: Living Conditions And Status Patterns In The Old South,* (Orlando: Academic Press, 1984). Kenneth L. Brown and Doreen C. Cooper, "Structural Continuity in an African-American Slave and Tenant Community," *Historical Archaeology* 1990, 24 (4): 7–19. Howson, "Social Relations and Material Culture."

6. David W. Babson, "The Archaeology of Racism and Ethnicity on Southern Plantations," *Historical Archaeology*, 1990, 24 (4): 20–28. Brown and Cooper, "Structural Continuity." Howson, "Social Relations and Material Culture." Otto, *Cannon's Point Plantation.*

7. Randolph B. Campbell, *An Empire For Slavery: The Peculiar Institution In Texas, 1821–1865,* (Baton Rouge: Louisiana State University Press, 1989).

8. Brazoria County Deed Records, Brazoria County Courthouse, Angleton, Texas. Jordan/McNeill/Martin Family Records, copies on file in the Archaeological

Research Lab. (A.R.L.), Department of Anthropology, University of Houston, Houston, Texas.

9. 1870 U.S. Federal Census: Agricultural Schedule for Brazoria County, Texas, copy on file at the Texas State Archives and Library, Austin, Texas.

10. Kenneth L. Brown, "Faneuil Family Research Notes," Notes are on file in the A.R.L. (MS in preparation). Cheryl Wright transcripts of interviews with Faneuil Family descendants, on file in the A.R.L.

11. 1870 U.S. Federal Census, Brazoria County Deed Records. Brazoria County Tax Records, 1848–1905, microfilm copies on file at the George Memorial Library, Richmond, Texas. Kenneth L. Brown, "John McNeill Family Research Notes," notes on file in the A.R.L. "J.C. McNeill Ledgers" copies on file at the A.R.L.

12. Brazoria County Tax Records, 1848–1905, microfilm copies on file at the George Memorial Library, Richmond, Texas. Jordan/McNeill/Martin Family Records on file at the A.R.L.

13. Brown and Cooper; "Structural Continuity."

14. Robert F. Thompson, *Flash Of The Spirit: African And Afro-American Art And Philosophy*, (New York: Random House, 1983). John W. Blassingame, *The Slave Community: Plantation Life in the Antebellum South* (revised and enlarged edition), (Oxford: Oxford University Press, 1979).

15. Ferguson, *Uncommon Ground.*

16. John N. Janzen and Reinhold Janzen, "Nkisi," in *Expressions Of Belief*, ed. Suzanne Gneub (New York: Rizzoli, 1988), 38–55.

17 Thompson, *Flash of the Spirit.*

18. Ibid., 106–8.

~

SALE AND SEPARATION
Four Crises for Enslaved Women on the Ball Plantations
1764-1854

Cheryll Ann Cody

Throughout the slave South, with each generation of planters, the fate of enslaved families and communities was inextricably tied to the economic and demographic lives of their owners. Herbert Gutman identified a pattern of "slave family and kin network destruction, construction and dispersal" related to the life cycle of the slave owner. Phase one, when the owner was a young adult was devoted to the construction of a labor force by gift, marriage and purchase. The impact of these policies on enslaved people was the destruction of existing familial and kin networks; Gutman rates this stage as one during which the stability of slave families was low. Phase two, which occurred when the owner was middle-aged, witnessed a "stabilization and reproduction" of the labor force through natural increase. The result of the stable phase for slaves was the "development of settled families and the emergence of new kin networks." Gutman describes this phase as one of high familial stabilization. The final phase, at death or retirement of the owner, saw the slave labor force dispersed by gift, sale and estate division. The impact on enslaved people was the breakup of families and kin networks formed during the second phase.[1]

Gutman's model correctly points to the link between the life cycle (or perhaps family cycle) of the owner and the stability of enslaved families. However, close examination of owner practices indicates that the model requires both modification and amplification. Gutman's definition of the three

119

phases needs refinement. Relying on the underlying assumption that owners accumulated slaves solely for the purpose of creating a slave labor force, Gutman fails to consider the use of slaves as marriage gifts to children. In fact, the dispersal of slave property came at two "transitions" in the life cycle of planter families, when children married and at death. Wealthy planters commonly presented large gifts of slaves and land at a child's marriage and additional legacies at death. Jane Turner Censer reports that nearly half of the sons and a quarter of the daughters of the North Carolina planters she studied received large gifts of property (land and/or slaves) from their parents. These gifts were designed to produce the financial autonomy of young adults at marriage.[2] Beyond splintering existing slave families and communities, some fathers specifically purchased slaves to provide gifts. South Carolina cotton planter Peter Gaillard presented each of his eight children with more than fifty slaves at the child's marriage. To meet this "demand" for marriage gifts, he purchased sixteen slaves in 1803, eighty-eight slaves in 1806 and seven more in 1808. Sixty-four of the eighty-eight purchased in 1806 were given to his sons, Tom and James on their respective marriages in 1811 and 1812.[3] The effects of estate dispersal on the stability of slave families and communities were felt not only upon the death of the owner, but also at the marriage of the owner's children. The greater the number of children provided with gifts of slaves, the more severe the breakup of enslaved families and kin networks. Thus, the demographic success of an owner, such as that of Gaillard could spell familial disaster in the slave quarter, and the use of slaves as marriage gifts to adult children, significantly reduced the duration of the second "stable" phase of Gutman's model.

Gutman's assumptions about the composition of slave units purchased and slave units sold or dispersed also needs to be examined. His model implies that slaves entered a plantation or farm as individuals, severing many if not all kin ties and that when estates were divided or sold, the individual was the unit of sale, not the family. Some studies confirm this practice, but others for South Carolina do not. In a study of the effect of sale and estate divisions on enslaved families in nineteenth-century Boone County, Missouri, James McGettigan found that enslaved people were sold most often as individuals with no regard to family bonds.[4] Husbands and wives were often separated (in 27 of 36 confirmed unions) and advertisements for sales rarely mentioned family ties or considered kin connections among enslaved people.[5] In addition to the separation of husbands and wives, Boone County slaveowners sold young children away from their parents, often dividing enslaved families among five or six buyers. Although most Boone County slaves (98 percent) were sold within the county, once separated it would be impossible for these families to maintain anything approaching their previous co-residential family life.[6] McGettigan concludes that economic and legal forces usually prevailed over humanitarian forces in the treatment of enslaved families.[7] Ann Patton Malone, both in her statistical analysis and case studies, notes estate divisions and gifts were among several sources of the large number of single people and female-headed households in nineteenth century Louisiana.[8] Treatment of enslaved people as individuals at the time of sales was not confined solely to the western regions of the cotton south. Additional studies of Burke County, North Carolina and Oglethorpe County, Georgia confirm the Missouri findings that family units were ignored by slaveowners at the time of estate division and sales.[9]

This practice stands in stark contrast with evidence on the treatment of enslaved families by South Carolina planters at the Gaillard plantations, at Good Hope and on the Ball family plantations.[10] Analysis of the marriage gifts of St. John's Berkeley Parish cotton planter Peter Gaillard to his children, suggests that Gaillard maintained nuclear families defined as parents and children under age fifteen as "inseparable" units. Once they became young adults, enslaved sons were far more likely than daughters to be separated from their parents and siblings. The greater "stability" of parent-daughter and female sibling ties appears to be the result of two practices. Young women remained members of the "inseparable" unit of their family of origin until they married and became "inseparable" members of their family of procreation, and elderly parents more frequently were defined as members of their daughters' household than that of their sons'.[11] Enslaved families at Orangeburgh District's Good Hope plantation escaped the potential ravages of estate dispersal when they were sold in 1859 to a single planter, who was to move them to Arkansas. Although the household and farm implements of Good Hope plantation were auctioned item by item, a single purchaser acquired all the slaves.[12]

Throughout this increasingly rich historiography, scholars have emphasized the values and practices of owners. Enslaved people are most often viewed as helpless victims in the financial calculations of their owners. This essay focuses on four crises for enslaved families and the efforts of wives and mothers to mitigate the worst effects of sales and estate divisions on their families. Evidence is drawn from a larger study of the demographic and familial lives of enslaved people at the Ball Family plantations of South Carolina's East Cooper River. Each case examined here reveals much about the relationship between slaves and their owners and the understanding each of these enslaved women had of their own ability to influence the survival of their families. Reactions range from desperation to sacrifice to sentimental appeals and finally frustration as each woman fought for her family in moments of crisis.

ISABEL'S DESPERATION

A close look at the tragic case of the polygynous union of Isabel and Chloe and their husband, Mathias, illustrates both the failure of slaveowners to understand the marital and familial structures of slaves and the tragic personal consequences of this oversight. The difficulty began, as was often the case for slave families, with the death of an owner and an attempt by the heirs to reach an equitable division of the property.

In the spring of 1765 with the death of John Coming Ball, his property in land and slaves was transmitted to his heirs. Ball named his oldest son, Elias (later known as "Wambaw" or the "Tory") as executor.[13] Among the property included in the estate was a group of slaves co-owned by John Coming Ball and his brother-in-law, Henry Laurens. The elder Ball had managed the slaves in co-partnership at Wambaw Plantation for nearly fifteen years. Laurens was well-occupied with his business in Charleston and left the division of the estate to young Ball with the request that he preserve the slave families intact.[14] On April 1, apparently after hearing about the pending division, Lauren restated his concerns about preserving slave families. He observed that his interest in maintaining families "was rather comparitive than absolute, my design being to avoid that inconvenience and I will say inhumanity of seperating & taring assunder my Negroe's several families which I would never do or cause to be done but in case of irresistable necessity. . . . "[15] Laurens suggested that he would give up his whole share in the slaves "in preference to an Act which has always shocked me too much to submit to it even in the Sale of New Negroes."[16] Nonetheless, Laurens noted that even with this gesture, slave families would be separated and "seven or eight families & some of them my best Negroes will be torn to pieces & probably cause great distraction amongst the whole."[17] He did not abdicate interest in the property.

The debate over the division of the Wambaw slaves quickly escalated into a dispute over the co-partnership, itself, the result of an estate settled fifteen years earlier. To press his case, Laurens argued that it should be up to him to do as he pleased with the Wambaw slaves because their value would still not total the amount due him from his father-in-law's estate which was divided in 1751.[18] Laurens felt he had the "right to expect some little indulgence in the division of Wambaw Negroes and effects" because he still was awaiting the title to Dockum plantation. Laurens further concluded that the disregard for the slave families was designed to cause him anguish and he ended his letter with this plea. "I don't know anything that could have been more contrived to distress me and embarrass my plantation agin more than this unnecessary division of Fathers, Mothers, Husbands, Wives, & Children who tho Slaves are still human Creatures and I cannot be deaf to their cries least a time should come when I should cry and there shall be none to pity me."[19]

After wrangling for nearly a year, and despite Laurens's emotional and self-serving plea, some slave families were separated at Wambaw. For one woman, Isabel, the division meant removal to Hyde Park Plantation and separation from her husband, Mathias. Mathias remained at Wambaw with another wife, Chloe. Within three months, Isabel returned to Wambaw and apparently murdered Chloe. From Wambaw, Laurens recounted the events leading to Chloe's death and his suspicions to Elias Ball.

> Upon my coming to this place I was inform'd of the sudden death of Chloe one of old Cain's family & that the Doctor who was called to her declared she died of poisin. Mr. Schad [Wambaw's overseer] & his Wife are both of the same opinion & from circumstances they suspect that she receiv'd a potion from a jealous Sister at Hyde Park named Isabel, who came here on Saturday Night & Chloe was seized with the disorder that killed her on the next day. They were both the Wives of Mathias & it seems Isabel had droped some threatnings towards Chloe which Mr. Schad will further relate to you & I make no doubt you will Inquire into this matter in a proper manner.[20]

Lauren's correspondence about the estate division and his account of Chloe's death offer several insights into owner attitudes and their conflict with African marriage systems. Throughout his letters, Laurens expressed concern for the familial bonds of slaves, as defined by a traditional nuclear family. He is quite explicit in stating his understanding of significant family bonds, "Fathers, Mothers, Husbands, Wives, and Children."[21] Laurens is also clear about why the potential separations disturb him. He is reluctant to cause pain to other humans, and reflecting what he believes were the broadly held values of the slaveowner community, Laurens fears that he will be embarrassed by the willful separation of slave families. At the same time, in his letter describing the death of Chloe and his suspicions of Isabel, he is very matter-of-fact in his reference to the polygynous union which lay at the heart of the conflict. "They were both the wives of Mathias," he writes, casually offering his explanation for Isabel's presumed actions.[22]

Isabel's actions perhaps are as readily understood. Unlike Chloe, she no longer lived on the same plantation as her husband, and no longer received the material, emotional and sexual benefits of the polygynous union. She saw Chloe as the immediate obstacle to her happiness, perhaps believing that the death of Chloe would result in her return to Wambaw or her reunion with Mathias at Hyde Park. Powerless to attack the true source of her pain in the persons of Elias "Wambaw" Ball and Henry Laurens, and given her understanding of her owner's attitudes on the separation of slave spouses, Isabel took what she saw as the action most likely to remain undetected and result in her reunion with Mathias. Although there are no surviving documents revealing the ultimate fates of Isabel and Mathias, their case stands as a vivid illustration of the persistence of African marriage systems among Carolina slaves and the potential for conflict with owners' decisions at the time of estate division.

NIPPE'S SACRIFICE

Thirty years later, slaves at another of the Ball plantations were confronted with a similar crisis of estate dispersal. One couple, Free Jack and Nippe, succeeded in preserving their family through a combination of owner benevolence, hard work and sacrifice. More importantly, they understood how owners would treat the kinship bonds of enslaved people when the estate was ultimately divided. With this understanding, they made the correct, albeit difficult choices.

John Coming Ball of St. James Goose Creek Parish died in 1792 without legitimate offspring. In his will he provided for the manumission of four slaves and the division of the rest of his property among the children of his two sisters.[23] Jane Ball, who had married her first cousin John Ball Sr., had five sons at the time of her brother's death, ranging in age from four to ten. Eleanor Wilson, a young widow in 1792, was to remarry the following year, but neither union produced offspring.[24] Thus John Coming Ball anticipated the division of his eighty-six slaves, among at least his five nephews:

> "I give my Negro Man Nat his freedom and all my wearing apparel. I give my Negro Woman Hagar and her child Charlotte their freedom. I desire my executors will have the latter educated and when she shall be old enough– placed out as an apprentice to a milliner or mantuamaker. I give my Negro man Jacky (son of Lucy) who is at present my Driver his freedom."[25]

But the rest of his slave property was to be administered by his executors until the heirs reached their majority. The impact of the death of an owner can be traced for the enslaved people belonging to "Poor" John Coming Ball at Back River Plantation. At his death in 1792 John Coming Ball had five heirs the sons of his sister, all of whom were minors. By the time the estate was divided, only two heirs survived and the estate of slave property was divided into only two portions. In this instance enslaved families were the beneficiaries of their owners' demographic bad luck; instead of the fracture of the community into five or more parts it was to be split into two.

Three surviving documents describe the estate's slaves between 1793 and 1811. In 1793 an inventory was taken of Ball's estate at Back River (later renamed Jericho plantation). Eighty-six slaves were listed valued at £3,965. The enslaved people were grouped by familial units and inseparable units were valued together. The four slaves who were manumitted in Ball's will, were each listed and evaluated separately. In 1799 a second list of the slaves at Back River was made. No valuations were assigned to the ninety-one slaves, but again family or household units were marked. A final list of slaves was drawn in 1811 which assigned slaves to each of the two divisions, valued each individual and demarked family units. Comparison of the three slave lists provides insight into the effects of the life cycle on evolving family structures, and the owner's tacit rules which influenced the stability of slave families at estate division.[26]

The family history of Free Jack and Nippe illustrates the recognition by slaves of the increased vulnerability of young males to separation from the family and the unique ability of this family to save their sons from sale and removal.

In 1793 Nippe was listed as the mother of four children, Cupid, Lucy, Phenda, and Betty. She apparently had no husband, but the 1799 list indicates that the father of Cupid and a younger child, Jack, was Free Jack. In 1799, Nippe's household included her two daughters Phenda and Lucy, who were both under twelve and Old Marcus, whose relationship cannot be determined. Cupid and N. (Nippe's) Jack were noted as sold. By 1811 Free Jack and Nippe's family had grown to include another daughter, Jane and two sons Cesar and Nat. But because the children of Free Jack and Nippe were young in 1793, they probably had not formed families of their own. When the estate was finally divided, the nuclear family remained intact. Nippe, Phenda and the three youngest children were given to division two. Old Marcus was given to division one.

Unlike all other enslaved families at the time of this estate division, Free Jack and Nippe were able to preserve their ties with their sons. On January 9, 1800, Free Jack entered into a bargain to purchase his two sons, Cupid and Jack for the sum of ninety pounds. Free Jack, who had continued to work at Back River as a paid driver was able to pay for the boys by a deduction from his wages and by law he held "said Negro Boys Cupid & Jack as his own proper good and Chattels free from all and every manner of claims."[27]

Although we do not know if Free Jack had purchased the freedom of his mother Lucy, or why she has disappeared from the record, it appears that Free Jack bought those members of his family that were most vulnerable to separation with an estate division, his oldest sons. When the estate was finally divided in 1811 the boys were adolescents, and had they remained the property of John Coming Ball's estate they would have been treated as individuals with no kin bonds. Indeed, of the twenty-three slaves listed alone, twenty were

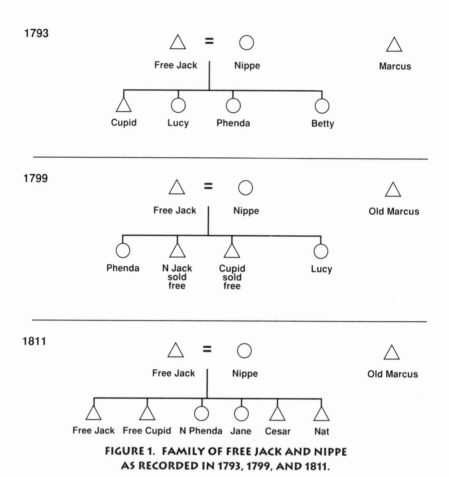

**FIGURE 1. FAMILY OF FREE JACK AND NIPPE
AS RECORDED IN 1793, 1799, AND 1811.**

young men and boys. Conversely, among the nineteen families noted with children, girls outnumbered boys thirty-nine to sixteen. Free Jack and Nippe's oldest sons would have been the most vulnerable. Their daughter, Phenda, who must have been at least eighteen, remained with her mother along with the younger children who were all under twelve. Ironically, in saving their sons from sale or estate division, Nippe sacrificed her own freedom. Twelve years after Free Jack bought their sons, Cupid and Young Jack, Nippe remained a slave.

DYE AND PATRA'S APPEAL

Eight years later the slaves belonging to John Ball Sr. were to suffer a far more cruel fate. Over two days in February 1819, the Ball family slaves were subjected to the most serious division, resulting from an estate dispersal. Following his death in 1817, John Ball Sr.'s property in land and slaves was sold. His will had set aside one plantation, Pimlico, for the use of his second wife, Martha Caroline and eight minor children. His two sons from a previous marriage saw their marriage gifts confirmed as legacies in the will. The remainder of the estate in land and property was to be divided among his heirs. The inventory of his estate in 1817 listed 669 slaves at seven plantations—Pimlico, Kensington, Midway, Hyde Park, White Hall, Belle Isle, and Marshland Farm near Charleston. On February 8 and 9, 366 of these slaves were auctioned, (197 male slaves and 169 female), grouped into 113 units which ranged in size from an individual to eleven people. Fifty persons were sold individually with men outnumbering women forty-three to seven.[28]

The sale and dispersal of the 366 slaves shows the strategies pursued by buyers in selecting slaves, and reveals the fragmentation of the six enslaved communities caused by an owner's death and a large sale of his property. One measure of the amount of fragmentation which occurred is the purchasing strategies carried out by the buyers. Forty-eight people bought slaves at the February auction. The number of units purchased by each buyer ranged from one to twenty-six, but most buyers, two-thirds, bought only one unit of slaves, and more than half of the single unit purchasers bought a single slave. Obviously, these single slaves were separated from all kin as well as their community. One buyer of a single unit bought the largest group of slaves which included eleven people. People who bought two units only rarely bought single slaves. While the four people who bought three units showed a preference for larger groups, most likely families, they bought only one individual and half the units purchased included five or more people. T. Scriven, who bought four units, acquired two "single" men, Glasgow and Ned, the family of Adam and Fatima and their two sons, William and Sancho, and Affy with her three children, Sancho, Belinder and Saby. When purchasing his six units, W. Lucas preferred single males, acquiring Saul, Jim, Dublin, Cork and Hector. He also bought the large family of Cesar and Elsy which included their six sons and two daughters.

The two largest purchasers in both total number of slaves and greatest number of units merit separate consideration. Both individuals were agents of John Ball Sr.'s two oldest sons, who as executors of the estate could not purchase land or slaves directly from it. J. W. Payne represented John Ball Jr. (Comingtee plantation) in the transactions, and M. Simons represented Isaac Ball (Limerick plantation). Payne bought sixty-six slaves in twenty-six separate units for $39,285, while Simons purchased sixty slaves in seventeen units at $37,791.

TABLE 1. SIZE OF SLAVE GROUPS PURCHASED BY NUMBER OF UNITS PURCHASED AT THE SALE OF JOHN BALL SR.'S SLAVES, FEBRUARY 8 AND 9, 1819.

Number of Units Purchased	Number of Owners Making Purchase	Size of the Slave Group											Total
		1	2	3	4	5	6	7	8	9	10	11	
1	32	18	1	2	4	0	3	2	0	1	0	1	32
2	8	6	1	1	2	1	1	1	2	1	0	0	16
3	4	4	2	1	2	1	1	2	1	0	1	0	12
4	1 (T. Scriven)	2	0	0	2	0	0	0	0	0	0	0	4
6	1 (W. Lucas)	5	0	0	0	0	0	0	0	0	1	0	6
17	1 (Isaac Ball)	5	3	1	4	0	1	1	1	1	0	0	17
26	1 (John Ball, Jr.)	13	3	2	5	1	1	0	0	0	1	0	26
Total	48	50	10	7	19	3	7	6	4	3	3	1	113

TABLE 2. MEAN SIZE AND COMPOSITION OF SLAVE GROUPS BY NUMBER OF UNITS PURCHASED AT THE SALE OF JOHN BALL SR.'S SLAVES, FEBRUARY 8 AND 9, 1819

No. of Units Purchased	No. of Owners Making Purchase	Total Number of Slaves					Slave Groups				
		Males	Females	All	Sex Ratio	Range	Mean No. per group	No. of units of single person	MSR[a] single person or sex	No. of Groups >1	MSR[a] groups >1
1	32	55	39	94	141	1-11	2.9	19[b]	360	13	146
2	8	30	32	62	94	1-9	3.9	7[c]	166	9	121
3	4	31	28	59	111	1-10	4.9	1	-[d]	11	137
4	1	6	4	10	150	1-4	2.5	2	-[d]	2	167
6	1	12	3	15	400	1-10	2.5	5	-[d]	1	233
17	1	26	34	60	76	1-9	3.5	7[e]	57	10	87
26	1	37	29	66	128	1-10	2.5	15[f]	467	11	103
All	48	197	169	366	177	1-11	3.2	56	272	57	124

[a] mean sex ratio; [b] one unit composed of 2 males; [c] one unit composed of 4 females; [d] all units single males; [e] one unit 4 females and one unit 2 females; [f] one unit 2 males and one unit 2 females

Both brothers, again through agents, bought land from the estate. John Ball acquired Kensington and Midway plantations and St. James Tract. Isaac bought Hyde Park plantation.

The two brothers apparently used very different strategies in selecting the units they purchased. John Ball favored single males and bought few enslaved families. Twelve (nearly half of the units he purchased) were of a single male slave. He also bought a single female. Males outnumbered females thirty-seven to twenty-nine among all the slaves he purchased. When buying families, John Ball preferred smaller groups, perhaps indicating that the parents were young. Only one family contained more than six members, the ten-person household of London and Dye. Isaac Ball favored family groups for the slaves he purchased. Five people were bought as individuals, while the remaining fifty-five were in larger groups. Four of the twelve groups included six or more members. Unlike his brother, Isaac Ball bought more females than males.

A total of ninety-four slaves were sold to buyers who purchased only one unit and although they remained with their immediate family, these slaves moved with no one else from their home plantations. Eighteen, primarily men, were sold as individuals to owners who bought one slave only and they were removed completely from family and friends. The large number of slaves sold as individuals was reflected in the mean group size for single units of 2.9 persons. Sixty-two were sold to owners who bought two units. Only six of these bondsmen were sold as individuals, the remaining fifty-six were associated with at least one other person, although not necessarily from the same home plantation. E. Broughton bought two men. Paul was from Marshland Farm and Pollydore from White Hall plantation. Schoolbred purchased Rose from Belle Isle plantation and March, who was listed at Kensington, Midway or Hyde Park. The mean unit size for people buying two units was 3.9, one person larger than the number of slaves who were bought by one-unit purchasers.

With one exception, slaves sold to buyers purchasing three units were in groups that included at least one other person, probably a family member. The preference of the four buyers for larger families produced a mean number of persons per group of 4.9. The policies of the remaining four purchasers have already been discussed in detail. With the exceptions of Isaac Ball, the desire for male slaves dominated the purchasing strategies.

By linking the individuals and units listed in the 1819 sale with the 1817 plantation inventories, the impact of the sale on slave communities can be determined. Familial units could be located with ease because they were bracketed or listed in order in the inventories. Individuals were more difficult to identify due to name duplication. Therefore estimates of the number of purchasers of slaves from each plantation must be considered minimums.

All plantations were severely divided by the sale. The thirty-nine slaves sold from Marshland Farm were bought by fourteen different people. Mrs. Ball bought six of these slaves, but her step-sons made no purchases. The enslaved communities at Belle Isle and White Hall were similarly fragmented. Thirty-one slaves from Belle Isle were sold to eight buyers including agents of both John and Isaac. The largest unit was the seven-member family of Isaac the driver and his wife, Betty, bought by T. Pinkney. The twenty-three enslaved people sold from White Hall went to nine buyers. Again, the largest unit was the six member family of the plantation driver, Cain and his wife Lucretia. The 213 slaves sold from Kensington, Midway and Hyde Park were purchased by twenty buyers. John and Isaac Ball bought most of their slaves from these three plantations, thus lessening the divisive effect on the slave community. Sixty-three of the slaves bought by John Ball were from the three plantations. He bought one male each from Belle Isle, Marshland Farm, and White Hall. Similarly, Isaac Ball bought most of his slaves from Kensington, Hyde Park, and Midway. He bought Jenny and her three children from Belle Isle, Jack and Jenny and their daughter Nancy, and Daniel, a single man, from White Hall.

Both John Ball (Jr.) and Isaac Ball used the opportunity of the sale of their father's slaves to increase their own holdings. Although a preliminary examination of their purchases indicates that each operated with a different strategy in the selection of his slaves, John Ball in his notation of the purchase in his own journal suggests that sentiment and paternalism lay at the heart of his decision. The slaves were bought, he wrote, "because they were related by connection with those that were owned by me before the sale."[29]

For John Ball to carry out this desire to reunite some of the slave families he owned with their kin, it was necessary for him to devise a legal strategy to make the purchase. One measure of the strength of his purpose then is the complexity of the actions he was required to take to successfully make such purchases. Because they served as executors of their father's estate, had participated in the inventory of this moveable property and had been named joint guardians for their stepbrothers and stepsisters, John Jr. and Isaac were prohibited by law from purchasing property at the sale of their father's estate. To circumvent this prohibition, each made an agreement with an agent to bid on and purchase a list of previously named slaves at the time of the sale and then resell them.[30] This legal subterfuge, as evidenced in both the Bill of Sale records for the State and the Miscellaneous Records of Deeds was further necessitated by the fact that their father's young widow, the recently remarried Martha Caroline

Swinton Ball Taveau, had filed suit to contest the power of guardianship over her children granted to her stepsons by her husband. The litigation was to proceed for seventeen years, and perhaps knowing the character and tenacity of their stepmother, John and Isaac deemed it necessary to document and clarify all actions concerning the estate.[31]

In deciding which slaves would be purchased to reunite kin, John Ball recognized slave kinship and family as having both breadth and depth, with a decided preference towards maintenance of the maternal lineage. Thirty-two of the sixty-six individuals can be identified as members of one extended family. For the purpose of the sale, these thirty-two had been divided into nine "separable" units and the potential existed that they could have been purchased by nine individuals splintering this group. The extended family group and the smaller divisions designated for sale are displayed in Figure 2. The sale units were probably composed of familial units that were deemed "inseparable" by the unwritten rules governing slave sales, and may have reflected the living arrangements of the slaves.

The sale units were composed of a variety of household types indicative of both the life cycle of enslaved people and the disruptive effects of high mortality on enslaved families. Three units were composed of two-parent nuclear families, headed by Old Smart and Patra, Driver Stephen and Easter, and Captain Peter and Flora. In addition, a young couple with no children, Billy and Beck; and a single mother and her female children, Beck, Dye and Lavinia were defined as units. A three-generational household headed by London and Dye and containing their unmarried daughter, Amey, and her seven children, including four unmarried young adults was the largest familial group. The remaining units were composed of the three adult sons of London and Dye, Windsor, London and Glasgow, each listed separately.

The composition of these family groups suggests that John Ball was attempting to reunite the families of the elderly slave sisters, Dye and Patra, perhaps at the expense of severing some ties among the younger generations. Three of the four sons of London and Dye were listed without families and two of their daughters with children have no spouse included in the "inseparable" sale unit. Neither of the adult children of Old Smart and Patra were listed with a spouse or children, but instead were included in the "inseparable" unit of their elderly parents. Four of Amey's children were adults and may have had significant relationships as well, though neither Hannah nor Sarah appeared as mothers in birth registers. The inclusion of the spouses of Easter and Flora in the grouping may indicate the success of skilled slaves, Driver Stephen and Captain Peter in maintaining their family ties. If these "inseparable" units were purchased to satisfy John Ball's desire to reunite kin, who then were the slaves in his

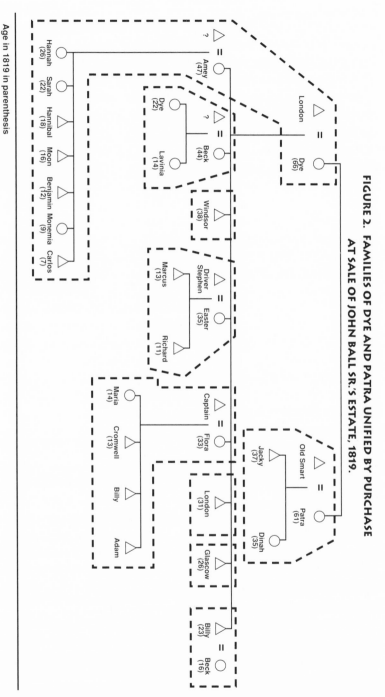

FIGURE 2. FAMILIES OF DYE AND PATRA UNIFIED BY PURCHASE
AT SALE OF JOHN BALL SR.'S ESTATE, 1819.

Age in 1819 in parenthesis
Sale units denoted by broken lines

possession who sought reunion? In 1810 John Ball had inherited the property of his bachelor uncle, Elias. With his brother, Isaac, John split the slave property according to those slaves who were working on each of his uncle's plantations.[32] But the division of enslaved families belonging to the Balls extended further back in time. In 1786, Elias II's slaves were divided among his children, with John Sr. (father of John Jr. and Isaac) and Elias III (their childless uncle) each receiving a quarter share. It was with this division that the four daughters of Windsor and Angola Ame were separated, though each had a family of her own.[33] Subrinagoddard (later known as Subrina), a sister of Dye and Patra remained with Elias III and was transmitted with her children to John Jr. in 1810. In purchasing a portion of the kin network of Subrina, John reunited three elderly slave sisters and their children and grandchildren. The decision to make this purchase indicates that the Balls recognized the broader kin associations of their slaves and in rare cases were willing to act to reunite kin.

The elderly women no doubt played a role in this reunification. Although the basis of their appeal is not known, these sisters were able to reunite their extended families and spare them the worst consequences of the estate division. They successfully prevailed upon the Balls when most others suffered far greater devastation of family bonds. Most Ball slaves who faced the auction block on those two winter days in 1819 could not look forward to the reunification of a broad kinship network, but rather saw both nuclear and extended families fragmented beyond repair. The fate of the family of C. F. Bachus and Hagar illustrates both the impact of the sale and some of the contrasts which may account for the success of some enslaved people and the failure of others to reunite and maintain extended kin. Like the sisters, Dye, Patra, and Subrina, Hagar suffered separation from her siblings with the 1786 estate dispersal. Hagar's four brothers were split among the four heirs and Hagar, her husband C. F. Bachus, and two young daughters remained an inseparable unit. Like Dye and Patra, C. F. Bachus and Hagar were transferred to Elias III and then to John Jr. in 1810. When facing the sale of John Sr.'s property, the identifiable kin group included C. F. Bachus, his four surviving daughters and four sons, and the children of his four daughters.

This three-generational kin group made up of eighteen individuals was divided into seven "inseparable" sale units composed of one two-parent nuclear family, Stephaney and Rose, one single mother and her children, Jenny, the elderly C. F. Bachus and his youngest daughter, Millee, the four brothers ranging in age from seventeen to twenty-six and three enslaved people sold as individuals; Celia, her eighteen year old son, Dick, and the twelve year old orphan, Sylvia.

FIGURE 3. SEPARATION OF THE FAMILY OF C. F. BACHUS AND HAGAR AT SALE OF JOHN BALL SR.'S ESTATE, 1819.

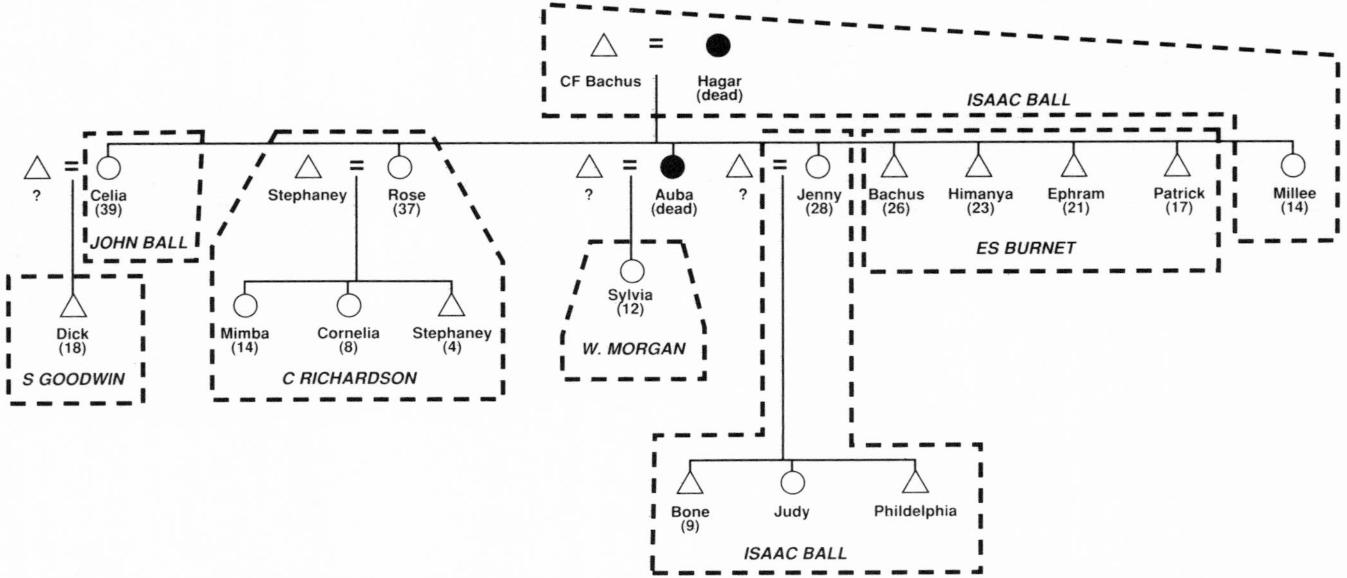

Age in 1819 in parenthesis
Sale units denoted by broken lines
Name of purchaser in italics

Six planters purchased units from this family, separating young Dick and young Sylvia completely from all kin. The nuclear family of Stephaney and Rose remained together as did the four brothers. Isaac Ball purchased both the family of C. F. Bachus and daughter Millee and Jenny and her children, and Celia was bought by John Ball. Although the Balls were well aware of the depth and breadth of kin connections as demonstrated in the case of the families of Patra and Dye, they demonstrated little regard for the extended kin of the deceased Hagar and her children. In two instances the Ball estate sold adolescents as individuals, although they permitted the four brothers to remain together. John Ball purchased the elderly C. F. Bachus and his two daughters, thus preventing total destruction of the old man's family, nonetheless the sale severely fractured this kin group.

BINKEY'S FRUSTRATIONS

Analysis of the impact of sales and separations on enslaved families usually ends with the auction and rarely are scholars able to reconstruct the impact of the sale on individuals after they are removed. In addition to geographic separation from family and friends and perhaps loss of personal property, some bondsmen also suffered a decline in status, when new owners demoted them to field work or had little need for their occupational skills. Drivers and house servants were particularly vulnerable to this loss of status. Artisans were less likely to suffer, though removal from a large plantation where one was a dedicated carpenter to a smaller one where one was required to work in the fields at least part-time, could similarly alter conditions of labor.

One enslaved family sold in 1854 from the estate of John Ball Jr. at Hyde Park plantation experienced sale, removal from the immediate community of extended family and friends and the loss of status. Unlike most enslaved people who suffered these losses, the response and ultimate fates of Jupiter and Binkey can be documented in the correspondence of their purchaser.

Born in 1802 at Limerick plantation, Jupiter was the second of ten children born to Caty Phillis and an unlisted father. Six of Jupiter's brothers and sisters survived to adulthood and all participated in the interplantational moves initiated by Isaac Ball when he relocated more than forty enslaved families among his properties on the East Cooper River. Binkey was the only child of Jenny and shared the first name of her maternal grandmother, Binkey. Binkey's mother had been twenty-two at her daughter's birth in 1806 and died between 1806 and 1810 leaving Binkey an orphan. In 1810 four-year-old Binkey was included in the nine-member household of Pompey and Peggy at Limerick plantation.

Jupiter and Binkey both remained at Limerick until 1818, when they were among the enslaved people moved across the river to Quinby. They had moved again to Hyde Park where, in 1823, their first child, a son Carolina, was born. Binkey was seventeen and Jupiter twenty-one. Six more children followed between 1825 and 1842, all born at Hyde Park. The family remained at that site until 1854 when Jupiter and Binkey and their four youngest children were sold to Charles and Louis Manigault who owned nearby Silk Hope plantation and two properties on the Savannah River, Gowrie and East Hermitage.[34] The familial unit at the sale included Jupiter (52), Binkey (48) and their children Tommy (20), Rebecca (18), Mary (14), and Harry (11). No record survives of the fate of Jupiter and Binkey's two oldest children Carolina (31) and Judy (23). Both Carolina and Judy had probably begun their own families and were sold in those familial units or separately. With that sale the record of their lives at Hyde Park ceases. Jupiter and Binkey first appear in Charles Manigault's correspondence with his son, Louis, on March 3, 1854 when he reported the family as runaways, who returned to their previous owner in an effort to avoid removal across state to the Savannah River plantations.

> I have just received a letter from Mr. Coward who informs me 5 of the newly Bo[ugh]t Negroes have run away from Silk Hope, because they dont like to go to Savannah River & he advises me to shew them that they belong to me. So I wrote him to send the entire Six down to me & I will start them off to you (as soon as he catches them). "Jupiter" the Father remains at Work at Silk Hope. All the rest of his caravan have "vamosed the ranch."[35]

Three days later, Charles Manigault reported,

> I got another Letter from Coward dated 3d inst. stating that all the Runaways were at his steps that morning with a note from old Mrs. Ball, stating that they went off because they were afraid of going to Savannah River. But on Friday Evg. last I wrote him that as they had runaway he must send them (all six) to me in turn I would ship the whole of them to you. He speaks highly of "Jupiter" as a highly Driver, who is sober, honest, & trustworthy who was intrusted with the keys of Cowards Brother when he managed "Hyde Park" Plantation.[36]

Manigault's threats to send the family to Savannah River were not empty and by March 10 he reported the arrival of the "troublesome" family. Charles Manigault offered some fatherly advice to Louis about handling Jupiter and especially Binkey, who seemed most willing to resist the move.

I must inform you that this old woman is very troublesome & has a bad influence on all the rest. And even Jupiter said something to me about his not being a field Hand (he has been a Driver, & Coward says a very good one). But so was Ishmael a Driver, & many others. Now he must go in the field, & his wife also, and I think if they two do one task between the two that will answer. The eldest Daughter, & the young man no doubt are prime. But the old woman (who is stated by Mr. Ball to be only 48) she must be brought to her bearings, & Jupiter too, & you just give them both a plantation talk & tell them that a good Negro makes a good master & the straight path is always easy, but the crooked path if full of trouble, & if either of them hang back you will put them in a boat & send them down to the Savannah Jail for a month or two, until they come to their senses, & I feel confident you will have [no] trouble, & you must act accordingly, & its best always in these cases to begin at once to put things straight with them. Mr. T. Bennet Lucas who bought 30 of them says my 6 are among the pick of them, & he wishes I'd let him have them at what I paid. If one Binkey wants to Bully you, carry her off yourself while the rest are at work in the field.37

For Jupiter and Binkey the sale to the Manigaults and the moves to Silk Hope and then the Savannah River plantations meant not only separation from family and friends, but a return to labor as field hands. Jupiter clearly resented the loss of his position of authority as a driver. Because skilled slaves received superior allocations of clothing on the Ball plantations, this loss of status also meant a decline in material conditions. According to Manigault, the return to the fields was suffered by other slaves when they were sold to him. Binkey apparently also felt a decline in status and a loss of privilege that had come with being the driver's wife. Of all the members of the family she appears to be the most willing to confront Manigault over her situation, first by running away and then verbally as suggested by Manigault's comment that his son should not tolerate her "bullying" him.

Manigault's advice in handling the problem of Jupiter and Binkey indicates some of the measures he took to force enslaved people to his will. The runaways are sent to a plantation more distant from their home plantation, although removal to the Savannah River sites may have been the intended fate of the family. He also suggests a lecture on behavior would be appropriate with the threat of removal to the slave jail in Savannah as an additional incentive to good conduct.

The precise actions taken to resolve the conflict between new owner Manigault and the family of Jupiter and Binkey were never revealed in the surviving correspondence. The story of Jupiter and Binkey ended with this note in an April 23, 1854, "List of Negroes at Gowrie and East Hermitage:"

Jupiter	½		50 Yrs.
Binkey	½	This Family,	43 Yrs.
Rebecca c.	P	from Ball's Estate,	17 Yrs.
Tommy	P	Cooper River,	20 Yrs.
Mary	½	at $550.	14 Yrs.
Harry			11 Yrs

All except Rebecca died of Consumption, Jupiter Tommy & Mary in
Charleston. Dr. Ogier's Charge.[38]

Binkey, like each of the women before her, sought to maintain her family in
a time of crisis and she relied on a variety of techniques, running away to gain
the support of a previous owner and verbal confrontation with her new owner.
None proved successful either in returning the family's previous elite status or
in avoiding the geographic removal from extended family and friends.

Each crisis described here saw enslaved women seize whatever means they
possessed to modify or reduce the worst effects of sales and separations. Isabel,
when confronted with separation from her husband was unable to attack the
source of her problem in the actions of her owner, but sought reunion by
poisoning her rival for Mathias, his second wife. Her actions stem from despair
and desperation and demonstrate that owners such as Laurens, who by their
words tried to maintain enslaved nuclear families, possessed a far from perfect
understanding of the kin systems of their slaves. Nippe apparently sacrificed
her own freedom in the interest of the freedom of her two sons. She and her
husband, Free Jack, understood the attitudes of the slaveowners and realized
that their sons were the most vulnerable to sale and separation. More than
twelve years passed after Free Jack set in motion his plan to free his boys without
him being able to free his wife and daughters. The actions of Free Jack and the
sacrifice of Nippe suggest that given the means, enslaved parents, mothers and
fathers, worked to protect their children and preserve their families. Dye and
Patra and their sister Subrina are most successful in appealing to sentiment and
paternalism not only to preserve some kin ties, but actually to reunite others
during the most serious estate sale endured by the Ball slaves. Binkey, totally
frustrated by the separation and loss of status suffered by her family following
a sale, tried to appeal to her previous owner and then in acts of confrontation
and defiance verbally confronted her new owner with her displeasure with the
work assignments of her family.

These women were not passive victims. Each drew upon whatever resources
they could muster to try to save their families. Sometimes some measure of
success was achieved, but more often than not, desperation, sacrifice, appeals
and frustration brought little result.

~
NOTES

1. Herbert G. Gutman, *The Black Family in Slavery and Freedom, 1750–1925,* (New York: Pantheon, 1976), 138.
2. Jane Turner Censer, *North Carolina Planters and Their Children, 1800–1860*, (Baton Rouge: Louisiana State University Press, 1984), 104–9, 138–41.
3. Peter Gaillard Plantation Accounts and Memoranda Book, 1783–1832, South Carolina Historical Society, Charleston, S.C.; Cheryll Ann Cody, "Naming, Kinship and Estate Dispersal: Notes on Slave Family Life on a South Carolina Plantation, 1786 to 1833,' *William and Mary Quarterly*, 39 (January 1982): 192–211.
4. James William McGettigan, Jr., "Boone County Slaves: Sales, Estate Divisions and Families, 1820–1865, Part I," *Missouri Historical Review*, 72 (1978): 176–97; James William McGettigan, Jr., "Boone County Slaves: Sales, Estate Divisions and Families, 1820–1865, Part II," *Missouri Historical Review*, 72 (1978): 271–95.
5. McGettigan, "Boone County Slaves, Part II," 285–6.
6. McGettigan, "Boone County Slaves, Part I," 194.
7. McGettigan, "Boone County Slaves, Part II," 295.
8. Ann Patton Malone, *Sweet Chariot: Slave Family and Household Structure in Nineteenth-Century Louisiana,* (Chapel Hill: University of North Carolina Press, 1992), 20–68, 205–17, 268–70.
9. See Edward W. Phifer, "Slavery in Microcosm, Burke County, North Carolina, *Journal of Southern History*, 28 (May 1962): 155 and Clarence L. Mohr, "Slavery in Oglethorpe County, Georgia, 1773–1865, *Phylon*, 34 (Spring 1972): 11–12.
10. Cheryll Ann Cody, "Naming, Kinship and Estate Dispersal" 192–211; Cheryll Ann Cody, "Kin and Community Among the Good Hope People After Emancipation," *Ethnohistory*, 41 (Winter 1994): 25–72.
11. Cheryll Ann Cody, "Naming, Kinship and Estate Dispersal."
12. *Good Hope Papers*, South Carolina Historical Society, Charleston, South Carolina; Cheryll Ann Cody, "Kin and Community among the Good Hope People."
13. Will of John Coming Ball, Ball Family Papers, South Carolina Historical Society, Charleston, S.C.
14. Henry Laurens (Charleston) to Elias [Wambaw] Ball (Hyde Park) 1 April 1765 *Letterbook of Henry Laurens*, Oct 30, 1762–Sept 10, 1766, Historical Society of Pennsylvania.
15. Henry Laurens (Charleston) to Elias [Wambaw] Ball (Hyde Park) 1 April 1765.
16. Ibid.
17. Ibid.
18. Will of Elias Ball, Feb 1750 approved Oct 1751, *Charleston Co. Wills* Book VI (1747–1752), South Carolina Department of Archives and History; Inventory of

the Estate of Mr. Elias Ball, Nov. 1751, *Charleston Co. Inventories,* WPA typescripts, vol. 79 (1751–3), 135–9. See also Henry Laurens (Charleston) to David Graeme (On board the *Mercury*) 23 January 1764, *Letterbook of Henry Laurens,* Oct 30, 1762–Sept 10, 1766, Historical Society of Pennsylvania and *The Papers of Henry Laurens,* editor, George Rogers, Jr., vol. 4 (1763–5) (Columbia: University of South Carolina Press, 1974), 141. Henry Laurens apparently purchased 400 acres at Dockum plantation from his brother-in-law, John Coming Ball, sometime between 1751 and 1754 and filed the record of the transaction with David Graeme, who was clerk of the Crown and Peace and of the Court of Common Pleas. The records were never officially filed, and as late as 1768, Laurens was trying to retrieve the documents.

19. Henry Laurens (Charleston) to Elias [Wambaw] Ball (Hyde Park) 1 April 1765 *Letterbook of Henry Laurens,* Oct 30, 1762 -Sept 10, 1766, Historical Society of Pennsylvania.

20. Henry Laurens (Wambaw) to Elias [Wambaw] Ball (Hyde Park) 2 May 1766, *Letterbook of Henry Laurens,* Oct 30, 1762–Sept 10, 1766, Historical Society of Pennsylvania. Joyce Chaplin, "Slavery and the Principle of Humanity: A Modern Idea in the Early Lower South," *Journal of Social History* 24 (Winter 1990): 306. Chaplin argues that Laurens' plea for the survival of the families of enslaved people provides evidence of his recognition of the humanity of African-American slaves. Unfortunately his words are at odds with the ultimate division of the estate and its tragic consequences for Chloe, Isabel and Mathias.

21. Henry Laurens (Wambaw) to Elias [Wambaw] Ball (Hyde Park) 2 May 1766.

22. Ibid.

23. Will of John Coming Ball, 1792, Ball Family Papers, South Carolina Historical Society, Charleston, S.C.

24. Anne Simons Deas, *Recollections of the Ball Family of South Carolina and Comingtee Plantation,* (Charleston, South Carolina Historical Society, 1978), 97–9.

25. Will of John Coming Ball.

26. "Copy of the Appraisement Made at Back River the 25th January 1793"; "List of Negroes Belonging to the Estate of John C. Ball, 5th February 1799," Ball Family Papers, South Carolina Historical Society, Charleston, S.C.; "A Valuation and Division of the Negroes Belonging to the Estate of John C. Ball Made at Backriver 23rd February 1811," Ball Family Papers, William Perkins Library, Duke University, Durham, N.C.

27. "Bill of Sale John Ball Executor for the Estate of John Coming Ball to Free Jack, 5 February 1800," *Miscellaneous Records of the State of South Carolina* vol. 3M, 442, South Carolina Department of Archives and History, Columbia, S.C.

28. "Will of John Ball, May 22, 1816," *Charleston Will Book E* (1807–18), 669–71, and "Inventory of John Ball, 14 Nov. 1817 to 1 January 1818," *Charleston District Ordinary Inventory Book E* (1802–19), South Carolina Department of Archives and History, Columbia, S.C.; "Sales on a/c of the Estate of John Ball Esqr decd . . . 29th February 1819," Ball Family Papers, William Perkins Library, Duke University, Durham, N.C.

29. John and Keating S. Ball Plantation Books, vols. 1–2, Ball Family Papers, Southern Historical Collection, University of North Carolina, Chapel Hill, N.C.

30. "Agreement between John Ball (Jr.) and John William Payne, July 9, 1819" and "Agreement between Isaac Ball and Maurice Simons, July 9, 1819" *Miscellaneous Records of the State of South Carolina,* vol. 4R, 244–8, "Bill of Sale for Slaves, 8 April 1819" *Miscellaneous Records of the State of South Carolina,* vol. 4S, 35–9, South Carolina Department of History and Archives, Columbia, S.C.

31. "A List of Negroes the Property of Elias Ball Made the 12th day of May 1784," "Appraisement and Division of the Negroes late the property of Elias Ball, 22 Jan 1787," Ball Family Papers, South Carolina Historical Society, Charleston, S.C., "Will of Elias Ball, 6 Dec. 1809," *Charleston District Will Book E* (1807–18); "Inventory of the Estate of Elias Ball, April 10, 1810," *Charleston District Ordinary Inventory Book E* (1802–19), South Carolina Department of Archives and History, Columbia, S.C.

32. "Inventory of the Estate of Elias Ball, April 10, 1810."

33. "A List of Negroes the Property of Elias Ball Made the 12th day of May 1784," "Appraisement and Division of the Negroes late the property of Elias Ball, 22 Jan. 1787."

34. See James M. Clifton, ed., *Life and Labor on Argyle Island: Letters and Documents of a Savannah River Rice Plantations, 1833–1867,* (Savannah Ga.: Beehive Press, 1979).

35. Charles Manigault (Charleston) to Louis Manigault (Gowrie, near Savannah), March 3, 1854, 175, in Clifton, *Life and Labor.*

36. Charles Manigault (Charleston) to Louis Manigault (Gowrie, near Savannah), March 6, 1854, 177–8 in Clifton, *Life and Labor.*

37. Charles Manigault (Charleston) to Louis Manigault (Gowrie, near Savannah), March 10, 1854, 179–80 in Clifton, *Life and Labor.*

38. "List of Negroes at Gowrie and East Hermitage," April 23, 1854, 185 in Clifton, *Life and Labor.*

~

"RAIS YOUR CHILDREN UP RITE"
Parental Guidance and Child Rearing Practices among
Slaves in the Nineteenth-Century South

Wilma King

"**A**t night let the negroes employ themselves as they please till the bell rings, without any interference," wrote the Marengo County, Alabama slaveholder Willis P. Bocock in his 1860 "Rules for the Overseer or Manager."[1] Although bondage determined the quantity of time enslaved families spent together, parents often defined the quality of that time. Not only was their charge especially crucial because the time that family members spent together was limited, but also because there was an ever-present possibility that slaveholders would remove children from the protective arms of their parents. It was important, therefore, for parents to teach their children fundamental survival skills at early ages. Despite their travails, many enslaved parents demonstrated an unfailing love for their offspring and socialized them to endure slavery by teaching them to work hard and to pay deference to whites while maintaining self-respect. These lessons constituted a major act of resistance to the demoralizing effects of slavery as children learned about their culture and how to survive as slaves.

Enslaved parents were often too weary from the demanding rigors of their labor to indulge their children; however, they tried to establish binding relationships with their offspring. Booker T. Washington's mother did not "give attention to the training of her children during the day," but she "snatched" a few minutes whenever possible to care for them. As a youngster, Frederick Douglass never saw his mother "by the light of day," because she worked on one plantation and he lived on another. Her occasional nocturnal visits suggest that she resisted separation from her son by traveling before or after work and possibly without permission. Both Douglass and Washington remembered their mothers for the sacrifices they made.[2]

The autobiographies of former slaves, Works Progress Administration (WPA) interviews, and letters from slaves to their owners in manuscript collections, abound with narratives of parental devotion to their families. For example, the narratives of the former slaves Mary Bell and Millie Barber are similar in that their parents were partners in "abroad" marriages. Their fathers' visits sometimes caused "confusion, mixup, and heartaches" when they traveled without passes and were caught by patrollers. In light of such risks, that parents made visits at all is testimony to their concern for the well-being of their children.[3]

The status of the Bell and Barber families was not unlike that of thousands of other slave families; however, the children of one South Carolina couple, Sampson and Maria, must have felt the sting of separation very keenly. Following an October 1847 visit to his wife and children, Sampson drowned while crossing a swollen river as he returned to the plantation owned by Charles Manigault. Perhaps the children did not fully understand the subsequent reasons for the confusion and heartache Sampson's death caused, but it is clear that Sampson cared about his family and went to great lengths to visit his wife and children.[4]

Parents, whether together or alone, taught their youngsters how to tolerate inhumane acts and degradation, to maintain their humanity, and to keep their spirits intact. They seized any opportunity to teach the youngsters behavior that was appropriate for a child and a slave. An 1833 letter from the Tennessean Hobbs to his wife in Virginia is testimony to his concern about parental guidance, given the difficulties of separation, especially from his daughter Elizabeth. Hobbs expressed an abiding interest in the child's growth and development. He wrote confidently of a singular dream, "I want Elizabeth to be a good girl."[5] Perhaps to be a "good girl" meant that she was to obey, help with chores, and do anything necessary to help mitigate the family's conditions.

Decades later, the slave Prince Woodfin forwarded a similar message from a Jamestown, California, gold-field to his wife back in North Carolina. His 1853 dispatch urged, "Rais your children up rite." He continued, "Learn them to be Smart and deacent and alow them to Sauce no person."[6] This was pertinent advice if children were to survive slavery. Courteous children would not cause offense nor would they bring reprisals upon themselves or their parents. In this context, "Smart" does not refer to an intellectual feat, but to industrious behavior.

Slaveowners expected enslaved children to work in a conscientious manner. They initially used youngsters to assist experienced adult workers, but, as they both grew older, children became substitutes for the adults and eventually replaced them. Ordinarily, children encountered white authority first-hand when they entered the work-force. Their parents shielded them from brutality whenever possible, but their protection was limited. During slavery, parents were as susceptible as their offspring when whites whipped adults and children alike. Nevertheless, along with the social value of cooperation with fellow slaves in the work place, parents taught youngsters how to perform their chores.

Through such lessons, children learned to deflect the lash from themselves or fellow slaves by completing their work satisfactorily or by helping others who lagged behind. The communal interest in protecting slaves from punishment surfaces in a song which warned:

> Keep yo' eye on de sun,
> See how she run,
> Don't let her catch you with your work undone

Hearing this admonition, children learned the value of collective efforts and the importance of completing their work in a timely manner. The additonal lyrics:

> I'm a trouble, I'm a trouble
> Trouble don' las' always

offer hope if their efforts failed. The message was useful for most occupations throughout the region.[7]

As a child, the North Carolinian Fannie Moore realized that her mother's nightly task of spinning and carding four cuts of thread (approximately 300 yards) was too demanding after a full day of toil in the field. Therefore, she helped her mother complete the job by holding the light, a flaming pine knot, so that she see could see how to spin the thread. "Sometimes I never to go bed," Moore recalled. The loss of sleep was less important than warding off punishments through mutual cooperation. Moore's sensitivity to her mother's predicament was not unusual among slaves.[8]

Slave women displayed a similar compassion for their sisters in bondage. Children observed such actions first hand on large plantations as they worked in "trash gangs"–predominately female agricultural labor units which included pregnant and lactating women as well as older slaves. In addition to serving as a "teaching-learning" experience, participation in the trash gang raised the consciousness of youngsters who imitated their elders.[9]

There were few distinctions made among field hands based upon gender; however, the same was not true when slaves occupied skilled positions. Only boys became artisans or craftsmen through apprenticeships or by working with others. The ex-slave John Mathews said he "learnt how to beat out de iron an' make wagin tires, an' make plows" after helping his father who was a blacksmith. His testimony notes the linkage between the work of adults and their offspring's future occupation.[10]

Girls could have learned the same techniques, but they did not have the opportunity. It does not follow that craft work was too strenuous for women, inasmuch as many women engaged in heavy labor such as plowing fields, hauling logs, and digging ditches. Childbearing was presumably the primary reason for their exclusion because, unlike field work which required more endurance than skill, it interrupted assignments that only skilled persons could complete. Without specific craft skills, women had fewer opportunities to travel and live away from their owners or to hire their own time and earn money to purchase personal items or their freedom.[11]

While older children learned agricultural routines or honed craft skills, those who were too young to work often remained in the care of other slaves—usually those too old or infirmed for other chores. Robert Shepherd of Athens, Georgia remembered "Aunt Viney," who cared for a large number of children while their parents worked. She served the children's meals in a "great long trough" in the yard, and she demanded strict attention to the routine. Otherwise, Shepherd said, "Aunt Viney would sure tear us up." Under such conditions, physical attention to children's needs was sometimes wanting, but seasoned caregivers compensated by sharing wisdom gained from life's experiences.[12]

Much of the advice for maneuvering through the maze of Southern etiquette and resisting slavery came from parents, grandparents, and fictive kin who had grown up in bondage. It is important to note that this advice was transmitted in this way, rather than through schools, child-rearing literature, or children's fiction of the mid-nineteenth century. Popular reading material of the day was not readily available to slave parents or their children. Moreover, availability of the material was of little consequence because most slaves were illiterate. Parents and adult slaves provided examples of acceptable behavior and passed survival tactics down to youngsters through oral lore.[13]

Slave parents insisted upon respect from their children who consequently learned to give deference to their elders. Prince Woodfin's edict "Alow them to Sauce no person" was not uniquely his own, but a view commonly held by many slaves. The Northern teacher Charlotte Forten observed that among the children on South Carolina's Sea Islands it was "the rarest thing to hear a disrespectful word from a child to his parent." The Mississippi planter Everard Green Baker appeared unfamiliar with such internalized customs when he wrote, "The young should be taught to be respectful & obedient to the older ones."[14] Furthermore, Baker insisted that enslaved adults be "kind and considerate to the younger ones." His suggestions show the limits of his understanding about what slaves did in their own time and the nature of their behavior within the slave community. Few slaves required advice on deferential behavior from outsiders.

Many slave parents demanded obedience from their children, yet they were not unreasonable in their demands. Their basic goal was to shield their children from harm by whites while demanding obedience, respect, and family unity. But the intricacies of slavery often perplexed children who found themselves in a struggle between plantation authority and parental influence. Parents insisted upon family loyalty and expected children to comply without reservation. An enslaved father impressed that lesson upon his son when he scolded: "You are my child and when I call you, you should come immediately, if you have to pass through fire and water." The simultaneous calls from the boy's father and his owner precipitated the harsh-sounding order. The child had responded to his owner rather than his father.[15]

If such situations recurred, a child would have to develop a strategy to pacify both a parent and owner. For example, a Cherokee freedwoman found a solution to a similar dilemma when her mother addressed her as Sarah and her mistress called her Annie when she was still a slave. Regardless of her response, the eight-year-old girl faced a whipping from her mother or owner. In the midst of this tug-of-war, Sarah said "that made me hate both of them." She admits her hatred, but did not mention fearing the women. "I got the devil in me," she said, "and wouldn't come to either one." Sarah found comfort in her grandmother who watched the dynamics between the women from a nearby porch. After the mistress died, the older woman explained that Sarah was abused because she was a constant reminder to the woman of her husband's infidelity.[16]

The disciplining of slave children was generally in the hands of their parents. Depending upon the size of the household, however, slaveowners sometimes exerted authority over the amount and kind of chastisement parents or others administered. For example, on August 31, 1864, the Tennessean John Houston Bills disapproved of the "unmerciful thrashing" Angelina gave her son Wilson, and Bills forbade "her interference with him again." Angelina, who apparently viewed his action as a usurpation of her parental rights, became "so boisterous & insulting" that Bills was "forced to correct her for the first time."[17] Bills's action appears to go beyond concern for the child and reflects his responses to a woman who exceeded boundaries defined by the patriarchal system. Perhaps Wilson did not understand the nuances of such intricate interpersonal relations between adult slaveowners and slaves, but he did not ask for an explanation. Early on, children learned not to question their parents along with the lesson that slaves did not challenge slaveowners.

Knowing when to speak, what to say, and to whom was an important resource for survival. Children who talked too much might unwittingly betray family secrets and incur punitive actions. The axiom, "Children are to be seen and not heard," was especially important because betrayal by a fellow slave was insufferable; its application served as a shield against youngsters who talked too much and unconsciously revealed plans or secrets which could result in punitive actions. Susan Snow, a youngster in Mississippi during the Civil War, learned the value of the saying after singing:

> Jeff Davis, long and slim
> Whipped old Abe with a hickory limb.
> Jeff Davis is a wise man, Lincoln is a fool
> Jeff Davis rides a gray and Lincoln rides a mule.

The first stanza of the ditty was innocuous; however, other lyrics contained more poignant social commentary.

> Old Gen'd Pope had a shotgun,
> Filled it full o' gum,
> Killed 'em as dey come.
> Called a Union band,
> Make de Rebels understand
> To leave de land,
> Submit to Abraham.[18]

Slaves sang the song, but Susan did not realize it was up "dey sleeves," meaning it was for their private entertainment. Susan sang it within earshot of her owner, who subsequently whipped her. The song gave pause to supporters of the Confederate States of America (CSA) because it predicted their defeat. Moreover, she sang about the CSA President, owner of a plantation and scores of slaves in Warren County, Mississippi, which adds another dimension of social criticism about slaveholders in the Magnolia State.[19] Learning when and where to sing the song proved more crucial than learning the song itself.

Slaveholders had clear ideas about the appropriate behavior for enslaved youngsters and made their expectations known through instructions to overseers. The rules were often not age-specific, but it does not follow that infractions by youngsters would be treated with leniency. Note the distinction in McDonald Furman's instructions to his overseer, "If a small negro runs away the meat of the family must be taken away or withholden until return." He added, "If a grown one [runs away] the meat of all must be taken away or witholden."[20] Although the runaways differed in age, the punishment remained constant. The comprehensiveness of most rules underscores the fact that much depended upon their interpretation and that slavery truncated childhood.

Writing in an 1852 issue of the *Southern Planter*, W. W. Gilmer commented specifically about the desirable behavior of slave children. He urged slaveholders to teach young servants not to run and hide from whites but "to stand their ground, and speak when spoken to, in a polite manner. . . . Talk to them; take notice of them; it soon gives them confidence."[21] It also "adds greatly to their value," he concluded. "Polite" slaves approached whites with bowed heads, downcast eyes, and lowered voices. Children's self-esteem was less important than creating the impression that they were intelligent and malleable servants who recognized their place in the society.

A former slave, Jacob Stroyer, commented about his owner's interest in creating subservience through an exercise given to youngsters. In anticipation of his arrival, the children bathed, groomed their hair, and dressed in their best clothes. Afterwards, Stroyer wrote: "We were then drilled in the art of addressing our expected visitors. The boys were required to bend the body forward with head down, and rest the body on the left foot, and scrape the right foot backward on the ground, while uttering the words, 'how dy Massie and Missie.' "[22] The girls curtsied and repeated the same words. According to Stroyer, this was considered acceptable behavior for a slave.

But there were no special ceremonies to teach Adelaide, a six-year-old servant girl, deference rituals at Hygiene, a small slaveholding household in Jesuit Bend, Louisiana. The plantation owner's wife insisted on deferential behavior, however, to reinforce the social distance between her three-year-old daughter Fanny and Adelaide. The woman always referred to her daughter as "Miss Fanny" when speaking to the slaves, whether they were children or adults. "Miss Fanny" gave "Old Reuben"–the man servant–a dime for Christmas in 1859.[23] The title "Miss" denotes differences in their status and suggests that slaves, regardless of size or age, owed deference to the child. Adelaide's response to this situation is unknown; however, a Juniper County, Mississippi, slave girl's reaction under similar conditions suggests the level of slaves' understanding of the deference ritual. When introduced to her "young mistress" the eleven-year-old Lu looked at the infant in her mother's arms and said, "I don't see no young mistress, that's a baby."[24]

The above examples come from different quarters, yet their common objective was to establish and maintain the "master-servant" relationship. White children learned to expect deference, and slave children learned to pay deference. Thomas Jefferson argued that white children imitated the "whole commerce between master and slave" from observing their parents interact with bond servants.[25] Afterwards, the children put on the same airs with smaller slaves. In many ways, power relationships existed between white and black children as they did between white and black adults.

Enslaved parents viewed compliance with the deference ritual as a way of avoiding slavery's punitive arm; they knew however that such compliance did not reflect their true feelings. Children, too, had to juggle public behavior and private convictions without upsetting the routine established by their owners. This kind of resistance required a degree of sophistication which further truncated childhood, because it compelled children to behave with a degree of maturity long before they reached adulthood. The need for such careful modulations of self suggests the dangerous position slave children occupied.

At early ages, slaves learned to adopt a demeanor, a "mask," to camouflage true feelings. The freedman Henry Bibb's comment, "The only weapon of self defence that I could use successfully was that of deception," illustrates the point.[26] During the Civil War, Mary Chesnut, an astute observer of antebellum society, mentioned the impenetrable expressions of domestic servants who appeared "profoundly indifferent" to war-related activities. Their detachment was so convincing that whites behaved as if the slaves were not present. "Are they stolidly stupid," Chesnut asked, "or wiser than we are, silent and strong, biding their time."[27] Such slaves were not dolts, but rather they cleverly concealed their interest in matters with a veneer of nonchalance.[28]

Slave parents seized every opportunity to teach their children how to make their demeanors conform to various social situations. Storytelling at nightfall is one of the oldest forms of entertainment, and it was not unknown in the slave cabins. What children heard and learned from the tales was of great importance to their maturation process. Bruno Bettelheim in *The Uses of Enchantment* argues that fairy tales serve a useful purpose whereby children gain wisdom through stories, "the purveyors of deep insights." Fairy tales fill the need for magic while instilling a belief that good will triumph over evil. It is possible that slave children working in homes among white children heard the tales. Jakob and Wilhelm Grimm published their famous collection of German folk tales including "Little Red Riding Hood" (1812) and "Snow White" (1815) well before slavery ended. Even so, it was not sufficiently widespread to displace African folk tales which served a similar purpose. [29]

Many African folk tales furnished slaves with behavioral models. Animal trickster tales, an integral part of the slave's oral tradition, taught lessons of survival and self-confidence. Irony and cynicism abound in these complex narratives of mythology and fantasy which entertain and educate. These lessons were not lost on the young.[30]

Animal tricksters have human properties; therefore, the powerful fox or wolf provided an easy substitute for a slaveowner or any other oppressor, while a meek rabbit or terrapin symbolized the oppressed party. Young slaves could readily identify with weak persecuted characters such as the helpless "Brer Rabbit," who faces danger yet endures. Brer Rabbit uses wit and guile to out-maneuver stronger and more vicious animals, but he is not content with survival alone and seeks to elevate his status in the eyes of others. Finally, the weak Brer Rabbit uses any means necessary to survive and overpower stronger animals. After an examination of African-American trickster tales, John W. Roberts asserts that "the sadistic elements of the trickster tales . . . aptly reflect a modern sense of moral outrage over slavery."[31]

Aside from the animal trickster tales, slaves told stories of "John," the human trickster, who is analogous to Brer Rabbit in antebellum stories of human deception. Slaves exchanged these tales in the same fashion as the animal fables. The structure of human trickster tales is similar to the animal stories, yet it differs in that John does not always succeed. Additionally, his triumphs are never as great as the animal trickster who wins love, kills adversaries, and elevates his stature at every turn. John is not Brer Rabbit's equal, but his shrewdness serves a purpose. Lawrence W. Levine contends that the tales were "the vehicle through which slaves rehearsed their tactics, laughed at the foibles of their masters (and themselves), and taught their young the means they would have to adopt in order to survive."[32] For the slave, survival was not so much a matter of acting like a trickster, as it was contingent upon not being a trickster's victim.

Parental lessons in survival included caution about the appearance of "trickster" sexual advances, and parents tried to prevent their children from falling victim to the serious offense of sexual abuse. Yet many former slaves claimed that their parents did not provide any sex education. Melville J. Herskovits' study of Dahomey details the instructions given to boys and girls as they approach puberty. The simulation of sexual experiences constitutes much of the training for boys who discuss and dramatize "love stories" in all male groups.[33] Of those instructions David Brion Davis writes, "Negro girls received from older women a well-planned sexual education, which included elaborate exercises and prolonged stimulation of the appropriate organs."[34] At the appropriate age, boys and girl engaged in stages of courting before consummating marriage. Dahomeans viewed this learning process as an essential part of their education.[35] Given the number of Africans coming into the New World with such knowledge, it is possible that they passed it on to their offspring just as they transferred other facets of their culture. Harriet Jacobs mentioned "the pure principles inculcated by my grandmother" in her narrative when writing about her own sexuality.[36] Perhaps former slaves interviewd in the 1930s, who denied receiving any sex education while enslaved, were uncomfortable with the subject and ended discussions by claiming ignorance. The avoidance of discussions regarding human sexuality was indicative of the era.[37]

Rather than open discussions, it is possible that slave parents used indirect ways of sensitizing their children about sexuality and resisting exploitation. Minnie Folkes remembered her mother saying: "Don't let nobody bother yo' principle; 'cause dat was all yo' had."[38] The meaning of "principles" used by Folkes and Jacobs is left to interpretation. By contrast, Lucy McCullough's mother said nothing, but there is little doubt about her intentions. The former slave recounted her mother's reactions after seeing her "cummin' crost de yahd en she say mah dress too short." The woman ripped out the hem and wove "more cloff on hit, twel it long enuf, lak she want it."[39] The added length was little protection against obvious signs of maturity, yet the mother believed it would shield her daughter a while longer.

The subject of sexual exploitation needs additional research because its major focus is upon slave women and white men. Illicit activities between white women and slave men have not been investigated thoroughly nor have incestuous relations among slaves. The study of sexual exploitation of young male slaves also remains in need of study. Contemporary publications on the subject often mention the Texan Rose Williams, whose owner forced the sixteen-year-old girl into a marriage, without raising questions about its impact upon her spouse, Rufus. Furthermore, Harriet Jacobs remembered the "despotic habits" of a slaveowner who frequently punished the young slave, Luke. Jacobs described the situation as the "strangest freaks" which she found "too filthy" to repeat. In all probability, Jacobs was referring to sexual abuse.[40]

Because of differences in interpretations and a general reticence about sexuality, it is difficult to know to what extent parents or others socialized children about their own sexuality. To be sure, some young females understood the special roles of expectant mothers and childcare through their daily contact with pregnant and lactating women in the trash gang. Children may also have heard conversations between the women and their elders, who added a retrospective dimension, about childbearing and parenting. Moreover, predominately female activities such as quilting, where women worked together in groups, could have facilitated the transfer of information. Fishing, hunting trips, or other exercises thought to be male activities probably served to socialize boys about sex roles.[41]

As children matured and became attracted to members of the opposite sex, there were occasions for them to woo and be wooed. Yet parents sometimes made decisions about when children, especially their girls, could entertain members of the opposite sex. At twelve years of age Laura Bell met Thomas, whom she admired, but her parents said she was too young to "keep company." Nevertheless, Laura and Thomas met secretly for "seberal years." Dicy Wind-field's parents would not allow her to court until she "wuz 'bout eighteen years ole." Even so, she and her special friend "wont allowed to go no whars together to 'mount to nothin.' "[42] In his study of sexuality in the slave community, Steven E. Brown concluded that young slaves, especially in Georgia, were "compelled to adhere to rigorous courtship strictures," including waiting until they reached the proper age. The testimony of former slaves suggest that age constraints on sexual activity knew no geographical bounds among slave parents. Concern about visiting among would-be lovers may have been connected to parents' fear of patrollers inflicting punishment upon those traveling abroad.[43]

Despite many obstacles, the promise of long-lasting fidelity was a reality for many slave couples who adhered to norms and values of their own. They avoided marrying family members and viewed extramarital relations as serious viola-tions of their moral code. Many slaves also resisted encroachments from interlopers. The historian Eugene Genovese hypothesized that married slaves "did not take white sexual aggression lightly and resisted effectively enough to hold it to a minimum." Many white men, according to Genovese, avoided "resistant women and dangerous men" and directed their attention toward "single girls by using a combination of flattery, bribes and the ever-present threat of force." It is unlikely that these same "resistant women and dangerous men" would take sexual aggression lightly regardless of the perpetrator's race.[44]

Given the numerous accounts of unwanted advances from black or white aggressors, "single girls" and other enslaved children must have witnessed overtures and taken cues from the "resistant women and dangerous men" around them. The former slave Ben Horry discussed a South Carolina driver who appeared to use his position as a way to exact sexual favors. "If omen don't do all he say," Horry remembered, "he lay task on 'em they aint able to do." He added, "My mother won't do all he say."[45] The child must have wondered why his mother refused the orders. And as a youngster, the South Carolinian Gus Feaster saw his mother engage in a physical confrontation with an overseer after she rejected his advances. Without any discussion from either of the women, children could form opinions about the appropriateness of the behavior that prompted such actions. The mere observance of such behaviors could introduce enslaved youngsters to examples of social behavior they could imitate.[46]

Slave children learned that engaging in premarital sex was not as serious an offense in the slave community as extramarital relations. Furthermore, they would come to see that premarital sex is not an accurate indicator of promiscuity. Sexually active couples often married and settled into long-lasting relationships. The young Tennessee couple, Willis and Martha, serve as only one example. After only two months of marriage, they became the parents of a baby girl. The nonplussed grandmother said Martha "makes quick work of it." Sensing her bewilderment, their owner comforted the woman by telling her, "such things often happen with the first born, but never afterwards." Willis and Martha's first child, Creasy, arrived September 30, 1854, while the others were born in 1856, 1858, 1860, and 1861. The slaveowner's words not only consoled the new grandmother but confirmed that stable marriages and the birth of additional children at fairly regular intervals often followed bridal pregnancies.[47]

Although neither the law nor the church protected slave marriages, there were long-lasting unions and many slaves exhibited distress at their disruption. The July 1849 letter from a South Carolina slave woman Lavina appealed directly to her owner about the separation of her daughter Aggy from her husband Jimmy. It is testimony to one family's devotion and belief in the sanctity of marriage. Lavina, a partner in a marriage of long duration wrote, "I am tormented. My conscience is bruised, my feelings are vex." Her agitation stemmed from Juddy using "Her sparklin black Eye [for] caching Other wimmins husbans" and their owner allowed Jimmy to remain with Juddy. Lavina asked, "Do you think it right in the sight of God?" Moreover, she suggested weighing "Jimmy and his deeds with this Magdalene Juddy all in one side [of a scale], and put justice, humanity and religion in the other."[48] Lavina's primary concern was Aggy. After stating her daughter's case in terms of Christian morality, the mother concluded: "Pray over it, Massa" and "View the Matter as u would if they were yore children."[49] Lavina regarded marriage as a serious commitment and probably passed that belief on to her daughter.

Lavina and other enslaved parents did all they could to help their children adjust to slavery until they were free. Perhaps their most difficult job was to ease the despair of separation. Regardless of the reasons—whether through sale, relocation, or hiring-out—separation had negative effects upon slave families for it removed family members from their places of birth and burial. In his study of African religions, John Mbiti explained the importance of the burial grounds when he wrote:

The grave is paradoxically the symbol of separation between the dead and the living, but turning into the shrine for the living-dead converts it into the point of meeting between the two worlds.[50]

The possibility of ever returning to the places and people that held special meaning was nil for most slaves. Hence, separations were among the most dreadful facets of slavery.[51]

When forewarned about separations, enslaved parents responded in different ways. Some of them told children stories about taking long journeys, while others interfered with imminent separations through acts of resistance such as running away. Having time to prepare for separations did not always ease the pain of separation. For example, Cornelius, a child owned by the Jennings family of Eden, Tennessee, remembered the day their owner sent her mother away. After more than a week to prepare for the parting, Cornelius said, "I cannot tell in words the feelings I had at that time." The former slave woman added, "My very soul seemed to cry out 'Gone, gone, gone forever.' "[52] Having no choice in the matter and not knowing what would become of their loved ones, slaves (such as Cornelius) were left feeling despair. This despair was further exacerbated if those being torn apart were denied the opportunity to say goodbye.

When faced with separating slave families, the Virginia slaveholder I. L. Twyman asked his brother-in-law John Austin to keep details of a pending 1848 slave sale to himself, otherwise the news, he declared, would "set them to crying and howling."[53] Twyman's delay in breaking the news to slave families simply postponed their reaction and relieved him of hearing their grief stricken cries for the moment.

Faced with impending separations from their children, slave parents sometimes sought viable alternatives to separations. Solomon Northup described the pitiable supplications from Eliza to traders at the New Orleans slave market. Her pleas for mercy differ from those of Lucy Skipwith, a slave mother owned by the Virginia planter John Hartwell Cocke. In 1859 Lucy begged Cocke not to sell her daughter who was accused of stealing $300 from the person to whom she was "indentured." Lucy argued that Betsey would be better off with her than growing up in an environment destined to bring about "her everlasting destruction." Ostensibly Cocke agreed, but he later explained: "I did not put Betsey with her mother to stop the sale of her but to better prepare her for sale."[54] Ironically, his faith in Lucy's parental influence worked to her advantage. Lucy, an unusual woman, could attribute the success in thwarting the sale to her extraordinary leverage with Cocke.

The reality of being sold and the affection between a parent and child are seen in the song "Mammy is Ole' Massa gwin'er to sell us?" The melancholy lyrics asked:

> Mammy, is Ole' Massa gwin'er sell us tomorrow?
> Yes, my chile.
> Whar he gwin'er sell us?
> Way down South in Georgia.[55]

In the following verse, the child bids a serene farewell and tells the mother "Don't grieve after me." Without a doubt the mother did not accept the separation with resignation. Mothers sometimes sustained themselves with the belief in a reunion after death.

If the family was separated, it was almost impossible to keep in touch with those left behind because of limitations on communication, illiteracy, lack of transportation, and ignorance of geography. Some slaves never saw or heard from each other again, yet they did not forget one another, as indicated by the 1833 letter from Hobbs. Although distressed the father reassured Elizabeth of his love when he wrote, "Do not think that because I am bound so fare that gods not abble to open the way."[56] He encouraged her to believe that God could and would ease their burdens. If earthly reunions were impossible, they knew heavenly rewards were possible.

An 1857 letter from a slave father in Georgia further underscores the pain of separation. "I wish to now," he wrote, "what has Ever become of my Presus little girl." He had "left her in goldsboro [North Carolina] with Mr. Walker" and had "not herd from her Since." The letter is moving, but it does not convey the emotional strain as strongly as Solomon Northup's description of Eliza's "exhibition of intense, unmeasured, and unbounded grief" when she was sold away from her children.[57]

Slaves were sometimes successful in removing themselves and their children from the institution of slavery. Children learned subtle acts of day-to-day resistance from observing slow and haphazard work habits that undermined production. At other times they received directives. The mother of a youngster in Tennessee told her daughter how to respond to abuse. "Fight, and if you can't fight, kick; if you can't kick, then bite." The mother warned, "I'll kill you, gal, if you don't stand up for your self." Perhaps this is a unique directive, but the slaves' propensity to wear a mask makes it doubtful.[58]

Some women resisted the demands placed upon them by refusing to have children, while others may have practiced infanticide. Some parents, resorting to such acts, may have preferred seeing the death of their children to seeing them live in bondage. There are documented reports of infanticide; however, care must be exercised in labeling unexplained deaths as infanticide. Recent investigations suggest that sudden infant death syndrome (SIDS) may have been the cause rather than a deliberate act.[59]

Some slave mothers and fathers were sorely distressed by seeing their offspring enslaved for life. After the birth of his daughter, Henry Bibb vowed never to father another child as long as he remained enslaved. Harriet Jacobs claimed that her heart was heavier than ever when she learned that her new-born child was a girl. She believed slavery was worse for women than for men because of the additional burden imposed by gender. Thomas H. Jones's laments are even more piercing: "I am a father and have had the same feelings of unspeakable anguish as I looked upon my precious babes," he cried, "and have thought of the ignorance, degradation and woe which they must endure as slaves."[60]

Many parents sought to remove themselves and their children from bondage. The majority of those who gained freedom before the Civil War did so by running away. The average runaway was a young, single man traveling alone. Slave mothers, regardless of status and age, were less likely to run away than childless women. It was easier for them to escape alone; consequently, parents sometimes inspired their children to flee. A part of every child's socialization was the preparation for freedom. The Missouri-born Lucy Delaney remembered that her mother "never spared an opportunity" to encourage her children to run away.[61] With this inspiration, Lucy was not reluctant to escape from bondage. By comparison, William Wells Brown was reluctant to run away and leave his mother and sister behind. "If we cannot get our liberty," his sister argued, "we do not wish to be the means of keeping you from a land of freedom."[62] Despite the differences in Delany and Brown's reactions to opportunities for freedom, their families encouraged them to run away alone. Enslaved parents helped their children to endure slavery and prepared them for surviving as free persons.[63]

Contrary to contemporary images of slave adults as "childlike," African Americans under slavery learned to handle situations involving violence, injustice, and arbitrary power at early ages. As a result of parental guidance and child-rearing practices, enslaved children learned to resist slavery and to maintain their integrity. When necessary, they donned the mask of compliance to hide their will to resist. Kate Drumgoold remembered her mother's persistence, and her recollections provide telling comments about the relationship between one enslaved woman and those who claimed to control her. Drumgoold recalled that their owner could never make her mother "feel like a slave." The woman's mettle provided valuable lessons about the importance of family and culture in acts of resistance. "She would battle with them to the last," the former slave recalled, "that she would not recognize them as her lord and master." Drumgoold, who followed her mother's example, concluded, "She was right."[64]

~
NOTES

1. "Rules for the Overseer or Manager," Willis P. Bocock Papers, Southern Historical Collection, University of North Carolina, Chapel Hill, N. C. (hereafter cited as SHC).
2. Booker T. Washington, *Up From Slavery: An Autobiography*, (New York: Bantam Books, 1967), 3; Michael Merger, ed., *Frederick Douglass: The Narrative and Selected Writings*, (New York: Random House, 1984), 19.
3. George P. Rawick, ed., *The American Slave: A Composite Autobiography*, 19 vols. (Westport, Conn.: Greenwood Press, 1972) 11: Missouri Narrative, Ser. 2: 27–8; 2: South Carolina Narrative Part 1, Ser. 1: 38–41. See Charles L. Perdue, Jr., Thomas E. Barden, and Robert K. Phillips, eds., *Weevils in the Wheat: Interviews with Virginia Ex-Slaves*, (Bloomington: Indiana University Press, 1980), 267.
4. Z. Haynes to Charles Manigault, October 25, 1847, Manigault Papers, Perkins Library, Duke. (hereafter cited as Duke).
5. Hobbs to his wife in Virginia, 1833, "Before Freedom Came Exhibit," Museum of the Confederacy, Richmond, Virginia.
6. Prince Woodfin to Nickles Woodfin, April 25, 1853, Nicholas Washington Woodfin Papers, SHC.
7. Perdue, *Weevils in the Wheat*, 88, 309.
8. Norman R. Yetman, ed., *Life Under the "Peculiar Institution": Selections from the Slave Narrative Collection*, (New York: Holt, Rinehart and Winston, Inc., 1970), 227.
9. Deborah Gray White, *Ar'n't I a Woman? Female Slaves in the Plantation South*, (New York: W. W. Norton, 1985), 94–5, 123; Jacqueline Jones, *Labor of Love, Labor of Sorrow: Black Women, Work and the Family, From Slavery to the Present*, (New York: Vintage Books, 1986), 16.
10. Ronald L. Lewis, "Slave Families at Early Chesapeake Ironworks," *Virginia Magazine of History and Biography* 82 (April 1978): 177. See Michael P. Johnson, "Work, Culture, and the Slave Community: Slave Occupations in the Cotton Belt in 1860," *Labor History* (hereafter cited as LH) 27 (Summer 1986): 325–55.
11. See Jones, Labor of Love, 18; Carole Shammas, "Black Women's Work and the Evolution of Plantation Society in Virginia," LH 26 (Winter 1985): 5–28; Leonard Stavsky, "The Origins of Negro Craftsmanship in Colonial America," *Journal of Negro History* (hereafter cited as JNH) 32 (October 1947): 428. Michael P. Johnson and James L. Roark argue that William Ellison, a South Carolina freedman, and subject of their monograph, owned a disproportionate number of slave boys. They suggest that he sold the girls to raise capital for more land and slaves while he kept the boys and trained them as skilled mechanics. *Black Masters: A Free Family of Color in the Old South*, (New York: W. W. Norton, 1984), 131–4.
12. Yetman, *Life Under the "Peculiar Institution,"* 64, 189: John Q. Anderson, ed., "A

Letter From a Yankee Bride in Ante-Bellum Louisiana," Louisiana History 1 (Summer 1960): 248; Bobby Frank Jones, "A Cultural Middle Passage: Slave Marriage and Family in the Antebellum South," (Ph.D. diss., University of North Carolina, 1965), 108; Thomas L. Webber, *Deep Like the Rivers: Education in the Slave Quarter Community, 1831–1865*, (New York: W. W. Norton, 1978), 10.

13. See Daniel T. Rogers, "Socializing Middle-Class Children: Institutions, Fables, and Work Values in Nineteenth-Century America," *Journal of Social History* 13 (Spring 1980): 354–66, for a discussion of the socialization of middle-class white children in the nineteenth century.

14. Woodfin to Woodfin, April 25, 1853, SHC; Charlotte Forten, "Life on the Sea Islands," *Atlantic Monthly* Part I (May 1864): 592; Everard Green Baker Diary, "Projects of Life," vol. II: 195, SHC.

15. Harriet A. Jacobs, *Incidents in the Life of a Slave Girl: Written by Herself*, ed. Jean Fagan Yellin (Cambridge: Harvard University Press, 1987), 9.

16. Yetman, *Life Under the "Peculiar Institution,"* 327.

17. John Houston Bills Diary, August 31, 1864, SHC; John W. Blassingame, *The Slave Community: Plantation Life in the Antebellum South*, revised ed. (New York: Oxford University Press, 1979), 178.

18. Yetman, *Life Under the "Peculiar Institution,"* 291–2.

19. See U. S. 8th Census, Slave Schedule, Warren County, Mississippi, National Archives, Washington, D. C.

20. "Rules for Government of Plantation," Cornhill Plantation Book, 106, McDonald Furman Papers, Duke.

21. W. W. Gilmer, "Management of Slaves," *Southern Planter* 12 (April 1852): 106–7; Webber, Deep Like the Rivers, 26.

22. Jacob Stroyer, My Life in the South (Salem: Salem Observer, 1885), 14–15.

23. Tryphena Blanche Holder Fox to Anna Rose Holder, September 5, 1858, November 15, 1858, Mississippi Department of Archives and History, Jackson, Mississippi.

24. Ophelia Settle Egypt, J. Masuoke, and Charles S. Johnson, eds., *Unwritten History of Slavery: Autobiographical Account of Negro Ex-Slaves*, (Nashville: Fisk University, 1954), 263; Jane Turner Censer, *North Carolina Planters and Their Children, 1800–1860*, (Baton Rouge: Louisiana State University Press, 1984), 147; Maxine Lorraine Clark, "Race Concepts and Self-Esteem in Black Children" (Ph.D. diss., University of Illinois, 1979), 17–22.

25. Thomas Jefferson, *Notes on the State of Virginia*, William Peden, ed., (New York: W. W. Norton & Company, 1982), 162. See Censer, *North Carolina Planters and Their Children*, 146–7.

26. Henry Bibb, "Narrative of the Life and Adventures of Henry Bibb, An American Slave Written by himself," in *Puttin' On Ole Massa: The Slave Narratives of Henry Bibb, William Wells Brown and Solomon Northup*, ed. Gilbert Osofsky (New York: Harper Torchbooks, 1969), 66.

27. Mary Boykin Chesnut, *A Diary From Dixie*, ed., Ben Ames Williams, (Boston: Houghton Mifflin, 1950), 38.

28. See Bertram Wyatt-Brown, "The Mask of Obedience: Male Slave Psychology in the Old South," *American Historical Review* 93 (December 1988): 1228–52.

29. Bruno Bettelheim, *The Uses of Enchantment: The Meaning and Importance of Fairy Tales*, (New York: Alfred A. Knopf, 1977), 26, 45–53. See Ruth Michaelis-Jena, *The Brothers Grimm*, (New York: Praeger Books, 1970).

30. Blassingame, *The Slave Community*, 127–8; Michaelis-Jena, *The Brothers Grimm*, 48. See Paul D. Escott, *Slavery Remembered: A Record of Twentieth-Century Slave Narratives*, (Chapel Hill: University of North Carolina Press, 1979), 18–35; Ariel Dorfman, *The Empire's Old Clothes: What The Lone Ranger, Babar, And Other Innocent Heroes Do To Our Minds*, (New York: Pantheon Books, 1983), 3–64; Robert Bone, *Down Home: A History of Afro-American Short Fiction from Its Beginnings to the End of the Harlem Renaissance*, (New York: Capricorn Books, 1975), 19–41.

31. Joel Chandler Harris, *Uncle Remus*, (New York: Schocken Books, 1972), 78–9; John W. Roberts, "Strategy, Morality, and Worldview of the Afro-American Spirituals and Trickster Tales," *Western Journal of Black Studies* (hereafter cited as WJBS) 6 (Summer 1982): 102–3; Lawrence W. Levine, *Black Culture and Black Consciousness: Afro-American Folk Thought from Slavery to Freedom*, (New York: Oxford University Press, 1977), 102–21; Ruth Polk Patterson, *The Seed of Sally Good'n: A Black Family of Arkansas 1833–1953*, (Lexington: University Press of Kentucky, 1985), 95–7.

32. Levine, *Black Culture and Black Consciousness*, 121–33; Wyatt-Brown, "The Mask of Obedience," 1242; Bettleheim, *The Uses of Enchantment*, 58; Charles W. Joyner, "The Creolization of Slave Folklife," in *The Afro-American Slaves: Community or Chaos?*, ed. Randall Miller (Malabar: Krieger, 1981), 131.

33. Melville J. Herskovits, *Dahomey: An Ancient West African Kingdom*, Vol. I (Evanston: Northwestern University Press, 1967), 278. Of the instructions Herskovits writes: At this time the process of enlarging and developing the lips of the vagina is begun. This may be done by massage, by the employment of mechanical devices, by applying chemical irritants derived from plants, by using ants, or by combining the use of several of these. Thus, it was stated that the Maxi people use a horn for this purpose, though in Abomey both special wooden instrument and the root of the indigo plant are employed, and in addition, ants of the type called zaxwa ("night warrior").

34. David Brion Davis, *The Problem of Slavery in Western Culture*, (Ithaca: Cornell University Press, 1966), 469.

35. See Herskovits, *Dahomey*, 281–2.

36. Jacobs, *Incidents in the Life of a Slave Girl*, 27.

37. Herbert G. Gutman, *The Black Family in Slavery and Freedom, 1750–1925*, (New York: Vintage Books, 1977), 82–3; Eric O. Ayisi, *An Introduction to the Study of African Culture*, 2nd ed. (London: Heinemann, 1986), 6; Thelma Jennings, " 'Us Colored Women Had To Go Through a Plenty': Sexual Exploitation of African-American Slave Women," *Journal of Women's History* 3 (Winter 1990): 46. See Maria Diedrich, " 'My Love Is Black As Yours Is Fair': Premarital Love and Sexuality in the Antebellum Slave Narrative," *Phylon* 47 (September 1986):

238–47; Catherine Clinton, *The Plantation Mistress: Woman's World in the Old South*, (New York: Pantheon, 1982), 69–70, 207–8.

38. Perdue, *Weevils in the Wheat*, 96.

39. Rawick, *The American Slave* 13: part 3, Ser. 2: 69.

40. Jacobs, *Incidents in the Life of a Slave Girl*, 192; Rawick, The American Slave, vol. 10, (Part 9), Supplement, Ser. 2: 4121–3. See Gutman, *The Black Family*, 84–5; Willie Lee Rose, ed., *A Documentary History of Slavery in North America*, (New York: Oxford University Press, 1976), 434–37; Linda K. Kerber and Jane Sherron De Hart, eds., *Women's America: Refocusing the Past* 3rd ed. (New York: Oxford University Press, 1991), 102–4.

41. White, *Ar'n't I a Woman?*, 94–95.

42. Rawick, *The American Slave*, 14, part 1, 99–102; vol. 10, part 5 Supplement, Ser. 1: 2385.

43. Steven E. Brown, "Sexuality in the Slave Community," Phylon 42 (Spring 1981), 3.

44. Eugene D. Genovese, *Roll, Jordan, Roll: The World the Slaves Made* (New York: Vintage Press, 1976), 423. See also Lavina to Dear Missis, July 1849, Lawton Family Papers, University of South Carolina, Columbia, S. C. (hereafter cited as USC).

45. Rawick, *The American Slave*, vol. 2 part 2, 298–326.

46. Ibid., 310; Gutman, *The Black Family*, 41–71.

47. Willis and Martha's marriage of twelve years ended with his death on September 16, 1862. See Bills Diary, September 30, 1854–September 16, 1862, SHC; Gutman, *The Black Family*, 60–6.

48. Lavina to Missis, July 1849, USC; Brown, "Sexuality and the Slave Community," 6; Blassingame, *The Slave Community*, 170–1; Genovese, *Roll, Jordan, Roll*, 481.

49. Lavina to Missis, July 1849, USC.

50. John S. Mbiti, *African Religions and Philosophy*, (Garden City: Anchor Books, 1970), 203.

51. See Norrece T. Jones, Jr., *Born a Child of Freedom Yet a Slave: Mechanisms of Control and Strategies of Resistance in Antebellum South Carolina*, (Middleton, Conn.: Wesleyan University Press, 1990), 37–63.

52. Egypt, *Unwritten History of Slavery*, 288.

53. I. L. Twyman to John Austin, October 4, 1848, Austin-Twyman Collection, Earl G. Swem Library, The College of William and Mary, Williamsburg, Va.; Gerda Lerner, ed., *Black Women in White America: A Documentary History*, (New York: Vintage Books 1973), 38; Leslie Howard Owens, *This Species of Property: Slave Life and Culture in the Old South*, (New York: Oxford University Press, 1977), 184.

54. Solomon Northup, "Twelve Years a Slave: The Narrative of Solomon Northup," in *Puttin' On Ole Massa*, 264–5; Randall M. Miller, *Dear Master: Letters of a Slave Family*, (Ithaca: Cornell University Press, 1978), 188–9.

55. Rawick, *The American Slave*, vol. 6: part 1, 211; Levine, Black Culture and Black Consciousness, 15; *Jubilee and Plantation Songs. Characteristic Favorites, As sung by the Hampton Students, Jubilee Singers, Fisk University Students, and Other Concert Companies* (Boston: Oliver Ditson & Company, 1887), 51.

56. Hobbs to his wife in Virginia, 1833, "Before Freedom Came Exhibit," Museum of the Confederacy, Richmond, Virginia.

57. Lester to Miss Patsy, August 29, 1857, James Allred Papers, Duke; Northup, *Twelve Years a Slave*, 245–6, 267–8, 280.

58. Egypt, *Unwritten History of Slavery*, 284.

59. Genovese, *Roll, Jordan, Roll*, 497; Elizabeth Fox-Genovese, "Strategies and Forms of Resistance: Focus on Slave Women in the United States," in *In Resistance: Studies in African, Caribbean, and Afro-American History*, ed. Gary Y. Okihiro (Amherst: University of Massachusetts Press, 1986), 157–8; Darlene C. Hine, "Female Slave Resistance: The Economics of Sex," WJBS 3 (1979): 123–7; White, *Ar'n't I a Woman?*, 86–8; Gutman, The Black Family, 80–2; Helen Tunnicliff Catterall, ed., *Judicial Cases Concerning American Slavery and the Negro*, (Washington: Carnegie Institution of Washington, 1926, reprinted by University Microfilms, Ann Arbor, Mich., 1969), 2:59. See Michael P. Johnson, "Smothered Slave Infants: Were Slave Mothers at Fault?" *Journal of Southern History* (hereafter cited as JSH) 47 (November 1981): 493–520; Todd L. Savitt, "Smothering and Overlaying of Virginia Slave Children: A Suggested Explanation," *Bulletin of the History of Medicine* 49 (Fall 1975): 400–4.

60. Stanley Feldstein, *Once a Slave: The Slave's View of Slavery*, (New York: William Morrow and Company, Inc., 1971), 56; Bibb, "Narrative," 81; Jacobs, *Incidents in the Life of a Slave Girl*, 77.

61. Lucy A. Delaney, "From The Darkness Cometh The Light or Struggles for Freedom," in Henry Louis Gates, Jr., general ed., *Six Women's Slave Narratives*, (New York: Oxford University Press, 1988), 15–6.

62. William Brown, "Narrative of William Wells Brown A Fugitive Slave written by himself," in *Puttin' On Ole Massa, 188.*

63. Brown, "Narrative of William Wells Brown," 187–8, 195–6. See Michael P. Johnson, "Runaway Slaves and the Slave Communities in South Carolina, 1799 to 1830," *William and Mary Quarterly* 38 (July 1981): 418; Judith Kelleher Schafer, "New Orleans Slavery in 1850 as Seen in Advertisements," JSH 47 (February 1981), 43; Benjamin Quarles, *Black Abolitionists*, (New York: Oxford University Press, 1969), 152–3; Larry Gara, *The Liberty Line: The Legend of the Underground Railroad*, (Lexington: University of Kentucky Press, 1961), 175–6.

64. Kate Drumgoold, "A Slave Girl's Story," in *Six Women's Slave Narratives*.

~

"IT'S A FAMILY AFFAIR"
Buying Freedom In The District Of Columbia, 1850-1860

Mary Beth Corrigan

I gnatius Tighlman of Georgetown was the only person freed under the terms of the Emancipation Act of the District of Columbia in 1862 to challenge his masters' claim to sole ownership of himself and his family, by filing a counter-petition to the three commissioners charged with awarding compensation to District slaveholders.[1] Tighlman disputed that his owners, the Sisters of Visitation, should receive $4,600, the sum sought for himself and Mary, his wife, as well as their seven children whose ages ranged from six months to seventeen years. Tighlman maintained that, in 1856, he and the Sisters negotiated a "contract" wherein the Sisters promised to manumit the entire Tighlman family, which then included five children, upon receipt of $500. During the ensuing years, one of these children died, three others were born, while the family maintained themselves "without expense to said sisters" and paid nearly $300 toward their freedom. Ignatius Tighlman argued that the balance of slightly more than $200 was the Sisters' just compensation and that he should receive approximately $230, the amount paid for Mary and the four oldest children. He thereby excluded the sum of $65 already paid for himself and maintained that no one should receive compensation for the three youngest children born after 1856.[2]

Characterizing the agreement as "their act of charity and benevolence" rather than a contract, the Sisters argued that the Tighlman family did not deserve freedom. Maintaining that they should receive the full $4,600, the Sisters

163

explained that they collected the money as a form of insurance "from loss provided [the Tighlman family] should fall back in sickness or distress on [the Sisters] for support as it was too small for consideration or price for Ignatius, his wife and children." They further argued that Ignatius made "a very lame effort to fulfill his portion of the agreement," as his payments amounted to only four dollars per month, derived from wages received almost solely from the Sisters over the six-year period. If members of the family were hired out, these slaveholders claimed that they would have received three to twelve dollars per month for at least four of them. The Sisters easily convinced the commissioners of the benevolence of the terms set for the Tighlmans' freedom and in turn received $2,100 for the entire family.[3]

In the urban areas of the United States, the perspective of the Sisters of Visitation and the commissioners was commonplace. Scholars have emphasized the reluctance of most masters who manumitted all or part of their holdings, even in cities where white and free black laborers supplanted slaves. Owners carefully weighed the economic interests of themselves and their families against their urban communities which discouraged the manumission of slaves likely to become indigent and recipients of public relief.[4] For this reason, most slaveholding states prohibited the liberation of slaves aged forty-five and over.[5] Upon considering manumission, urban slaveholders never forgot their economic circumstances but, like the Sisters of Visitation, were also mindful of their communal obligations to ensure that their former slaves would become self-reliant once freed.

Historians have unwittingly absorbed the assumptions expressed by the Sisters of Visitation of Georgetown in 1862. Nearly one hundred years later in 1960, Clement Eaton argued that slave hiring and the payment of wages to slaves was "an important step toward freedom," as the system cultivated self-reliance. Slaves negotiated with their employers for a share of their wages, worked industriously, and applied frugality as they sought the funds to secure their freedom.[6] As such, Eaton maintained that slave hiring countered the ill-effects of the slaves' dependence on their masters. Because historians now understand that slaves throughout the South bargained continually to secure privileges from their masters, raised crops on their own provision grounds, and haggled to sell wares in local markets, few would now agree that hired-out slaves saved money and exchanged goods more competently than other slaves.

Even so, the characterization of hired-out slaves as especially self-reliant persists among historians, largely because scholars have minimized the role of the family among slaves who, through hard work and scrimping their pennies, purchased their own freedom. Recent studies have stressed the access to freedom which slave hiring afforded particular slaves, but neglected the communities and families behind manumission efforts.[7] This oversight is not especially surprising, as no one has systematically examined the role of family and community among the slaves who were most likely to purchase their freedom, that is, those who worked in urban areas. Family was no less central to the slave community and its economic activities in the cities than the country. As such, "self-purchase" was a family endeavor rather than an individual enterprise. More than any other activity, the purchase of freedom attested to the success of slave families and communities in urban areas to balance their own economic needs, their masters' demands, and their thirst for freedom.

Slaves in Georgetown and Washington City at once depended upon and supported their kin and communal networks as they struggled to secure their freedom. Although he headed the effort, Ignatius was not alone in earning the cash required for his family's liberation. Undoubtedly, able-bodied members of his nuclear family assisted, but members of his extended family and the community probably helped as well. All the while, however, Ignatius and Mary Tighlman did not abandon their family obligations, as they provided for the well-being of their seven children, endured the death of a son, and probably also met their responsibilities to their siblings and parents.[8] Undoubtedly, commitments to kin depleted the financial resources of slaves interested in purchasing their freedom, but such bonds were reciprocal as their kin contributed to the purchase of their families as well.

The relationship of the Tighlmans to their community was typical, as families were the foundation of the free black and slave community in Washington City and Georgetown. Despite legal restrictions, slaves married, frequently to free blacks. Their marriages tied both slave husbands and wives to a system of mutual and reciprocal obligations with their children, parents and siblings that buffered the impact of illness and pregnancy. Like free blacks, slaves also endeavored to provide food, clothing and shelter to kin and to tie them to the broader African-American community, particularly through their participation in churches.[9]

During the 1850s, slaves in Washington City and Georgtown surmounted tremendous obstacles to family formation common to all urban slaves. Nearly all slaves in these cities nurtured family relationships outside of their masters' household, in large part because few whites supported large numbers of slaves within a single household. In Washington City and Georgetown, three out of four of the urban slaveholders held close to half of the District's slaves in holdings of fewer than three slaves.[10] As a result, few slaves lived with more than one or two members of their family. Slaves negotiated with their masters to secure release time from their work, permission to visit their family and friends, and, in some cases, separate residences from their masters. Any measure of independence enhanced a slave's ability to maintain family ties. Ultimately, masters could sunder these relations, as they could revoke privileges, sell or hire out their slaves. Freedom was thereby the best protection of the cherished family ties of slaves.

The District's free black and slave community zealously sought the liberation of its individual members. Such aspirations were intertwined with the goals of families, as freedom sanctioned their ties and released them from the intrusions of their masters. The legal recognition of marriage was far more than a symbolic right, because it ensured that husbands and wives themselves determined the stability of their own marriages. Free status also removed the threat that sale, transfer, or hiring out would sunder family relationships. Since women conferred status to their sons and daughters, the manumission of women ensured the freedom of children born thereafter. Free blacks also bargained with and sought employers so that they exercised greater control over their own economic resources, including their time, than slaves. Moreover, free blacks were able to establish their own residences without the meddling of their employers. Liberated from interference into their marriages, occupations, and residences, free blacks determined which family members worked, raised children, and cared for the old and infirm. At best, a few slaves could claim such independence within their own households as a privilege, not as a right.

In the years prior to the Civil War, urban slaves in the District of Columbia were no less anxious to secure their freedom than their forebears. In April 1848, seventy-seven slaves from Washington City and Georgetown, including men and women with special hiring and live-out privileges, circumvented legal means of acquiring freedom, and set sail on the *Pearl*, a schooner captained by an abolitionist sailor, in an attempt to run away to Philadelphia. Riots erupted on city streets, mobs burned the offices of an anti-slavery journalist to the ground, and local officials imprisoned abolitionist Congressman Joshua Giddings who defended the ship's captain during congressional session. However, the unsuccessful runaways, who were sold to dealers in Charleston, New Orleans, and elsewhere, bore the brunt of local whites' wrath. It is difficult to ascertain whether District slaveholders granted privileges with less frequency as a result of the *Pearl* incident, but memories of the event reminded slaveowners of their servants' recalcitrance and slaves of the serious repercussions of a foiled escape.[11]

Anxieties that the cities of the District would become an asylum for free people of color were far sharper among whites than apprehensions of mass flight by slaves. Through the first half of the century, a high demand among employers for free black workers, especially as domestic servants, attracted a continuous stream of migrants from Maryland and Virginia into the District. With urban denizens, these former slaves built durable churches and schools that welcomed more newcomers and established ties with free blacks and anti-slavery activists in the North. By 1850, there were more than ten thousand free blacks in the District, constituting twenty percent of its population and outnumbering slaves by more than three to one.[12] As the Maryland and Virginia legislatures moved to exclude free blacks from their states, District whites who feared an influx of displaced African Americans endeavored to curb their migration by bolstering the Black Codes and undermining the economic foundations of the free black community.[13] Immigrant men and women increasingly competed with free blacks for positions as laborers and domestic servants, and thereby discouraged free blacks from migrating into the capital.[14] Their diminished economic strength affected slaves, since they shared communal resources.

The increasingly competitive labor market reinforced the division of labor among men. In 1850, one out of nine free black men worked as skilled laborers in Washington City and Georgetown, but this figure understates the extent which white craftsmen, who occupied more than twenty-three out of twenty-four skilled positions, shut free blacks out of the trades. Closed out from steady, skilled positions in the cities during the 1850s, five out of six free black men worked as either unskilled urban laborers, personal servants, or without a regular occupation.[15] As a result, most free black men labored in the cities whenever possible but necessarily accepted short-term jobs in the countryside where they found work with relative ease.

During the 1850s, the majority of free black women worked as personal servants of some kind and provided a wide range of services for their employers which included bringing water in from the wells, building and tending the fires of the household, mending and washing clothing, cleaning fixtures grimy from the dust and mud of the roads, raising poultry, tending gardens, buying produce and meat at the markets, baking the daily bread, and cooking meals for their owners. Meanwhile, these servants often cared for their employers' and their own children. By 1860, few free blacks lived within white households who increasingly favored immigrant servants. As a result, free black women often worked continuously as day servants, but accepted odd jobs such as preparing a banquet and washing to make ends meet.[16]

Work shaped the roles of free blacks in their families and communities. Men provided their kinswomen and children with food, clothing, and cash. The peripatetic nature of men's work enabled them to maintain ties with kin and friends in the countryside. For their earnings and contacts, free black men commanded obedience within their families. Largely because women were a constant presence within Washington City and Georgetown, child care was primarily their responsibility. Even though they could depend upon the economic assistance of their kinsmen, women forged strong networks to alleviate the dual burdens of work and child care. Women whose work schedules enabled them often reared the sons and daughters of women whose employers required their services during the day. In addition, these women's networks were essential sources of companionship to women whose husbands and lovers were often away.

The work and family roles of slave men and women were similar to free blacks, but their masters determined when, where, and for whom they worked. Like free black men, slave men often worked in both the countryside and cities. A large number worked as farmhands whose duties included transporting goods for sale two or three times weekly to the markets. Other slave men worked in both the rural and urban households of their masters. Building repair and maintenance, for instance, consumed the energies of slaves skilled in carpentry, whitewashing, or other trades in both the countryside and cities. Several masters employed their slave men, not as farmhands or marketers, but as butlers, waiters, or carriage drivers within urban households. Few masters occupied their slave men on a continuous, year-round basis so that slave hiring was common. As a result, slave men worked in numerous ways for a variety of different employers, most often determined by their masters, throughout Washington City and Georgetown as well as on farms in Maryland and Virginia.[17] The slave trade was always an alternative for owners unable to find regular work for their slave men.

The work of slave women was arduous and tied them closely to the workings of their masters' households. During the 1850s, the overwhelming majority of slave women worked as house servants and performed the same types of tasks as free black women in Washington City and Georgetown.[18] Yet, even when hired out or living out, slave women did not sustain themselves on task work as free black women often did. Masters and employers generally required their servants to labor within a single household six days per week. Work began with the preparation of breakfast and frequently did not end until bedtime. All the while, slave women cared for their own and their masters' children. Busy for most of the week, slave women had far less geographical mobility than slave men or free blacks.

The rigors of slave work shaped the family and communal roles of men and women. The movement of slave men between city and countryside enabled them to maintain contacts with family members from the countryside, but a master's decision to transfer, trade, or hire out, often unexpectedly interfered with family relationships. This instability only intensified slave women's dependence upon their free and slave kinswomen. Given the rigors of their work schedule, slave women relied upon kinswomen who frequently helped with child care. At the same time, this camaraderie was especially important to women with husbands, brothers, and other kinsmen, as their masters often prevented frequent or consistent visits.

The family relationships of few urban slaves were immune from the agenda of their masters. As they prepared for their adult work roles, teenage slaves could almost count upon intrusions from their masters. Before age ten, slave boys and girls assisted their mothers and employers with light household chores. Accordingly, there were an equal number of slave boys and girls living in Washington City and Georgetown. As slave boys approached their teens, masters compelled most of them to leave their families and communities to work in the countryside. The mechanisms for accomplishing this end were tried and true. Some masters sold their slaves, while others hired them out to planters. Slaveholders who maintained both rural and urban households merely transferred slave boys from the city to the country. Likewise, masters forced teenage women raised in the countryside to work in the cities. This movement between city and country was so swift that the proportion of women among teenage slaves in the cities was close to adult slave women, who outnumbered men by two to one (Table 1). Teenagers physically separated from their mothers and other kin who raised them necessarily began to find new ways of maintaining and building family relationships. Most accomplished this goal, but they risked estrangement from their parents and siblings.

At no time in a slave's life was he or she free from the anxiety of the disruptions caused by sale or hiring out. As long as adult slaves remained healthy and productive, slaveholders were likely to retain them, but there were absolutely no guarantees. If owned by an insolvent master or part of an estate, a slave's future was especially shaky. Owners were far more likely to use the slave hiring system to diminish their obligations to slaves. Prior to the Civil

TABLE 1. Sex Distribution by Age, Slave Population in the District of Columbia, 1860.

Age	Male (M)	Female (F)	Total	Ratio F/M	% Slave
0-9	353	361	714	102	22
10-19	360	617	977	171	31
20-39	307	558	865	182	27
40++	192	437	629	228	20
Totals	1,212	1,973	3,185	163	100

Source: U.S. Bureau of the Census. The Population of the United States in 1860. (Washington, D.C.: Government Printing Office, 1864), 586–7.

War, slave hiring was so prevalent that owners often expressed the value of their slaves in terms of their wages. At the end of the 1850s, one out of every six slave men and women between the ages of eighteen and forty-five worked for employers other than their owners.[19] Hiring arrangements transformed negotiations between all masters and slaves, as slaves who dwelled and worked within their masters' households often received wages.[20]

In Washington City and Georgetown, slave hiring profited most owners and generated low returns for their slaves during the late antebellum period. Although filed during the war, the petitions to the Board of Commissioners for Emancipation demonstrate long-held practices regarding slave hiring. Most owners who discussed their slaves' wages did not mention how they were divided between master and slave. Regardless, the general tenor of the claims indicates that few masters hired out their slaves without receiving a substantial portion, if not all, of their wages. Claimants commonly referred to their slaves' earnings as benefits to them, in terms of their "yields" or the amount of wages "clear of expenses." Several owners calculated the value of their slaves as a product of their yearly wage and remaining productive years. In this manner, Susanna Hughes valued her slave Anna Fisher at $936, as she brought $72 annually, a sum the owner expected to receive for the next thirteen years when her term ended. Meanwhile, other owners enumerated the distribution of wages between themselves and their slaves. Rebecca Williams of Georgetown claimed that she received sixty dollars per year from both Charity Ambush and Sarah Mason, with the remainder, "above five dollars per month," belonging to each of them. Samuel Stevenson yielded Williams a dollar per day when he worked as a bricklayer and twelve dollars per month when he worked as a waiter at the National Hotel during the winter; the excess he retained for himself. E.H. Callis of Prince George's County, Maryland, claimed that Lewis Hanson's work in the anchor shop at the Navy brought a dollar per day "besides what is alotted to him."[21]

Given the widespread receipt of wages by their slaves, masters and employers frequently withdrew from their customary obligations to house, feed, and care for their servants in sickness. Particularly among domestic servants, masters and employers provided "found," but minimized their obligations whenever possible. Joseph Bryan paid his live-in slave Delia eight dollars per month for her contribution to the household, but this sum also covered the expenses of her two young children. Martha Wilson travelled from Georgetown to her master's residence in Montgomery County, Maryland, when her employer of eight years would not reduce her workload or tend to the illnesses of herself and her eight-year-old son. She received little sympathy from her master, whom she last served twenty years before.[22] Because of the ambiguous nature of their masters' responsibilities, several slaves devoted much of their slender resources to sustaining themselves and members of their families.

Domestic servants, including a large number of slave men and nearly all slave women, worked as part of their masters' or employers' households so that a room, often in the basement of the house, somewhat compensated for the low, if any, wages received by these slaves. Waiters, butlers, and servant men garnered between ten and fifteen dollars per month, whereas servant women typically earned between eight and ten dollars per month. Even a skilled bondswoman, like Lucinda Broom, "an excellent cook, washer and ironer as well as pastry cook and confectioner," was hired at a mere twelve dollars per month. Youth or old age brought the rate of the wage down to around six dollars per month, the amount received by fifteen-year-old Josephine Harris and fifty-five-year-old Harriett Johnson. Young children likewise reduced the amount of wages brought in by slave women to as little as five dollars per month, like Sarah Fairfax and Mary Loggins, mothers of two-year and eight-year-old girls respectively, who "hired out with the incumbrance of child."[23]

Under this work system, skilled slaves, who were almost always men, could bargain with their masters and employers as if they were wage laborers. When negotiating wages, skilled free wage laborers relied upon the value of their product, their years of training, and the scarcity of their services to secure high wages. However, a hired slave's efforts to earn more cash were often in vain if his or her master benefited from the net increase. Nonetheless, the ability to secure high wages was still valuable to slaves. Regardless of who retained the wages, an indispensable skill was a bargaining chip for slaves that helped secure concessions from their masters, including a greater share of their own wages but also self-hiring and live-out privileges as well as extended release time to visit kin and trade goods at market. If not necessarily augmenting the income of slaves, higher wages might have yielded a measure of independence that enabled them to meet their economic, parental, and other private obligations to kin.

For all slaves, self-hiring was an esteemed privilege. Even though masters received large portions of these slaves' wages, the right to select their own employer protected them from unreasonable work demands and gave them greater control over their time. Largely because of the greater specialization in their labor, slave men acquired self-hiring privileges with greater ease than slave women of Washington City and Georgetown. Mary Ann Clark, who owned Edmond Stewart, a hostler, and Nace Foster, a carpenter, permitted them to secure their own employers on the condition that they each turn over $120 per year to her. Meanwhile, Sam Martin, once a farmhand, worked as a cart driver whereby he bought and sold wares throughout the countryside and the cities. His master required that he turn over five dollars per week and board himself. Severn, a fifty-seven-year-old woodsawyer, "had his own time," earned one dollar per day, paid his master two dollars per week, and received from him fuel and shelter which he shared with his wife.[24]

Slaves in the District's cities commonly secured live-out privileges. In large part because of the peripatetic nature of men's work, men were more likely than women to establish residences independent of their masters and employers. Slave men who practiced a craft or traded goods in local markets did not necessarily work near their employers' or masters' domiciles so that there was not as much incentive to tie them to a household as a domestic servant, for instance. Moreover, slaves employed as wagonners, cartmen, and coachmen frequently traveled short distances as they conveyed goods and passengers between the cities and surrounding countryside. Farmhands often traded the produce cultivated on their masters' or employers' farms in one of the city markets and sometimes stayed overnight in the cities.

As much as their work regimen allowed, slave men and women marketed wares in Washington City and Georgetown. Because slave men frequently traveled between the city and countryside, they profited more than slave women from the market trade. With access to agricultural goods, farmhands, market-ers, and wagonners sold goods for themselves while representing their masters at the market. Often, these slave men became hucksters, acting solely on their own behalf during their own time, particularly on Saturdays and Sundays. Even on those days, household chores and the responsibilities of child care were likely to constrain slave women from journeying to the countryside and back to the city. As a result, women's opportunities at these markets were limited, and they were principally consumers rather than sellers at these markets.

As in other slave societies, the marketing activities of slaves in Washington City and Georgetown largely depended upon the independent endeavors of slaves in the countryside. Often, masters allocated land to their slaves for their own use. Most grew crops such as corn, turnips, and soybeans, but many also grew staples such as rice and, in the Chesapeake, tobacco. Without study of agriculture in Southern Maryland and Northern Virginia, it is difficult to estimate the importance of slave provision grounds in the area surrounding the District. Nonetheless, the extent of slave marketing in Washington City and Georgetown indicates the importance of these allotments to rural and urban slaves alike.[25]

Slaves often stole commodities from their masters to enhance their earnings. Like poor whites and slaves in other regions of the South, the slaves of the District believed that their work added value to their masters' goods and that they thereby shared ownership in those commodities. In 1859, while riding along the C & O Canal, a New England traveler encountered this producer ideology. The barge captain always responded to the whistles of Montgomery County merchants, which signaled the readiness of free black and slave men to trade commodities such as "corn or oats, a few dozen of eggs or a ham or even a pig tied by one leg" for extra money. At one stop, the captain purchased a 150–pound pig. Indifferent to whether the merchants were slave or free, the canal boatman reasoned that the merchants were not stealing, as their masters and employers contended, but only seeking their just compensation, as "the one that worked and raised an article ought to own at least a share in it and probably the fellow was not getting more than his share."[26]

Domestic servants, whether slave or free, likewise pilfered goods from their masters and employers. In some cases, they stole the products of their labor, like roast meat, bread and cakes. At other times, they took produce and meat before their preparation. Unlike farmhands, though, servants perpetrated their crimes within close view of their employers, who had ready access to any cellars or vaults that served as hiding places. One householder found that his servant had the assistance of a friend, who took goods left on a window sill.[27] To a limited extent, masters and employers conceded to their slaves and servants, offering them chickens, apples, cakes, and the like in addition to wages and board.[28] Yet, several shared the view of *The Republic* that "many of those who go out to service do so with the intention of stealing enough to support several idlers dependent upon them."[29]

Of greater concern was the quality of goods sold at the market by petty hucksters, who supposedly sold stolen goods of suspect quality. In addition, they camouflaged their foul-smelling meat with saltpeter, used inaccurate measures, and routinely sold over-ripe fruit. Whites also maintained that domestic servants employed such measures. In one column, *The National Intelligencer* decried the use of saltpeter on pork and thievery by domestic servants, or "sable ones," without explaining the connection between the crimes.[30] Throughout the 1850s, Washington City and Georgetown officials raised the license fees collected from hucksters, built stalls at the markets and collected fees from their rightful occupants, standardized measures for loaves of bread, and restricted access to the wharves along the Potomac River in an effort to improve sanitation within the markets themselves as well as to ensure the quality of market goods.[31] Nonetheless, the demand for cheap wares was unceasing, as the "people who carried their own baskets," poor whites and blacks, could scarcely afford to give up their market activities.[32]

Markets offered an arena for kin to visit each other outside their masters' view. In some cases, they were the only places that family members could meet. On December 2, 1859, a Georgetown slave named Sarah Maranda Plummer wrote her father concerning her thwarted attempts to try to see him. Aware of the demands of his employer and his visits to her mother, she hoped to visit him in Hyattsville, Maryland, but as "some of the family were sick i could not get off." Desperate, Sarah looked for her father in the city market on Sunday, one day after her grandmother spotted him, but missed him.[33] Especially on Saturdays, the busiest days, slave and free black men congregated at the markets. Several local whites regarded these men as loiterers at best. After policemen arrested five blacks on a Saturday night outside the District's largest market, known as Center Market, *The Washington Sentinel* commented that the "parties of ill-mannered and rude idlers, at that place, have long and justly been regarded by purchasers, as breathing and cigar-smoking nuisances."[34]

Cash, produce, and other wares accumulated by slaves provided the material basis for family activities. Food was central to family visits. Slaves commonly partook of Sunday meals together. Free kin, like John and Elizabeth Brent, could facilitate such gatherings because they maintained their own residence. On weekdays and weekends, Elizabeth's sisters and brothers, who were slaves in Georgetown, visited and ate supper with them. Elizabeth's parents, slaves who, frequently on Saturdays, travelled from the countryside to Center Market, dined and lodged with the Brents.[35] Slaves also used food as gifts which were important reminders of absent kin. In closing her letter to her father, Sarah Maranda Plummer asked for celery, eggs and "a good slip of that grape vine."[36] Slaves also used their cash, food, and other wares to sustain pregnant, ill, or infirm family members. Burials of deceased family members also constituted a considerable expense.

Even unskilled slave men worked and resided independently from their masters more frequently than slave women. They counted on men to secure and maintain their privileges which, in turn, enabled men to provide companionship and to produce their own goods, exchange them in the markets, and earn extra cash to supplement wages. Generally unable to venture far from their masters' households, slave women participated in the markets with limited success. Often, families relied on the extra cash earned at the market to supplement the meager wages and rations provided by their masters and employers. Such income supported the activities of families, fostered hopes of buying freedom, and was thereby almost as essential to slaves as food, shelter, and clothing.

During the 1850s, the purchase of freedom represented the most effective legal means for free blacks and slaves to liberate their entire community. There were a myriad of ways that slaves bargained with their masters for freedom. Whether the manumission was deeded or willed, slaves who won their freedom outright continually sought manumission as a reward for earning high wages, obedience, and affability.[37] If pledged manumission by will, slaves performed their duties conscientiously to prevent masters from rewriting the will and reneging upon any vows of freedom. Such last testaments were never rock-solid, as well-intentioned, but deceased and insolvent, masters could hardly interfere with the sale of slaves, including those pledged their manumission, if the proceeds paid the debts of the estate.

To slaveholders considering manumission, the character of their slaves mattered less than their productivity. District slaveholders used manumission to divest themselves and their families of slaves who were unable to contribute either wages or service to their households. Typically, District masters held on to their young slaves and manumitted their older slaves. Slaves under the age of nineteen, more than a half of the District's bonded population, comprised only a third of the slaves whose deeds of manumission were registered in 1856, 1858, and 1860 (Tables 1 and 2).

Slaveholders' concern for profits accounts in large part for the varying patterns of manumission between men and women. Able to secure high wages as laborers, slave men were manumitted at an older age than women. By the time slaves were in their twenties, masters were more likely to free men than women, although the absolute number of manumissions by deed among men and women was roughly equal. Women's share of manumission deeds was far below two to one, the margin which they outnumbered men within the slave population as a whole. Masters generally held their slave men until a later age to exploit their ability to garner wages for as long as possible. As slave men aged and were likely to develop disabilities, masters frequently freed them. There were two times as many manumissions of men as women above the age of thirty-five (Tables 1 and 2).

Because of their work roles and reproductive cycle, masters manumitted

TABLE 2.   Sex Distribution by Age, Slaves Manumitted by Master's Deed* in the District of Columbia, 1856, 1858, 1860.

Age	Male (M)	Female (F)	Total	Ratio F/M	% Slaves Deeded Manumission by Master
0-9	9	9	18	100	24
10-18	2	6	8	300	11
19-35	15	19	34	127	45
36-45	10	5	15	50	20
Totals	36	39	75	108	100

* With sums of less than $20 transferred to owner.

Source: Manumission and Emancipation Record, v. 4, RG 21, National Archives, Suitland, MD.

their women at a relatively young age. Teenage women were three times more likely to be freed than teenage men. Some slaveholders undoubtedly manumitted some of these domestic servants to reduce the cost of maintaining their households, but this motive was more than likely intertwined with an unwillingness to assume care for slave children. Masters thereby freed teenage and young adult women at the beginning of their childbearing years and often with their young child(ren). In the late 1850s, one out of five of the slave women were deeded their manumission at the same time as one or more of their children. Correspondingly, two out of three slaves under nineteen won their freedom with their mother. If retained as a slave through her childbearing years, a slave woman was less likely to be freed than a man. Because trustworthiness was a premium, masters often employed servants, even with infirmities, into their old age (Tables 1 and 2).[38]

Few masters relinquished highly productive workers without asking a high purchase price, but nonetheless a significant number of slaves, frequently with their family members, raised money to secure their own freedom. In the late 1850s, one out of every four slaves who had been deeded their manumission won their freedom because either they or family members paid their masters for their liberty (Table 3). Only a handful of slaves were able to accumulate sums of money much greater than $500 for their own purchase, and most masters could probably receive much greater sums for able-bodied, adult slaves.[39] The slaves of the least value and most costly to their masters, particularly older men and women in their childbearing years, were also the most likely to purchase their liberty. Beyond the cost of the purchase, the families of these slaves pledged their economic support of them, once freed. Especially for older or disabled slaves, steady work was difficult to find so that their freedom entailed economic risks for the kin who pledged to support them. This prospect hardly diminished the thirst for freedom among slaves and their families.

TABLE 3.   Manumissions Deeded by Kin or After Self Purchase in the District of Columbia, 1856, 1858, 1860.

	Frequency	% Manumission Deeds
By non-kin	79	73
By non-kin upon slave's purchase of freedom	17	16
By kin	12	11
Totals	108	100

Source: Manumission and Emancipation Record, v. 4, RG 21, National Archives, Suitland, MD.

Buying freedom hardly served the interests of masters alone, as slaves effectively acted upon their overwhelming desire for freedom. Regardless of their cost to their masters, slaves could not purchase their freedom without skilled negotiating, planning, and saving. By bargaining for their own purchase, slaves encountered the ever-present threat that their sale, transfer, or hiring out might separate them from kin and hoped to acquire greater autonomy in pursuing their economic fortunes and family relationships. Typically, slaves entered into an agreement with their masters and subsequently paid them in installments. They were freed upon their last payment, and no sooner, as the partial fulfillment of these arrangements did not protect the slave from sale and the subsequent abrogation of the compact.[40] Through these arrangements, slaves communicated the earnestness of their quest for freedom to their masters, offered them compensation, and thereby secured manumission.

Such negotiations with masters entailed risks, as many slaves in the District, to no avail, paid their masters small sums for their own liberation. Such difficulties were easy to understand. Accumulating the cash for freedom was enormously challenging to slaves, given the low returns from their wages and marketing and their commitment to the support of all their family members. Several, like twenty-six-year-old Charlotte Gustus and forty-six-year-old Maria Maddox, rendered partial payments on long-standing agreements to their masters without culminating the transaction and securing their own manumission. From 1858 until her emancipation, Charlotte paid $300 to her master, far short of her ultimate goal of $625. Meanwhile, Maria's master received only thirty-five to forty dollars in the twelve years following their initial arrangement.[41] Both freed in 1862, Maria and Charlotte unwittingly wasted their money which could have otherwise been used to care for their children and other members of their family.

The fate of Charlotte's and Maria's endeavors suggests the difficulties of purchasing freedom in the District of Columbia, so that "self-purchase" was seldom an individual endeavor. Nonetheless, a significant portion of manumissions deeded in the late 1850s, approximately one out of six, were won by slaves who handed over sums of $150 to $900 to their masters (Table 3). Generally unable to count on steady provisions of food, clothing and shelter from their masters, few slaves could save the funds from their earnings and support their families without the assistance of family and friends.

Slaves' participation in a predominantly free African-American community was critical. Able to travel without seeking the permission of their masters and in full control of their earnings, free blacks supported slaves who sought to buy their freedom and thereby chipped away at slavery and contributed to the liberation of their entire community. Alethia Tanner, who purchased her freedom in 1810, was a model to others within the African-American community. By the time of her death in 1864, she had bought and liberated twenty-two friends and kin, including some of the District's most prominent free blacks. The relative prosperity of Tanner's family was essential to her success, as kin probably contributed cash to assist her cause. At the very least, her family enabled her to devote her earnings toward the freedom of slave kin and friends.[42]

Special privileges were essential to the success of several men who purchased their freedom. Able to pick up extra work and exchange wares in the countryside, approximately half of the adult slaves granted their freedom upon their own purchase were men, and they generally raised greater sums of money than women.[43] Slave men whose work regularly took them in and out of the city developed ties with kin and friends over a broad geographical area, and men with special privileges could strengthen their bonds with less interference from their masters. If unable to contribute directly to their savings, the families of these men probably supported their economic activities in other ways, for example, by providing shelter or exchanging goods with them. Lemmon Shelton paid his master $900 over a two-year period, during which he resided on his own in the cities, to receive his liberty in 1860. Likewise, forty-three-year-old Thomas Jackson lived out in Washington City and purchased his freedom at $400.[44]

The manumission of women guaranteed that their progeny would be born free; thus, slaves and free blacks supported the efforts of slave women to purchase themselves. Families often placed a priority upon freeing young women before their children inherited their status as slaves. In addition, women with child care responsibilities, who were anchored to a limited space, encountered additional obstacles when trying to raise the money toward their freedom. Because their cash earnings were meager, few women could accumulate cash without the assistance of their husbands and other kinsmen. Accordingly, thirty-two-year-old Eliza Johnson raised $375 with the assistance of her friends and conveyed the sum to her master who freed her in mid-1856.[45]

Several of the slave women who raised the money for their manumission took advantage of their masters' desire to diminish their slaveholding obligations and won the freedom of their children as well. In early 1858, Henrietta Milburn transferred $300 to her master for the freedom of herself and three children, aged between two and six years old. Later that year, Sarah Stephenson secured freedom for herself and her six children, whose ages spanned from four to eighteen years, for the sum of $150. Of course, not all slave families in Washington City and Georgetown were as lucky as Sarah and her children.[46]

However, slave women and their children could hardly count on their masters to manumit them together. Many slaveholders in Washington City and Georgetown retained paternalistic attitudes toward slave children, and their attitudes clashed with the goals of slave families. While considering slave children a burden, some masters demonstrated contempt for their slaves' ability to raise their own sons and daughters and thereby retained children whose parents had been freed or sold.[47] As he prepared to free his adult slave, Agnes Bryant, Thomas Carbery revealed his lack of confidence in Agnes. In early 1856, Carbery set Agnes' eight-year-old daughter, Mary, free, but reserved the right to "retain custody of said child Mary" until she reached age twenty-one and further stated his intention to name a guardian in the event of his death. This quasi-manumission of Mary set the stage for Carbery's manumission of Agnes, who, two months later, finished paying him the sum of $250 for her own freedom.[48] It is unclear whether Carbery intended Mary, while under his guardianship, to reside with her mother immediately or at a later point, but he was attempting to protect her from the possible destitution of Agnes, whose husband Henry had recently died and probably raised most of the payment before his death.

Once freed, a slave could devote his or her resources to secure the freedom of kin and thereby promote the freedom of future generations. Often, free blacks, rather than slaves, were the primary agents in securing the freedom of a slave. During the late 1850s, free blacks in Washington City and Georgetown often owned slaves with the ultimate intention of manumitting them.[49] Kin manumitted one out of every ten slaves with deeds registered in 1856, 1858, and 1860 (Table 3). Like slaves, these prospective free black buyers often paid their kin's slave owners in several installments over a period of several months or years, but free blacks sometimes hired the time of their enslaved kin and thereby brought them closer to their ultimate goal.[50]

Free black slave owners frequently retained ownership in their family members. As long as certificates of freedom were fifty dollars each, many of these families could not afford to register their freedom. Meanwhile, these slaves acquired most of the benefits of freedom, as whites recognized them as free. While the legal ownership of slaves buttressed the owner's authority, the actions of free black masters reflected their desire to unite their families within a single household, to ensure liberty for their progeny, and, in some cases, to save a family member from sale to a faraway place.

In the late 1850s, free black owners of slaves in Washington City and Georgetown who manumitted their kin were overwhelmingly men who purchased their wives and their children. Often, these free black owners held their wives as slaves so that their children were born slaves. In 1855, Nathaniel Jackson freed his family whom he bought six years earlier for $800, including his wife Eliza and his children, thirteen-year-old Eliza Ellen, eleven-year-old

Joanna, and eight-year-old John Henry, as well as the two youngest children born after Jackson purchased his family.[51] Richard Griffin, manumitted in October 1858 at age nineteen, knew no other master than his father, Thomas Griffin, as Richard was born a slave after Thomas bought his wife.[52]

Among the handful of known cases, free black women owners of slaves invariably purchased one of their children. Obviously, these women were slaves when their sons and daughters were born and subsequently secured funds to buy them. In 1854, Emily Duncan completed her payments to the master of her eighteen-year-old daughter and, in turn, freed her. In 1856, Martha Ann Sewall of Washington City manumitted her daughter Sarah Ann, while Betsy Roberson retained ownership of her son John, whom she purchased in 1846 at age ten, until District emancipation in 1862.[53] These women were probably unmarried; without the assistance of a husband, they probably secured help from other kinsmen and kinswomen.

Sometimes the purchase of a slave often spared a family member from sale to the South. In such cases, free blacks and slaves pooled large sums of money and traveled long distances to thwart the separation of their family. Jacob Ross, a whitewasher from Georgetown, negotiated with the owners of his wife and daughter, both held in Lexington, Virginia, to purchase them. In 1856, he paid $601 at a public sale for his forty-year-old wife, Keziah. Almost four years later, he purchased his sixteen-year-old daughter Frances Ann for $701. By 1860, Jacob, Keziah, and Frances Ann formed a common household, although the District Emancipation Act freed both of these women two years later.[54]

In all likelihood, the Ross family received help from the broader African-American community which frequently raised the large sums of money required by owners about to sell their slaves south. Such an endeavor often entailed risk. In April 1855, the Washington City police broke up a meeting of twenty-four black men, including four slaves, ostensibly for their violation of codes concerning their public assembly. These men were members of a benevolent society, organized to "relieve the sick and bury the dead," and were discussing ways of purchasing Eliza Howard, whose master wished to sell her for $650. The papers siezed from the police raid indicated that the men had collected somewhat less than forty dollars, which included a large contribution from U.S. Congressman Gerrit Smith. Each of the twenty-four congregants endured some time in the watchhouse. With the exception of one slave who received a whipping and four free men sent to the workhouse, the men paid a fine of more than $5.50 each. The total of their fines, equaling more than $110, was more than three times the amount collected for Howard's freedom.[55]

The strong connections to the northern anti-slavery movement forged by the African-American community of Washington City and Georgetown were critical to free blacks desperate to secure large amounts of money to purchase kin. In 1857, Earro Weems labored to secure the funds for the freedom of his nineteen-year-old son Augustus, "the last of the family in Slavery." When sold to Alabama, Augustus cost $1,100. It is difficult to determine exactly how Weems accumulated the funds, but he raised a considerable portion in Philadelphia with the help of the noted abolitionist William Still. Expecting a similarly high return in New York State, Weems gave up $500 to furnish payment for the freedom of the wife of Henry Highland Garnett, another prominent free black in Philadelphia. Weems received assistance from internationally-renowned abolitionist Frederick Douglass in Rochester and Syracuse, but the trip was not fruitful, because most potential benefactors were away for the summer. As a result, Weems turned to one of his friends in Washington City who borrowed $180 at the bank and in turn lent the sum to Weems. His friend required repayment within three weeks, and Weems beseeched William Still for assistance. Even with the possibility of insolvency, Weems expressed joy and gratitude to William Still, "I am expecting daily the return of Augustus, and may Heaven grant him a safe deliverance and smile propitiously upon you and all kind friends who have aided in his return to me."[56] While few free blacks duplicated Weems's quest to retrieve a family member from the deep South, Weems's love and devotion to his son was characteristic of free blacks and slaves in their struggle to free their kin.

In his ongoing struggle to unite his family throughout the 1850s, Emanuel Mason exemplified Weems's qualities, but also depended upon the determination of his owner, Sarah Forrest of Prince George's County, Maryland, to minimize the costs of her slaves. In the early 1850s, Mason, a carpenter, nearly died from rheumatic fever. Forrest sought a buyer who would pay $100 for him. As there were no takers, she offered him his freedom for $300 which he paid in several installments. Because she owned his entire family, Forrest remained a nuisance to Mason. Once he regained his health and freedom, he established a house on Capitol Hill and began to hire out his wife by the year. In addition, Emanuel and his wife secured live-out privileges for their young sons and daughters until they reached an economically productive age, between eight and ten years old.

Emanuel's children soon knew that the arrival of Forrest or one of her agents signified the return of the oldest of them to the farm. In 1859, Emanuel Mason's troubles multiplied when his eight-year-old and youngest son, Ben, fled when Forrest's representative arrived to take him away from his parents. The police descended upon the house, did not find the boy, and subsequently arrested Emanuel for harboring a fugitive, as he would not disclose the boy's whereabouts. He spent ninety days in prison for his alleged crime, and remained there until he could secure the funds necessary to pay prison costs of over $160 and the interest that later accrued. *The National Era*, an anti-slavery organ located in Washington City, pled for leniency. They also reported that Sarah Forrest sold Emanuel's wife, whose new master was asking $230 for her freedom, and the community was organizing to raise the funds. Early in 1860, Emanuel's imprisonment ended without his payment of the fine, as President James Buchanan pardoned him on the grounds that Emanuel was ignorant of his son's whereabouts.[57]

Emanuel Mason was not alone in his silence; the members of his family and the African-American community at large also demonstrated the importance of maintaining family ties and protecting them from the intrusions of masters. Emanuel might not have known where his son went, but at least some members of his family, if they were not harboring Ben themselves, knew where he was throughout the entire period of Mason's imprisonment. Maintaining an impenetrable cordon of silence, no one divulged Ben's hiding place, even though the information would have abbreviated Mason's imprisonment. The potential consequences for Ben's defiance of his master were more terrifying to the entire family than Emanuel's imprisonment. As punishment, Ben could have been sold anywhere in the South. Instead, he went into hiding, probably until the beginning of the war.[58]

From the time of his manumission through his imprisonment, Emanuel Mason demonstrated a fervent and unstinting loyalty to his wife and children. As a carpenter, Emanuel earned the cash necessary to hire out his wife and secure a residence near the Capitol in Washington City. Such arrangements enabled him and his wife to bargain with Forrest to secure live-out privileges for his children and a modicum of independence for his family. In this regard, the Masons were hardly exceptional, as most slaves continually sought ways of maintaining a niche for themselves and their families. The stakes were especially high when the earnings of slave and free black men enhanced the privileges or prospects for freedom for family members. The balance between work and family roles was delicate, as their jobs often took men from outside the District. A passionate devotion to their kin, rather than economic self-interest, motivated them to maintain their families in the District and to free them from the intrusions of slavery as much as possible.

The free blacks and slaves of the District of Columbia would not have made much progress in securing freedom for their kin and uniting their families without the support of their community. Especially in times of emergency, members of the African-American community quietly, and with a plucky determination, supported the endeavors of slaves and their families to secure freedom, and thereby made possible what no slave could do alone.

METHODOLOGY

The data on manumissions was derived from the Manumission and Emancipation Record held at the National Archives in Suitland, Maryland. The National Archives has retained manumission registers dated 1802–63 (1847–54 are missing) which were created by the U.S. District Court for the District of Columbia, which had original jurisdiction over the capital. All slaveholders were required to register manumissions with a justice of the peace, not necessarily at the District Court. As a result, these extant registers do not provide a complete record of manumission in the District, but probably reflect the general patterns of manumission. I have therefore avoided using these records to derive the rate of manumission among slaves in the population as a whole, but have used them to assess the ways that slaves secured their manumission, especially if deeded.

I derived a database to assess the age and sex distribution of slaves manumitted during the years 1856, 1858, 1860, and 1861. This procedure also highlighted cases where families assisted in the purchase of kin. Every slave in each record of manumission constituted a single case. Ultimately, the database included 144 manumitted slaves. The fields included the date, information on the master, the manumitted slave, as well as details on the manumission: on the master(s), number, sex, color, surname (as match to slaves), and jurisdiction; on the manumitted slave, relationship to master, sex, color, age, occupation; on the manumission transaction itself, type, amount of purchase, number of slaves manumitted, surnames (as match to other slaves), and relationship to other slaves on record.

NOTES

I would like to thank Ira Berlin, Roderick MacDonald, Larry Hudson, and other participants of the Rochester Conference for their encouragement and astute readings of this essay. Although impossible to incorporate all of their insights here, I will consider their questions and reservations as I work on my study of the African-American family in the District of Columbia between 1850 and 1865.

1. Following the outbreak of the Civil War, the destruction of slavery was swift in the District of Columbia. Congress provided for abolition in the capital almost eight months before the Emancipation Proclamation. See "An Act for the Release of Certain Persons Held to Service or Labor in the District of Columbia," U.S.,

Statutes at Large, Treaties, and Proclamations, vol. 12 (Boston, 1863), 376–78; Ira Berlin, Barbara J. Fields, Thavolia Glymph, Joseph P. Reidy, and Leslie S. Rowland, eds., *The Destruction of Slavery* ser. 1, vol. 1, *Freedom: A Documentary History of Emancipation, 1861–67* (New York: Cambridge University Press, 1985), 157–84.

2. Tighlman paid the Sisters $298.75. Ignatius Tighlman excluded himself when requesting compensation, probably because the commission disallowed claims from other slaves who sought restitution of the sums transferred to their owners for their own manumission. Filed on August 15, 1862, more than two months after his master's claim, Tighlman's petition can be found in Petition 569; Records of the Board of Emancipation in the District of Columbia, 1862–63 (National Archives Microfilm Publication M520, Roll 4); Records of the U.S. General Accounting Office, Record Group 217; National Archives, Washington, D.C. (Hereafter, cited as Records of the Board of Emancipation in D.C., 1862–63 [M520, roll], RG 217, NA.)

3. The commissioners accepted the Sisters' argument in large part, although they did not entirely dismiss Ignatius Tighlman's claim. Judging that the Tighlman family was worth $2,387.10, the commissioners subtracted the amount of $298.75 that Ignatius had paid and awarded the Sisters $2,088.35. He received nothing. U.S. Congress, House of Representatives, "Emancipation in the District of Columbia," *House Executive Documents,* 38th Cong., 1st sess., No. 42, 49; Petition 569, Records of the Board of Emancipation in D.C., 1862–63 (M520, roll 4), RG 217, NA.

4. Even in areas where the anti-slavery movement was strong, most slaveholders distributed their slaves to family members before manumitting them. Both the states of New York and Pennsylvania turned to indentured servitude as a means of dealing with newly freed blacks who could not maintain themselves.

    See Gary Nash and Jean Soderlund, *Freedom By Degrees: Emancipation in Pennsylvania and Its Aftermath* (New York: Oxford University Press, 1991), especially ix–xv, 41–73, 137–166; Vivienne Kruger, "Born to Run: The Slave Family in Early New York, 1626–1827" (Ph.D. diss., Columbia University, 1985), 724–886; Shane White, *Somewhat More Independent: The End of Slavery in New York City, 1770–1810* (Athens and London: University of Georgia Press, 1991), 28–30.

5. In 1796, the Maryland legislature provided that no slave can be freed "unless the said slaves shall be under the age of forty-five, and able to work and gain a sufficient livelihood and maintenance, at the time the freedom shall commence." In the same session, Maryland lawmakers defined penalties for idleness among free people of color. When establishing the District's government in 1801, Congress provided that all Maryland laws remained in effect in the the the areas of District ceded by Maryland. This area alone constituted the capital after 1846, when Virginia retroceded Alexandria. See Worthington G. Snethen, *The Black Code of the District of Columbia* (New York: American and Foreign Anti-Slavery Society, 1848), 7, 26–27, 29–30.

6. Clement Eaton, "Slave Hiring in the Upper South: A Step Toward Freedom," *Mississippi Valley Historical Review* 46 (March 1960): 663–78.

7. The omission of family in the consideration of slave hiring hardly discounts the

findings of two recent studies by T. Stephen Whitman and Douglas Egerton who have explored the impact of slave hiring system upon the consciousness of master and slave. T. Stephen Whitman maintains that a hired slave's ability to earn "extras" and ultimately freedom yielded a harder working labor force at the Maryland Chemical Works in Baltimore, which could not hold onto free laborers. See "Industrial Slavery at the Margin: The Maryland Chemical Works," *Journal of Southern History* 59 (February 1993): 31–62.

In his study of Gabriel's Conspiracy of 1800, Douglas Egerton found that Gabriel, like many slaves with extensive privileges, resented his merchant-employer more than his planter-owner. See "Gabriel's Conspiracy and the Election of 1800," *Journal of Southern History* 56 (May 1990): 191–214.

8. I have been unable to ascertain the occupations of any member of the Tighlman family. The Sisters of Visitation owned a large tract of land on the outskirts of Georgetown so that it is likely that Ignatius received his wages as a farm laborer and traded the goods produced for the Sisters and his family in one of the markets. Meanwhile, Mary and the oldest daughter probably worked as domestic servants.

The participation of the Tighlmans in the broader African-American community has been easier to discern. As members of the Holy Trinity Church, the Tighlman family contributed time, if not money, to members of their community. Records of two of the children's baptisms can be found in the Baptismal Register, 1835–1858, Box 19, Folder 3, Holy Trinity Church Archives, Manuscript Division, Georgetown University, Washington, D.C.

9. The ideology of kinship among the urban slaves in the District of Columbia was similar to plantation slaves. See Herbert Gutman, *The Black Family in Slavery and Freedom, 1750–1925* (New York: Pantheon Books, 1976).

10. This statistic is derived from a sample taken of the Slave Schedules, District of Columbia, Census of Population (National Archives Microfilm Publication M432, roll 57), Seventh Census of the United States, 1850, Records of the Bureau of the Census, Record Group 29, National Archives, Washington, D.C.; and Slave Schedules, District of Columbia, Census of Population (National Archives Microfilm Publications M653, roll 105), Eighth Census of the United States, 1860, Records of the Bureau of the Census, Record Group 29, National Archives, Washington, D.C.

11. In addition to local newspapers, see John H. Paynter, *The Fugitives of the Pearl* (Washington, D.C.: The Associated Publishers, 1930) and, in condensed form, idem., "The Fugitives of the Pearl," *Journal of Negro History* I, (Jul. 1916): 243–64; Harriett Beecher Stowe, *A Key to Uncle Tom's Cabin*, 394–425; *Congressional Globe*, April 20, 1848, 656; *Congressional Globe, Appendix*, April 20, 1848, 500–510; *Congressional Globe Appendix*, April 25, 1848, 518–24; Daniel Drayton, "Personal Memoir of Daniel Drayton," and John I. Slingerland, "Captains Drayton and Sayres: Or, the Way in Which Americans Are Treated, for Aiding the Cause of Liberty at Home," in *Slavery, Race and the American Courts* Ser. 4: *Slave Rebels, Abolitionists, and Southern Courts, vol. 2*, ed. Paul Finkelman (New York: Garland Publishing, 1988), 440, 490–3.

12. *The Seventh Census of the United States: 1850* (Washington, D.C.: Robert Armstrong, 1853), 232–5.

13. In 1851, the Washington City Council increased the required fee for a certificate of freedom from twenty to fifty dollars and reduced the number of white freehold sureties from five to one. In addition, the council doubled the size of the police force at least in part to control the activities of free blacks. For copies of the Black Codes, see James Sheahan, *General Laws of the Corporation of the City of Washington* (Washington, D.C., 1853), 244–54; Worthington G. Snethen, *The Black Codes of the District of Columbia*, 38–9, 45–6; Kenneth G. Alfers, "Law and Order in the Capital City: A History of the Washington Police, 1800–1886," *GW Washington Studies*, 5 (Washington, D.C.: George Washington University Press, 1976), 13–4.

    Despite their fears, Georgetown officials did not take similar measures. The Georgetown code of 1845 which required no fee and two white sureties for a certificate remained in place. See Snethen, *The Black Codes of the District of Columbia*, 54. For the reaction of Georgetown residents to the measures of the Maryland and Virginia legislatures, see *The Georgetown Advocate* (Georgetown, D.C.), March 13, 1851.

14. The population of foreign immigrants in the District nearly tripled between 1850 and 1860. For the 1860 census figures, see *The Population of the United States in 1860* (Washington, D.C.: Government Printing Office, 1864), 588. For a petition to Congress from 250 laborers seeking the displacement of black workers, see "A.G. Keller *et al.* to the House of Representatives and the Senate of the United States, March 10, 1852," HR 32A G5.6, Committee on the District of Columbia, Records of the U.S. House of Representatives, Record Group 233, National Archives, Washington, D.C.

    For a discussion of immigration in other Southern cities, see Ira Berlin and Herbert Gutman, "Natives and Immigrants, Free Men and Slaves: Urban Workingmen in the Antebellum American South," *American Historical Review* 88 (December 1983), 1175–1200. On Virginia and Maryland legislatures during the 1850s, see Ira Berlin, *Slaves Without Masters: The Free Negro in the Antebellum South* (New York: Pantheon Books, 1974), 355. The reaction of District whites can be gauged in "Memorial of the Mayor, Board of Aldermen, and Common Council of Georgetown, D.C.," Senate 31A-H4, Committee on the District of Columbia, January 8 through July 8, 1850, Records of the U.S. Senate, Record Group 46, National Archives, Washington, D.C.; *The Georgetown Advocate* (Georgetown, D.C.), March 13, 1851.

15. These figures are derived from data taken from the free schedules of the 1850 manuscript census. Compilers include the African-American Communities Project, Smithsonian Institution, Washington, D.C.; the Center for Washington Area Studies, George Washington University, Washington, D.C.; and Lois Horton. James Oliver Horton, director of the African-American Communities Project, generously allowed me to use this data. (Hereafter, cited as AACP data.)

16. According to the 1860 census, more than three out of five free black women worked

and half of these women as washers. Among immigrant women, one out of four worked, and the majority of these women as live-in servants. AACP data.

17. Records of the Board of Emancipation in D.C., 1862–63 (M520, rolls 1–6), RG 217, NA.

18. The work of slave women has been derived largely from reading advertisments in *The National Intelligencer* (Washington, D.C); *The Evening Star* (Washington, D.C.); slaveholders offered descriptions of the work performed by their slaves in Records of the Board of Emancipation in D.C., 1862–63 (M520, rolls 1–6), RG 217, NA; and The Laura Jones Crawford Diary, 1859, Manuscript Division, Library of Congress, Washington, D.C.

19. When compiling the slave census in 1860, enumerators recorded whether the slave was hired out for Georgetown and Washington City (with the exception of wards 4 and 5). This figure is derived from a sample taken of the Slave Schedules, DC Census (M653, roll 105), RG 29, NA.

20. A large number of owners seeking compensation under the terms of the District Emancipation Act of 1862 calculated the value of their slaves on the basis of their wages. As an alternative, these owners could have used tax assessments of 1860. Perhaps the inflated wages of 1862 were a more profitable basis of calculating assessments than the pre-war value of these slaves. Several claimants noted the payment of wages to servants who boarded and worked within their households, Records of the Board of Emancipation in D.C., 1862–63 (M520, rolls 1–6), RG 217, NA.

21. See especially Petitions 263, 790, 846, Records of the Board of Emancipation in D.C., 1862–3 (M520, rolls 3, 5–6), RG 217, NA.

22. Petitions 322 and 371, Records of the Board of Emancipation in D.C., 1862–3 (M520, roll 3), RG 217, NA.

23. Petitions 341, 353, 389, 458, 533, Records of the Board of Emancipation in D.C., 1862–3 (M520, rolls 3–4), RG 217, NA.

24. It is difficult to compare the wages of free blacks and slaves, because the wages received by free blacks are not easily discernible from extant records. Nonetheless, Severn was probably earning higher wages than most free black men, especially those near his age. With manumission impossible at age fifty-seven, Severn's living arrangement was probably a reward for his lifelong contribution to his master's household. Petitions 367, 554, 882, Records of the Board of Emancipation in D.C., 1862–3 (M520, roll 3–4, 6), RG 217, NA.

25. During the eighteenth and nineteenth centuries, slave women were a strong presence in the markets of Barbados, Jamaica, Louisiana and elsewhere. See especially Ira Berlin and Philip D. Morgan, "Introduction," and Hilary McD. Beckles, "An Economic Life of Their Own: Slaves as Commodity Producers and Distributors in Barbados," in *Slavery and Abolition* 12 (May 1991): 1–67.

While the workload of women from Washington City and Georgetown undoubtedly constricted their participation in the markets, the women who worked on the farms outside the District were domestic servants with their own child care responsibilities as well. Probably, they did not have much opportunity to travel to the cities and sell produce. In this significant way, the economic activities of District slaves were distinctive from other slave societies.

26. Ella E. Clark, ed. "Life on the C & O Canal: 1859," *Maryland Historical Magazine* 55 (June 1960): 117–8.

27. *The National Intelligencer* (Washington, D.C.) December 23, 1848.

28. The Crawford Diary, Library of Congress.

29. *The Republic* (Washington, D.C.), September 12, 1850.

30. *The National Intelligencer* (Washington, D.C.) December 23, 1848.

31. To date, no one has closely examined the debate concerning the regulations of the marketplace in Washington City and Georgetown. The material for such a study is vast, and would illuminate class relations within these southern cities. Critical to my thinking on the impact of market regulations has been E.P. Thompson, "The Moral Economy of the English Crowd in the Eighteenth Century," *Past and Present* 50 (February 1971): 76–136.

There was only one attempt to regulate specifically the market activities of slaves. In 1806, the corporation of Georgetown prohibited the selling of any goods by slaves on Sundays. There is no comparable ordinance in Washington City; Snethen, *The Black Codes of the District of Columbia*, 50–1. On the addition of stalls to Center Market, see W.B. Bryan, *A History of the National Capital*, 335; for laws regulating markets, see *Laws of the Corporation of Washington* (51st, 54–55, 57th Councils), 1853–54, 1856–60; *The National Intelligencer* (Washington, D.C.) July 23, 1844; May 3, 1850; May 8, 1850; February 2, 1852; April 19, 1852; April 4, 1853; September 12, 1853; November 28, 1853; May 15, 1854; October 12, 1854; December 25, 1854; October 15, 1855.

32. *The National Intelligencer* (Washington, D.C.) August 1, 1855.

33. "Letter from Sarah Maranda Plummer to Adam Plummer, December 2, 1859," in *The Mind of the Negro as Reflected in Letters Written During the Crisis, 1800–1860*, ed. by Carter Woodson (New York: Negro Universities Press, 1926), 526.

34. *The Washington Sentinel* (Washington, D.C.) October 10, 1854.

35. Paynter, *The Fugitives of the Pearl*, 1–16, 37–46.

36. Sarah Maranda Plummer to Adam Plummer, December 2, 1859, idem.

37. Before deeding manumission, masters commonly requested between five and twenty dollars from their slaves. For this essay, I have not considered such cases as purchases of freedom.

38. In 1856, 1858, and 1860, there were five women manumitted by deed with their children: Battany with Bunion, Martha Francis, Rosann, and Diner on June 10, 1856; Maria Stewart with Henry and Kate on June 5, 1858; Harriett Kane with George, Mary Frances, Albert, Charles, and Harriett Ann on June 10, 1858; Lucinda Lewis with Leah and Caroline on July 17, 1860; Anastasia Loundes with Catherine, John, Anna, William, Thomas, and Albert on October 15, 1860. Manumission and Emancipation Record, v. 4, Slavery Records, Records of the United States Circuit Court for the District of Columbia, Record Group 21, Records of the United States District Court for the District of Columbia, National

Archives, Suitland, Md. (Hereafter, cited as Manumission and Emancipation Record, v.4, RG 21, NA.)

39. The assessments of the Board of Commissioners provide a rough guide to the value of slaves, as petitioners identified their slaves by sex, age, and gender. Owners received greater compensation for men, but few slaves between the ages of eighteen and thirty-five were assessed far below $500, unless there was an infirmity. Their values in 1855, even 1860, were probably much higher, as the market price of slaves plummeted with the prospect of abolition. U.S. House, "Emancipation in the District of Columbia," 1–79.

40. In 1827, William Claggett sold his slave Richard who had transferred all but sixty-five dollars towards his freedom. Claggett did not apprise Abraham Van Meter, Richard's new owner, of their agreement. Richard petitioned for his freedom. The court decided that, because of his ignorance of Claggett's and Richard's arrangement, Van Meter was under no obligation to recognize the agreement. *Negro Richard v. Van Meter*, Cranch Circuit Court Reviews, vol. 3 (December 1827), 214.

41. Few masters, like the Sisters of Visitation in their original petition, admitted their receipt of cash from their slaves to the commissioners of emancipation, but many had undoubtedly collected such sums over several years. In 1858, Charlotte Gustus' master, William Edes, bought her to rescue her from imminent sale South and provided that she return her purchase price to secure her freedom. He maintained that he should receive only $325 from the commissioners who awarded him $547.50, nearly the full amount he first paid for her. Petitions 281 and 319, Records of the Board of Emancipation in D.C., 1862–3 (M520, roll 3), RG 217, NA.

42. "Special Report of the Commissioner of Education on the Condition and Improvement of Public Schools in the District of Columbia," *House Executive Document 315*, 41st Congress, 2nd Session, 196–7. For references to Alethia Tanner, see Constance McLaughlin Green, *The Secret City: A History of Race Relations in the Nation's Capital* (Princeton: Princeton University Press, 1967), 16; Ira Berlin, "The Revolution in Black Life," in *The American Revolution: Explorations in the History of American Radicalism*, ed. Alfred Young (De Kalb, Ill.: Northern Illinois University Press, 1976), 367; Mary Beth Norton, Herbert Gutman, and Ira Berlin, "The Afro-American Family in the Age of Revolution," in *Slavery and Freedom in the Age of the American Revolution*, eds. Ira Berlin and Ronald Hoffman (Urbana: University of Illinois Press, 1986), 189.

43. Manumission and Emancipation Record, v. 4, NA.

44. The manumission registers indicate that forty-year-old Henry Brown and forty-three-year-old Harry Thomas paid $500 and $200 respectively for their freedom, but give no clues concerning their occupation and hiring status; Manumission and Emancipation Record, v. 4, RG 21, NA.

45. Manumission and Emancipation Record, v. 4, RG 21, NA.

46. Manumission and Emancipation Record, v. 4, RG 21, NA.

47. As an extreme example, Cornelia Munson named her infant slave Dolly who by

the time she was three years old "was a pet in the family." Petition 812, Records of the Board of Emancipation in D.C., 1862–63 (M520, roll 6), RG 217, NA.

48. Deeds of Manumission, Thomas Carbery to Mary Bryant, February 28, 1856, and Thomas Carbery to Agnes Bryant, April 23, 1856, Manumission and Emancipation Record, v. 4, RG 21, NA.

49. Carter Woodson maintained that most of these slaveowners were "motivated by philanthropy," but the majority were plantation slaves bought for a profit; *Free Negro Owners of Slaves* (Westport, Conn.: Negro Universities Press, 1968), v. See also Michael Johnson and James Roark, "Strategies of Survival: Free Negro Families and the Problem of Slavery," in *Joy and Sorrow: Women, Family, and Marriage in the Victorian South, 1830–1900*, ed. by Carol Bleser (New York: Oxford University Press, 1991), 88–102.

50. Alberry Moxley, a barber, arranged to buy his wife and one of his five children for $450 from Sally Matthews. His payments began in 1862 and were scheduled to end in 1863. During that period, he hired his wife for the sum of $2 per month; Petition 28, Records of the Board of Emancipation in D.C., 1862–63 (M520, roll 6), RG 217, NA.

51. Manumission and Emancipation Record, v. 4, RG 21, NA.

52. Ibid.

53. Ibid.; Petition 460, Records of the Board of Emancipation in D.C., 1862–63 (M520, roll 4), RG 217, NA.

54. In 1860, Jacob Ross's household included Keziah, listed as forty-six-years old, and Frances, twenty-six; Free Population Schedules, District of Columbia, Eighth Census of Population, 1860, (National Archives Microfilm Publication M653, roll 101), Records of the Bureau of the Census, Record Group 29, National Archives, Washington, D.C., 86 (Hereafter, cited as D.C. Free Population Schedules, 1860 [M653, roll], RG 29, NA.) Petition 468, Records of the Board of Emancipation in D.C., 1862–63 (M520, roll 4), RG 217, NA.

55. *The National Era* (Washington, D.C.) April 19, 1855.

56. Letter from Earro Weems to William Still, September 19, 1857, in *The Mind of the Negro*, ed. Carter Woodson, 579; Earro Weems manumitted his son on August 7, 1858, Manumission and Emancipation Record, v. 4, RG 21, NA.

57. Mason had the sympathy of several whites of Washington City, who took his case to the Pardon Attorney of the United States. I am indebted to John Kelly for pointing out this source to me. See Emanuel Mason Abstract, Case A-251, Pardon Case files, Office of the Pardon Attorney, Record Group 204, National Archives, Suitland, Md.; *The National Era* (Washington, D.C.) June 30, 1859.

I have been unable to locate manumission records for Emanuel Mason's wife. Her name also does not appear in the records of the Board of Commissioners for Emancipation. A fifty-year-old woman named Eliza is listed with Emanuel Mason in the 1860 census, and I suspect that she is his wife. If this were Mason's wife, her appearance in the free census did not clearly indicate free status, however, as many slaves who are hired out or owned by free blacks were listed as free. D.C. Free Population Schedules, 1860, (M653, Roll 104) RG 29, NA.

58. It is impossible to be certain of Ben's fate, but it is unlikely that he worked for Sarah Forrest again, as there was no indication in any account of the incident that she recovered the boy. Chances were she gave up on the case, and the war subsequently interfered with her ability to recover any of her slaves.

Under special provision of the District Emancipation Act of 1862, slaves who worked in the District and whose masters failed to file a claim for them were able to claim their freedom. Two of Sarah Forrest's slaves, nineteen-year-old Eliza Mason and eighteen-year-old John Mason, who were probably children of Emanuel Mason, thereby petitioned for their liberty. On July 19, 1862, she wrote:

> I do not want my servant Eliza Mason back and will gladly accept your offer, but
> I believe her brother John will return if let alone, but if he will call on me and
> say he is unwilling to come back of course there will be no use in trying to keep
> at home, so I suppose you could fix the papers for both if necessary . . . .

Petition filed by John W. Mason, July 28, 1862, Records of the Board of Emancipation in D.C., 1862–63 (M520, roll 6), frames 891–976, RG 217, NA.

~

SYMBOL, MEMORY, AND SERVICE
Resistance And Family Formation In Nineteenth-Century African America

Sharon Ann Holt

Fannie Moore was enslaved; she was owned, along with her mother and siblings, by a cruel and violent North Carolina woman. Fannie's mother suffered over and fought with her owners about lashings meted out to her children until, one day, while at work in the field, she had a saving vision of Jesus Christ. Her joy issued in a shout, and she was summoned before her mistress to account for her outbreak. As her daughter recalled many years later:

> My mammie jes grin all over her black wrinkled face and say: "I's saved. De Lawd done tell me I's saved. Now I know de Lawd will show me de way, I ain't gwine a grieve no more. No matter how much yo'all done beat me an' my chillun de Lawd will show me de way. An' someday we nevah be slaves."[1]

With these words, Fannie Moore's mother challenged her mistress simultaneously to three distinct fights. By celebrating her salvation she affirmed the freedom of her soul despite the enslavement of her body. If she actually spoke the words as her daughter recalled them, she compounded her offense by very artfully implying that her mistress herself was not saved and could never be. Under the "someday" of God's ultimate care, Fannie's mother exulted, there would be no slaves. If slavery did not enjoy God's favor, then, by implication, slaveholders did not either; they would reap the justice due to the unrighteous.

Fannie's mother also directly challenged the power of the mistress's violence. The strength of her now-saved soul, she averred, and her certainty of Jesus' superior power and particular love, would provide more comfort than the mistress could inflict pain, even by lacerating the children. Fannie's mother therefore not only questioned her mistress's righteousness, but she also stole away the intimidating power of the whip, for which power, presumably, the white woman had risked her hopes of salvation in the first place.

But the rebellion did not end even there. Fannie's mother, though denied because of her enslavement the legal right to protect or claim her own children, precisely did claim them in her jubilant speech, and declared that her love had the force to invalidate the mistress's power to injure them. Though we cannot know for sure, there is no sign that Fannie herself was present at the interview between her mistress and her mother. If Fannie was present, then the mother's dramatic show of independence must have been gripping for Fannie. If, as seems likely, Fannie was somewhere else, then her mother must have recounted the episode to her. Fannie had often seen her mother thus, recalling that, "De 'ol overseeah he hate my mammy, case she fight him for beatin' her chillun. Why she get more whuppins for dat den anythin' else."[2] The showdown with their mistress, which ended when the mother absorbed yet another beating in silence, and then returned to the fields singing, surely reaffirmed and strengthened Fannie's pride and faith in her mother's ultimate authority over her and willingness to protect her. By thus boldly announcing her conversion and her indifference to her mistress's cruelty, Fannie's mother offered her children a vision which linked family feeling, religious joy, and spiritual liberty. Their mother's vision offered the children a symbolic freedom from the lash which she had been unable to gain for them in actuality.

Such symbolic acts involving family affiliation, acts which intricately braided issues of work, culture, resistance, and family, abound in the records of the slave experience. What did they mean? When, where, and how did slaves link resistance to family feeling? How significant were such moments for them? What follows if we posit that slaves cherished these ephemeral liberties, that they defended them, retold, and remembered them? What can we learn about resistance, about family, and about culture, through an understanding of these complex moments?

The first question that arises is whether it is even appropriate to call these activities resistance. Should they be understood as survival tactics, or are they just signs of residual aversion to accommodations the enslaved had in fact already made? Making such distinctions partially obscures the reality that survival and aversion could also nurture a sense of accomplishment and an independence of spirit antithetical to the ideology of enslavement. Because family loyalties survived despite the depredations of white hegemony, whenever African Americans displayed the power of their family ties, they were simultaneously mocking the vanity of white tyranny.[3] But the term "resistance" implies acts which, in addition to sustaining hope and pride, include a certain level of conscious aggression. This essay argues that moments like Fannie Moore's mother's confrontation with her mistress indeed constituted real resistance. The argument is based upon contrasts in the ways African Americans structured and valued family ties in slavery and freedom.

At least three broad systems of affirming and defending family ties were available to both slaves and freedpeople, systems which I call "symbolic affiliation," "family memory," and "mutual service." Under slavery, symbol and memory had greater potency and appeal, while after Emancipation, mutual service took pride of place. In each period, African Americans subtly but significantly shaped the meaning of family ties and the expectations laid upon family members in order to direct the strength of their families against precisely those forms of oppression that were most crucial to sustaining white prerogatives. The specific assaults African Americans faced varied from place to place, and certainly changed between slavery and freedom, and the details of their resistance shifted accordingly, but the essential format—organizing and behaving as families in ways which frustrated white beliefs and desires—remained a constant. Shaping family life to confront oppression was, indeed, a form of conscious resistance.

Acts of "symbolic affiliation" are acts which unsettled slaveowners by testifying to the family ties which the laws of slavery refused to honor. Often slaves made their case obliquely through the kinds of exaggerated deference and disguised mockery which it was difficult for slaveowners to punish. Slaves could also act out their family feelings by openly taunting their owners, and by inverting cherished slaveowner values to the advantage of the enslaved.[4] Fannie Moore's mother leaned upon Christian faith, mocking her mistress with the impotence of violence against love. Another young slave, named Wesley, took direct and paradoxical advantage of a threatened whipping to begin courting his eventual wife, Minerva Jane. Their daughter, Laura Bell, later recalled that,

> Marse Mack's overseer, I doan know his name, wus gwine ter whup my mammy onct, an' pappy do' he ain't neber make no love ter mammy comes up an' takes de whuppin' fer her. Atter dat dey cou'ts on Sadday an' Sunday an' at all de sociables till dey gits married.[5]

Perhaps too tongue-tied to openly court Minerva Jane, Wesley made the best of a gruesome opportunity. This shy lover adroitly subverted the purpose of the whipping, turning the white man's exercise of dominion into a drama of the slave's own masculine pride, strength, and courage. And the incident was cherished in their daughter's memory, reflecting honor on mother and father, and giving pride to their child.

The power of Wesley's action exists not only in his having thwarted the overseer directly, but also in the creative and symbolic quality of his sacrifice. Taking a whipping is more than a symbolic act, certainly. Parents might do it for their children, adults for aging parents, and husbands for wives, because a stronger person's stepping in could actually save the life of a more vulnerable one. But the fact that this community of slaves, including the young woman who was thus spared, understood Wesley's sacrifice as an act of courtship suggests another context of meaning beyond the strictly concrete service he provided.

Within the legal framework of American chattel slavery, romantic union between slaves was strictly instrumental, encouraged for the purposes of creating slave property and mitigating the slaves' desires to flee. Any benefits which accrued to slave families themselves were, from the master's point of view, incidental. Though individual masters might be more solicitous in these matters, legally speaking, unions between slaves could be encouraged, ignored, or dissolved at a master's pleasure. Wesley and Minerva Jane "misappropriated" the white man's indifference and cruelty, turning the whipping into an almost mythic enactment of enduring love.[6] They cast aside the overseer's presumably central role, as the intended humiliation of the female slave became her apotheosis, her elevation to the place of one worthy to receive a lover's sacrifice. The slave couple thus successfully dramatized right before the overseer's eyes the two things slavery demanded that he absolutely deny: the young man's masculine pride and courage, and the couple's fidelity. Probably he sensed, without fully understanding, the meaning given to the whipping ordeal by the slaves, and while the quarter tended to its wounded members, he was left to fend off his misgivings and embarrassment as best he could. Thus could a symbolic act of affiliation be at the same time a drama of resistance.[7]

Another couple's affirmation of romantic love took place against the backdrop of pervasive uncertainty rather than direct violence, but also has a certain quality of parable. Exter Durham, a North Carolina slave, gave his wife, Tempie Herndon, a wedding ring which he had whittled out of a red button; she wore it for fifty years, long after freedom, until it wore thin and fell off in a washtub.[8] This couple had fairly cordial relations with Tempie Herndon's owners, who offered them some old household furnishings and a few bags of seed when they left in 1865 to farm on their own account. In the context of their particular enslavement, the wedding ring was a quiet, persistent rebellion, a public and visible sign representing their pride in a marital bond which existed as a private matter, on sufferance, not as a protected legal certainty.

For Tempie Herndon and Exter Durham, the ring was a symbol of the power of their own will, openly advertised to slaveowners. In a larger sense, their story also partakes of a classic American myth. Set against the background of the nineteenth-century American cultural drama pitting wealth against virtue, this enslaved couple appears as an archetype of the simple, sturdy purity and the liberation of love from lucre so idealized by romantic white contemporaries.[9]

By demonstrating loyalty and claiming the prerogatives of kinship before their owners' very eyes, slaves could enact for themselves, and teach their children, the central importance of their family ties. Such acts of rebellion proclaimed the enslaved community's definition of a good husband or wife, revealed the nurture available from parents, and decreed the loyalty expected of children. Slaveowners exaggerated their own absolute authority when they refused to honor family ties among slaves, and they dramatized their paradoxical certainty that their slaves, being less human than themselves, had weaker family sensibilities. Some owners even comforted their troubled consciences with the belief that their slaves looked to them as family surrogates. But by creating and claiming family feelings unrecognized by the laws of chattel slavery, slaves both supported each other and undermined their masters' fictions. Acts of familial affiliation were symbolic rebellions when they could project such multiple tentacles of meaning, reaching into the hearts of those involved, challenging or scorning the power of slaveholders, fostering pride among the enslaved, and rooting themselves in the surrounding culture, both black and white.[10]

Family memories were at least as important for nurturing family feeling under slavery as were acts of symbolic affiliation. Since 1976, when Herbert Gutman published his history of African-American families, scholars have mostly acknowledged familial patterns in the given names of slaves. Recent work on slave surnames only confirms the conclusion that many slaves preserved their own family trees and family names, and did not simply adopt the surnames of successive slaveowners.[11] Scholars have also argued that passing on a father's name to a son or daughter helped sustain knowledge of and respect for slave fathers. But naming patterns had broader implications than those pertinent to paternity. One family historian has suggested that "early generations left clues for others to follow . . . just as surely as if they had been in a wooded wilderness and had notched trees along the way or laid a line of colored stones . . . the trail was in the names . . . they chose for their children."[12] First names may indeed have been passed down precisely to signal to descendants the shadowy presence of a unique family line and thereby to thwart the anonymity that chattel slavery was supposed to produce. While one need not exaggerate the amount of conscious rebellious intent involved in a practice which can be explained at least in part by invoking affection and respect, there is no greater empirical warrant for denying the possibility than for embracing it.

Consider Caroline, daughter of Frankie, sister of Isabella, William, Frederick, and Alexander, who lived as a slave in Granville County, North Carolina until 1865. She and her husband, Robert, raised nine children, all born in slavery, including four named Frank, Isabella, Frederick, and Alexander. Between 1855 and 1865, at least four different slaveowners in two counties held members of this family, but after Emancipation they found each other and were reunited, settling on neighboring farms in Granville County. One hundred and twenty-odd years later, their great-granddaughter identified Caroline in an 1840 debt transaction because Caroline had named her children after her mother and siblings—the clue was the names that coincided, but not just by coincidence.[13]

The account records of the Freedman's Savings Bank (1865–1874) provide a rich resource for measuring slaves' genealogical craft, a resource which has not yet been fully mined.[14] Information given on the account forms also offers some clues as to how useful name recall was in sustaining a sense of family membership and family pride. Upon opening an account, depositors were asked to provide very detailed information about their past, including their former owner's name, their own place of birth and last residence, names of parents and siblings, names of spouses and children, and sometimes the fates of all these kin as well, all of which would be set down on the account form by a Bank officer. Many of the account records have been lost, and those that survive are irregular in format and not consistently filled in. But those which offer extensive information can be very instructive about the breadth, detail, and strategies of preservation characteristic of slave family memory.

Austin Latham, for example, was freed in Pitt County, North Carolina, and was fifty years old in 1869 when he went to open his bank account in New Bern. He knew the first names and surnames of both his parents, though they had been sold away during his infancy. Of brothers, he said, "Don't know that I have any," but he named his two sisters, Maria Clark and Celia Clark, noting that they were last known to live in Washington County, North Carolina, on the plantation of James Clark, where Austin had been born. Reconstructing the story from this single document, it is fair to surmise that Latham's father and his mother, also named Celia, had had different masters, his father perhaps owned by someone named Latham. Both parents were sold away, leaving the sisters and the baby Austin behind with their mother's owner. Maria and Celia Clark probably cared for the boy until he too was sold sometime before

Emancipation to a James McDaniel in Pitt County. Though he went to Pitt County alone, Latham carried in his memory his father's full name, his mother's full name, and what intimate visions of them had survived to be reinforced by his sisters. Austin Latham's wife was also sold away from him and they had had no children, so the family Latham claimed was a family which had survived, despite separation and sale, in memories passed from parents to daughters to son.[15] Family memory had resisted the depredations of slavery, and had kept Latham from being altogether without roots.

Dilla Warren, another former North Carolina slave, was also in her fifties when she opened her Bank account. Like Austin Latham, Mrs. Warren had been left with family memories instead of family members. Her husband, her mother, and two brothers had been sold, presumably all at once, seventeen years before the war. One of two sisters had been sold thirty-five years before, her father sold thirty years before, and of her fifteen children, twelve had died as infants or youngsters, two had been sold away, and one, whose bounty she was depositing, had died in the Union army.[16] One brother had been accidentally killed by lightning, leaving only one surviving sister, whose whereabouts were unknown. But, despite their affliction and grief, these people left evidence in naming patterns of their loyalty and family feeling. Dilla Warren's father, Ned Clark, had a namesake in her brother, Ned Clark. Mrs. Warren in turn passed versions of the name to two of her own sons, Ned Clark Warren and James Clark Warren. Her son Andrew was named for her brother, Andrew, and her mother, Harriet, and lost sister, Ann, were memorialized in a daughter, Harriet Ann, who had been sold away. This chain of memory had concrete significance as well, as Mrs. Warren noted on her deposit slip that, in the event of her death, she desired that her money be paid to "Edward Paxton, son of my dec'd brother Andrew Nixon."[17] Death, sale, tragedy, and multiplying surnames (Clark, Nixon, Warren, Paxton), even taken all at once, had not brought about the disintegration of this family.

By passing information across generations and by encoding family memory in the names of children, the Latham/Clark and Warren/Clark/Nixon/Paxton families had held together, despite sale and death, outlasting the most pressing and destructive of social circumstances by practising this memory-based art of family relations. A thorough examination of the Freedman's Bank records would almost certainly identify many similar families and confirm that, as Herbert Gutman noted many years ago, "slavery had not obliterated familial and social memory. . . Naming practices linked generations of blood kin." Whether those practices and memories sustained slave identity, directed the inheritance of family goods, or guided runaways along the roads back to the old places, family memory helped keep the slaves' world intact.

Symbols of family affiliation and feats of memory were practical matters of great importance in the lives of enslaved African Americans. Slave affirmation of family ties takes on even greater significance when the view shifts to the period after Emancipation. The coming of freedom changed the meaning and the duties of family membership but did not break the link between family feeling and resistance to oppression. Comparing the duties of family membership in the two periods highlights the centrality of that link. After Emancipation, African Americans continued to need the strength of family ties in the struggle to turn legal freedom to advantage. The duties expected of kin changed to reflect the new economic and productive imperatives of that struggle, as opposed to the symbolic and commemorative necessities of their former condition. Changing the expectations for family members enabled African Americans to continue to use family affiliation to resist oppression.

The dramaturgy visible in the symbolic actions of slaves seems largely to have disappeared after Emancipation. Throwing defiance into the face of whites was risky enough under slavery, when white owners had had incentives to preserve their own comforting fictions as well as the lives of their slaves. After Emancipation, taunting became virtually suicidal. The drama did not disappear overnight; indeed the records of the Freedman's Bureau indicate a widespread joy among freedpeople in displaying bright-colored clothing, headgear, and "uppity" manners, ordinary pleasures made sweeter by previous prohibition.[18] Severe repression by whites, and the general passivity of the Bureau in the face of planters' violent forms of "labor discipline," helped to silence freedpeople's enthusiasm and drive their dramaturgy underground.

For the former slave, freedom meant at least two things immediately: the opportunity to reunite the scattered family and the chance, indeed the necessity, to farm on one's own account. These two conditions of freedom broke upon the people simultaneously, and inevitably became linked. Becoming and remaining a member of the family quickly came to mean participating in the family's practical exertions, taking part in its attempt to rise. Such "mutual service" ultimately replaced symbol and memory as the *primary* token of family membership. Symbol and memory did not disappear, but they no longer carried the principal power to make or unmake family connection; that power devolved onto service.

Participation in the economic efforts of a family could be as variable as the acts of symbol and memory had been, and as emotionally compelling. In one woman's case, substantial economic and family labor defined her marital identity, overriding legal formalities. Her name was Caroline. She had been born a North Carolina slave, and married Barney Richardson four or five years after Emancipation. After he died, she married John Haskins, and had been widowed ten years when she was interviewed in 1937. She gave her name as Caroline Richardson, rather than Caroline Haskins, and her narrative suggests her reasons for doing so: she and Barney Richardson had "had three chilluns, who am all dead now. We worked an' slaved till we bought dis house, an' paid for it, den in 1918 he died."[19] Though no children survived from their union, the years and the extensive personal and economic labors she had shared with Richardson seem to have been more salient in defining her identity than the formality of a second, evidently childless and largely property-less marriage. She was, in effect, claiming membership in the Richardson family on the basis of shared enterprise, of mutual service.

Services did not need to be directly economic to matter in the definition of family. Elizabeth Johnson Harris, child and grandchild of North Carolina slaves, acknowledged her gratitude to one of her early schoolteachers by making her, symbolically, a family member. Young Elizabeth Johnson's first formal schooling took place at a "private home school" conducted by Sarah Drayton in the living room of her parents, a Rev. and Mrs. Samuel Drayton. Years later, Mrs. Harris named a daughter Fannie Drayton in honor of that first school-teacher. Schooling had affected Elizabeth Harris profoundly; she remembered and recorded all the names, both maiden and married, of her teachers, and she saw to it that her own children completed their secondary education, no small task in the late-nineteenth-century South.[20] Her own memoir, written in manuscript toward the end of her life and dedicated to her children, bears witness indirectly to her devotion to education. The entirety of her childhood, youth, and married life is compassed in the first half of the fifty-odd page manuscript, and the remainder, minus a page or two of summation at the end, is devoted to detailing one weekend visit she paid to one of her sons at college. The very proportions of her narrative suggest that formal education stood second only to religion in her pantheon. In the context of this passion for education, her daughter's name suggests that, in gratitude for Sarah Drayton's vital service, Elizabeth Harris indeed meant to invite her former teacher into her family circle.[21]

Service, in these two cases, could override considerations of formal kinship to affirm or even initiate family membership. Conversely, bonds between close kin could fracture in the absence of service, and family members could virtually disappear not just from the immediate scene but even from memory. The genealogy of the McGhee family of North Carolina, descendants of slaves Caroline and Robert, reveals numerous branches which relocated to the North in the early twentieth century, about whom no information could be discovered in the 1980s among the North Carolina McGhees. Henry McGhee, born in

1890, grandson of Caroline and Robert, was untraceable because, "It is said that he left Henderson [North Carolina] after 1925 and went North somewhere." Henry's brother, Hervy McGhee, married and had a daughter, whose name was known to the North Carolina McGhees, but the family genealogist noted only, "It is said that Hervy died in New York where he lived with his daughter, Ernestine." A sister Phyllis married a man who "took his family to live in Delaware, where Phyllis died," and virtually nothing is known of their children. Mary Frances McGhee married and raised children in Granville County, but died in Pennsylvania, living with children who had moved there. "It is not known," commented the family historian, "if she has any descendants living today, because contact has not been kept with any of them."[22]

These losses were not solely the result of the costs of communication across distances. Some sense of family membership could be maintained even through small and irregular acts of service. Mary Faison Reavis, another daughter of the McGhee clan, moved to Baltimore, Maryland in the year 1912–1913. She hosted her uncle when he came for cancer treatment at Johns Hopkins University, and her sister, when she came to attend Morgan State College in 1913. Details of this period of her life are known to the North Carolina kin, but no more such services or details are recorded after a later move from Baltimore to Trenton, New Jersey. The family historian notes only, "It is believed she died there [in Trenton]. She had only one child, a daughter, whose status is not known."[23] Mary Reavis had kept her place in the family so long as she had been in a position to participate in its networks of service and survival. Outside of those networks, her presence faded.

One South Carolina father, Josh Richie, also kept his place in his family and community through a dramatic, though irregular, service. Estranged from his wife, he left his home community of Promised Land to take up work on the railroad. There was no stop in Promised Land, but when Richie's train passed through on its way somewhere else, he would fill a bucket with food, and "just set that bucket down on the ground while the train was still moving." The food was for his own family or for "whoever was there at the time, for who needed it." In later years, after he had settled in New York, Richie made a point of sending boxes of candy and fruit to his sisters, who were still in Promised Land.[24]

A Tar Heel couple, Berle and Mariah Barnes, offered reverse testimony to the importance of service in sustaining family membership. Their son, Charlie, whom they confessed had always been a worry to them because of his "wild ways," had gone North, as had all their other children. But Charlie alone had sent money back to his struggling parents, and his loyalty in this matter had bred in his parents a special additional regard for him. Charlie Barnes died up North, and Mr. and Mrs. Barnes could not afford to have his remains shipped home. Berle Barnes suffered deep grief, and perhaps even physical pain, as he noted that his heart "ached jes' like toothache" over this inability to do right by his loyal son. Eventually Charlie appeared to his father in a dream, assuring Berle that he was safe in heaven, and Berle was comforted. The couple mentions no other children by name in their narrative, suggesting that, despite his distance and because of his attentiveness, Charlie may have become, in a certain sense, their only child.

The point here is not that family members got lost. African-American families had lost members long before they had had any say in the matter. What makes these stories remarkable is the contrast between families under slavery, in which individuals could hold in memory a network of relations with people whom they themselves might never have known, and families after Emancipation, who could lose track even of children and siblings once they were removed from a network of mutual service. This remarkable change in the standard of family membership coincides with and reflects the change from enslavement to freedom. Analysis of the contrast between enslaved and free families can help us to decipher the relationship between family membership and resistance.

It is crucial to emphasize that both enslaved and free families had symbolic acts, memorials, and acts of service at their disposal, and that families on both sides of the moment of Emancipation used all three techniques, and probably many more, in building and sustaining their families. Enslaved kin did provide service to one another out of affection and concern; cooks smuggled extra rolls or meat to their homes in the quarters, families fed both runaways and short-term fugitives hiding in nearby forests or swamps. Young adults would tend garden patches for aging parents; those elders might in return see to the safety of the grandchildren while the parents were at work in the fields. These services testified to family connection every bit as much as the symbolic gestures and recurrent names. By the same token, families after freedom embraced symbols of display and titles of authority, and by song, lesson, and story initiated their children into the family history. The point here is not that either enslaved or free families used one or the other style exclusively; it is exactly to argue that African-American families used these styles differentially, consciously, purposefully, and in response to specific forms of oppression. Enslaved or free, African Americans chose in each circumstance to privilege those rules and duties of family membership which best served to disconcert their oppressors and blunt the attacks they knew would come, while establishing the strongest families they could.

The structure of slavery privileged symbolic claims of family membership over acts of direct service to kin as a strategy of resistance. Since the formal rights of kinship were forbidden to slaves, any slave's claim to family membership was, almost by definition, an act of defiance. Therefore, symbols and memory, besides having the direct benefit of sustaining kinship links across death, separation, and sale, could also function as deliberate insolence. Under slavery, the function of mutual service was more ambiguous, since feeding, working for, sheltering, clothing, and healing one's kin also contributed to the value of those kin as slaves, and thereby lined the master's pocket. Perhaps more importantly, a standard of service could not stretch to encompass the relatives most crucially in need of familial recognition, those whose ability to contribute to family well-being was frustrated by distance, or eliminated by sale or death. Slavery did not so much diminish the practical or emotional importance of service *per se* as it put the reliability of service beyond the control of slaves themselves. That enslaved kin took advantage of available opportunities to help each other was a fact of life. But, since family members could not be held *responsible* for their ability or inability to provide direct assistance, enslaved families could not judge family loyalty only on the basis of service. They had to elaborate non-service standards, which included memory and symbolic acts of affiliation, by which to adjudge family loyalty.

Enslaved people must have struggled continually to separate doing for their loved ones from contributing to the profits of their oppressors, and there are hints in the record about those struggles. Maternal infanticide and the nurture of runaways, for example, were two acts of service that defied the interests of masters; and both also illustrate the awful predicament of enslaved kin as they tried to thwart the potential for slaveowners to reap the benefits of slaves' familial devotion. Maternal infanticide, which did occur during the period of slavery, though we cannot know how often, captures with agonizing precision the tangled nature of service in the context of enslavement. Granting the freedom of death to a beloved child indeed resolved the tension between providing service to a loved one and making profit for the master, but at a hideous cost. Anguished reflection on motherlove as a motive for infanticide appears in nineteenth- and twentieth-century black women's writings, as it must have in the talk of contemporary slave communities, suggesting that revulsion from these acts was mingled also with pity and understanding.[25]

Many more of the enslaved blended service and resistance by feeding and sheltering runaways or those temporarily hiding in nearby swamps and forests. Some runaways or "hideaways" might have taken to the woods precisely to rejoin kin from whom they had been separated, making the act of feeding and sheltering them doubly significant. As was the case with infanticide, the power of clandestine service to represent family loyalty lay in its intended defiance rather than in its quality as a service. Sustaining an escaping or hiding member of the community was a service act which undermined rather than supported the system of enslavement; therein lay both its importance and its dangers.

In short, enslavement gave families few good options for investing service to kin with unmistakably rebellious intent. Service was not less salient than symbol because slaves needed service less, but because service did not readily lend itself to the expression of defiance. For slave families, service was more geared to sustenance, symbolic acts to resistance.[26]

Emancipation transformed the meaning of mutual service within black families. After 1865, freedpeople could marry, legally claim and protect both children and elders. This new context of family life dissipated much of the defiance previously attached to memory and symbolic affiliation. After Emancipation, instead of working to dismantle black family structure and frustrate family feeling, whites turned to establishing exploitative economic relations, pressing poverty upon the freedpeople by seeing to it that the former slaves did not acquire land, did not escape debt, did not leave the rural South, and did not receive education. Blocking the economic and social advance of the former slaves became the crucial focus of white domination in the post-Emancipation years, and black dependence and impoverishment the measure of its success. In this new context, family memory became a matter of little concern to whites, while mutual service, which significantly improved a family's economic prospects, disturbed them indeed.[27] Networks of mutual service allowed African-American families to avoid or minimize the unequal patronage relations sought by whites; mutual service also increased the productivity of labor-intensive, hand-tool farming, helping farm families to stay out of debt and to accumulate the small surpluses essential to long-term prosperity.[28] For the same reasons, namely its growing importance in sustaining economic independence, mutual service moved ahead of symbol and memory in defining loyalty and membership in black families.

Jacob Thomas, a North Carolina freedman, perhaps summed up the change most pointedly. He told his Federal Writers Project interviewer, "Dar's dis much [to say for slavery], we ain't worried 'bout livin' den lak we does now, an' dar's dis much fer bein' free, I has got thirteen great gran'chilluns an' I knows whar dey ever' one am. In slavery times dey'd have been on de block long time ago."[29] As Thomas noted, the locus of the main struggle had shifted; slaves, lacking control over their intimate kin, had worked ceaselessly to exhibit and sustain family ties and had claimed as members all those who could be held within the circle of memory. Freedpeople, able to settle with kin and to record their births and deaths, worked together to overcome the obstacles to material survival which were placed in their way. To those who contributed materially went the honor of family membership, with all the rights and privileges pertaining thereto. Those who drifted out of the circle of service could find they had also drifted beyond the circle of membership.

This conception of nineteenth-century family structure suggests some interesting questions about African-American family history in the twentieth century. If providing service was the key to family membership in the postbellum years, how did families sustain ties and loyalty through the years of Northward migration? Did memory and symbol rebound in importance as kin began again to reach for each other across great distances? Or were customary service networks simply adapted to accommodate the Northern cousins? Might those who departed have left to escape the demands of service as much as to follow the promise of Northern employment? Some new understandings of the Great Migration might emerge from a reconstruction of the texture of service exchange between urban migrants and their rural families.[30]

In the changing structures of African-American families, form has followed function. These families faced a dual task; they had first to insulate members from immediate anticipated hardship, and second, to strengthen the entire community and equip it to surmount the oppressions of any given moment. To enable families to meet these two needs, the structures of family membership varied from slavery to freedom and were linked to strategies of resistance. Among enslaved families tormented by abuse, separation, and sale, symbolic acts of affiliation combined with remarkable genealogical recall to build a vision of family survival and to create channels for the expression of pride and rage. After Emancipation, acts of service contributed, by interfering with landowners' efforts to impose debt peonage on their labor force and by helping to create homesteads where families could set down roots.

Before and after Emancipation, in other words, to fulfil one's obligations to one's family meant to be at all times actually or potentially in rebellion. African-American family norms have not been simply cultural artifacts; they are not only matters of taste, adaptation, or tradition. African-American family norms must be understood as an expression of political will as well. Within a framework shaped by personal desires and by the need to survive, African-American families have consistently sought, encouraged, and rewarded behavior which seriously challenged both the racial ideology and the concrete power of white society.

～
NOTES

1. George P. Rawick, *The American Slave: A Composite Autobiography* (Westport, Conn.: Greenwood Publishing Co., 1977) vol. 14, part 2, 130.

2. Rawick, *The American Slave*, vol. 14, part 2, 130.

3. For the enslaved, flaunting family ties may have also been a relatively safe way to defy or embarrass a white master. Since many slaveholders relied upon high fertility among their slaves to increase their holdings, it was somewhat less likely that they would punish displays of stable conjugal affection.

4. See Thomas L. Webber, *Deep Like the Rivers: Education in the Slave Quarter Community, 1831–1865* (New York: Norton, 1978), 247 for a theoretical statement concerning slave ability to invert white teachings. See especially chaps. 6 and 7 for discussion of the impact of such inversion on the issues of religion and racial superiority.

5. Rawick, *The American Slave*, vol. 14, part 1, 101.

6. Peter Linebaugh advances this usage of "misappropriate" in his study of the struggle of seventeenth- and eighteenth-century English working people to defend customary work rules against merchant capitalists who sought to impose the standardization of the wage. The English courts, speaking on behalf of merchant capital, used "misappropriate" as a synonym for "theft." Linebaugh uses the word to connect the bitter battles between working people and capitalists over the rules of property with those over the definition of crime and the customs of punishment. Linebaugh argues that embattled workers would deliberately mistake or "misappropriate" capitalists' language of crime to challenge and to mock it, and ultimately to express their own sense that capital accumulation itself was "theft." I borrow Linebaugh's usage here to emphasize that enslaved workers too could deliberately transform the meaning of a seemingly "self-evident" act of mastery into an ironic failure which redounded to the moral credit of the victim. See Linebaugh, *The London Hanged: Crime and Civil Society in the Eighteenth Century* (London: Penguin Books, 1991).

7. It seems also that the couple added a delicate deception of their master to the open thwarting of the overseer. After telling the story of the whipping and courtship, Mrs. Bell added, referring to her mother, "I'se hearn her tell 'bout how [Wesley] axed Marse Mack iffen he could cou't mammy an' atter Marse Mack sez he can he axes her ter marry him." The overseer, evidently, did not tell the master of the whipping, perhaps confirming the contention that the overseer was uneasy about it. Nor did the master notice the full-blown courtship which grew out of the ordeal. He assumed he was giving Wesley and Minerva Jane permission to begin what, quite without his sanction, they had already virtually completed.

8. Rawick, *The American Slave*, vol. 14, part 1, 287. Mrs. Durham's owners apparently went to some trouble to put on a formal wedding for this couple, and Mrs. Durham

remembered the occasion as a grand one, though not without moments of humiliation. Her wedding veil was made from an old net window curtain, and after the black minister had finished the ceremony, her master insisted on "having his fun" as she called it, by forcing the couple to "jump the broom," backward. Exter Durham, who, according to his wife, had "had a dram," fell sprawling on his back, and "Marse George" enjoyed his joke very much, emphasizing that it meant Exter would be a henpecked husband. Moreover, no amount of slaveholder interest in the wedding itself changed the fact that Exter Durham had to leave early the next morning to return to his own master's place.

9. Exter Durham's gift of the ring echoes in interesting ways a decisive moment in the sentimental twentieth century play by Richard Morris, *The Unsinkable Molly Brown*. That romance, set at the turn of the twentieth century, but written and staged in the early 1960s, is adapted from the true story of Leadville Johnny Brown, a young, impoverished nineteenth-century farmer who marries Molly, an immigrant Irish country girl. He offers her the only ring he can afford, a band from a cigar. Their happy union nearly disintegrates under the pressure of later spectacular wealth and the consequent respectability Molly tries to enforce upon an unwilling Johnny. In a bid to bring into their lives as tycoons the simpler, sturdier, yeoman values from which they sprang and from which they had always taken their strength, Johnny presents Molly with a new ring, made of real jewels in the shape of the long-lost cigar band. The Durham and Herndon union, founded on virtue alone, survived without such renewing decoration. See *The Unsinkable Molly Brown*, Lyrics and Music by Meredith Wilson, Book by Richard Morris (New York: G.P. Putnam's Sons, 1960).

It is also interesting to note that Protestant Christians define a sacrament as "an outward and visible sign of an inward and spiritual grace." By that definition, the Durham marriage was every bit as much a sacrament as that of their owners. The theology of sacrament roots the enslaved couple in the most sacred precincts of Protestant Christianity, while their story's echoes of *Molly Brown* position them as iconic parallels to that sentimental sermon on the purest strain of American virtue. Though these connections must be viewed primarily as literary embellishments, they also suggest a context within which the ordinary behavior of African Americans can be assigned a proper significance within the construction of our national mythologies.

10. Victoria Bynum discusses the role of women in undermining the fictions of white men in the late antebellum years. She sees the "unruly" behavior of women, across class and race, as a central element in the weakening of "patriarchy." While I do not find her whole argument persuasive, I am drawing on her insight into the vulnerability of unstable cultural norms in making this analysis. See Victoria Bynum, *Unruly Women* (Chapel Hill: University of North Carolina Press, 1992).

11. Gutman noted the significance of naming practices in solidifying family memory among slaves beginning in the eighteenth century. He wrote, "Enslavement had radically altered the lives of these eighteenth- and nineteenth-century Africans and Afro-Americans and made it impossible for them to recreate the kin groups central

to all West African societies. But slavery had not obliterated familial and social memory. . . . Naming practices linked generations of blood kin." Herbert Gutman, *The Black Family in Slavery and Freedom, 1750–1925* (New York: Pantheon Books, 1976), 93.

12. Barnetta McGhee White, *In Search of Kith and Kin: The History of a Southern Black Family* (Baltimore: Gateway Press, Inc., 1986), 6.

13. White, *Kith and Kin*, 6.

14. See "Signatures of Depositors to the Freedman's Savings Bank," New Bern, Raleigh, and Wilmington, N. C., National Archives, microcopy 816, roll 18.

   There is a crying need for a name and location index of these records to make them more accessible to researchers. Entries were made as people presented themselves, and so the blanks are in no systematic order at all. Reconstructing the financial efforts of individual people requires coordinating two different National Archives microfilm sets: account records, which hold names and family information, and deposit records, which record deposits and withdrawals. Often the records which survive in the two microfilm series do not match, making the task altogether impossible. A full, definitive index would make it possible not only to follow individual and family transactions, but also to cross-reference census and tax records pertaining to the same people with the information held at the bank. For a concise history of the Bank see Abby L. Gilbert, "The Comptroller of the Currency and the Freedman's Savings Bank." *Journal of Negro History*, 57 (April, 1972).

15. Freedman's Bank Account Records, depositor number 1379.

16. Mrs. Warren recorded the exact ages, to the month, of all twelve of her children who died as youngsters.

17. Freedman's Bank Account Records, depositor number 1333.

18. U. S. Department of War, Bureau of Refugees, Freedmen, and Abandoned Lands, *Reports of Outrages, North Carolina, 1865–1866*. National Archives Record Group 105.

19. Rawick, *The American Slave*, vol. 14, part 2, 201.

20. See James D. Anderson, *The Education of Blacks in the South, 1860–1935* (Chapel Hill: University of North Carolina Press, 1988), especially chaps. 4 and 6, on the paucity of secondary schools for African-American students.

21. Elizabeth Johnson Harris, MS memoir of the period 1867 to 1923, in Manuscript Archives, William R. Perkins Library, Duke University, Durham, North Carolina, especially 3–4 and 11–12.

22. White, *Kith and Kin*, 134, 126, and 143.

23. White, *Kith and Kin*, 70.

24. Elizabeth Rauh Bethel, *Promiseland: A Century of Life in a Negro Community* (Philadelphia: Temple University Press, 1981), 178.

25. See Grace Nichols' poem "Ala," in *Ain't I a Woman: A Book of Women's Poetry from Around the World*, ed. Ilona Linthwaite (New York: Peter Bedrick Books, 1988), 145; Toni Morrison, *Beloved: A Novel* (New York: Alfred A. Knopf, 1987) and Angelina Weld Grimke, *Rachel: A Play in Three Acts*, "The Closing Door," and

"Goldie" in *Selected Works of Angelina Weld Grimke*, ed. Carolivia Herron (New York: Oxford University Press, 1991), 123, 252, 282.

26. Alex Lichtenstein argues that theft by slaves precisely did challenge the master's power by proposing a counter-ideology of property to that of the master class. Since slaves overwhelmingly seem to have stolen food, Lichtenstein's argument suggests a third way that the service of feeding could take on symbolic significance. I would argue that, exactly in Lichtenstein's terms, it is the act of expropriation which constitutes the defiance, not the presence of food, just as it is not the gift of food itself, but the gift of food to a runaway, which is relevant in distinguishing routines of self-succor that also serve masters' needs, and the kinds of service which challenge masters. See Alex Lichtenstein, " 'That Disposition To Theft, With Which They Have Been Branded': Moral Economy, Slave Management, and the Law," *Journal of Social History* 21:2 (Spring, 1988): 413–40.

27. African American's memories of kinship ties to white families clearly remained disturbing to whites throughout the period of freedom, and may have grown more disturbing rather than less over time.

28. For discussion of the relation of family labor and small surpluses to long-term prosperity, see Sharon Ann Holt, "A Time To Plant: The Economic Lives of Freedpeople in Granville County, North Carolina, 1865–1900," Ph.D diss., University of Pennsylvania, 1991, or Holt, "Making Freedom Pay: Freedpeople Working For Themselves, North Carolina, 1865–1900," *Journal of Southern History*, May, 1994.

29. Rawick, *The American Slave*, vol. 14, part 2, 351.

30. Nicholas Lemann suggests that the networks are sustained, sufficiently even to allow for return migration. He acknowledges, however, that returners so far have been a minuscule proportion of the total number of migrants. See Nicholas Lemann, *The Promised Land: The Great Black Migration and How It Changed America* (New York: Knopf, 1991), especially chaps. 4 and 5.

~

"SHE MAKE FUNNY FLAT CAKE SHE CALL SARAKA"
Gullah Women and Food Practices Under Slavery

Josephine A. Beoku-Betts

She make funny flat cake she call "saraka." She make um same day ebry year, an it big day. Wen de finish, she call us in, all duh chillun, an put in hans lill flat cake an we eat it. Yes'm I membuh how she make it. She wash rice, an po off all duh watuh. She let wet rice sit all night, an in mawnin rice is all swell. She take dat rice an put it in wooden mawtuh, an beat it tuh paste wid wooden pestle. She add honey, sometime shuguh, an make it in flat cake wid uh hans. "Saraka" she call um.[1]

T he recollections of Katie Brown, a former slave from Sapelo Island, Georgia, whose grandmother prepared a special rice cake for her family on particular Muslim fast days, illustrate ways in which marginalized cultural groups can utilize their own resources to create a separate world to express their cultural identity. By invoking recollections about her family's observance of Muslim religious practices, Katie Brown showed that even under the oppressive conditions of enslavement, her family was able to maintain a collective identity independent of the dominant culture. By describing this event in the context of women's nurturing and caregiving roles in the family, her testimony also sheds light on ways in which black women contributed to the formation and continuance of African-derived cultural practices, an often neglected issue in the study of African influences on African-American culture.[2]

This paper contributes to this discourse by examining the significance of African-derived food practices under slavery and the role of Gullah women in the formation and continuance of these traditions.[3] I argue that while cooking as work performed by women in the home has not received much analytical attention because of its invisibility and devaluation by society as a so-called natural role for women, an examination of this aspect of women's work under slavery can show ways in which this activity was used to promote resistance and forge an alternative framework of cultural expression under severe conditions of oppression. As members of the slave community, enslaved women contributed to devising and transmitting alternative ways of expressing their culture by using common but resourceful strategies such as particular methods of cooking and styles of flavoring, the procurement and preparation of healing foods from herbs and wild plants, and the preparation of foods in observance of religious rituals. Through teaching by example and providing constant recollections of their past through storytelling and other oral traditions, women also contributed to strengthening the collective identity of the community of slaves. An examination of the role of enslaved black women in the daily preparation of food in slave households and households of white plantation owners also illustrates how they used this particular work activity to influence the integration of African food practices in present-day Southern food traditions.

Evidence for this analysis is drawn from testimonies of former slaves conducted by the Federal Writers' Project in the 1930s. While these testimonies should be read as cautiously as any historical oral records, they provide a unique source of documentation for the analysis and reinterpretation of the diverse roles of women under slavery, and allow us to examine the various strategies women used individually and cooperatively with other women and men to survive the institution of slavery.[4] Based on a recent ethnographic study I conducted with Gullah women in Sea Island communities in Georgia and South Carolina, I shall illustrate at various junctures ways in which some of these practices have been maintained in present-day Gullah culture.[5]

To focus on food practices from the perspective of women's lives is not to imply that men did not have a valued role in this process. The purpose is to validate the continuance of African-derived food traditions as a form of resistance against oppressive cultural practices, and the particular role of women within this process.

The evidence is clear that under slavery both men and women played a vital role in the procurement of food for their families. For example, the task and garden system of labor which was widely practiced in coastal South Carolina and Georgia, permitted slaves some extra time to produce food for family subsistence from gardening, hunting, and fishing, and to produce/generate surplus goods for exchange in the underground economy they created.[6] Enslaved men were more likely than women to directly participate in this network of exchange, because they were relatively more mobile and commanded more skills that could be exchanged on the market. Men were also less constrained by routine caregiving roles in the family.[7] Nonetheless, while many men played a key role in providing for the daily well being of their families, few studies reveal cases of men taking daily responsibility for cooking in the slave household, other than at times of family emergencies. Although most men knew how to cook, food preparation tended to be gender specific in the slave household, with men viewing certain chores as women's responsibility, and women largely respecting these gender role boundaries.[8]

In the division of labor, much of the work men performed in the management of food practices was oriented towards outdoor activities, such as hunting and fishing, preparation of meat and seafood for smoking and barbecues, as well as using cash earned from sales of goods/produce or from stolen goods to procure gifts of food for family subsistence. Women on the other hand were more often responsible for transforming this food into a cultural form through the activity of cooking.

Although slaveowners provided food for their slaves, access to food and the quality of the slave diet was governed by climate, topography, size and location of the plantation, size of the slave family, labor conditions on the plantation, and the affluence and character of the slaveowner.[9] The main sources of food for slaves were weekly rations of corn and pork (sometimes supplemented with molasses, other salted meats and starchy vegetables), and fresh vegetables from small garden plots many were allowed to cultivate. They also hunted and went fishing (depending on labor conditions on the plantation), and stole either food or non-food items.[10]

Slave testimonies reveal that enslaved families depended on the foods they cultivated or stole from their masters to supplement their diets and men and women equally cooperated in these activities. Much of the work involved in cultivating their garden plots, which varied in size from a quarter acre to as much as twelve to fifteen acres, was done at night or at weekends when the slaves had some extra time.[11] Charlie Grant of Marion, South Carolina, and Sylvia Cannon of Florence, South Carolina, respectively, recalled that:

> Oh, yes, de slaves had dey own garden dat de work at night en especially moonlight nights coarse de had to work in de field all day till sundown. Mamma had a big garden en plant collards en everythink like dat you want to eat.[12]

> Coase dey let de slaves have three acres of land to a family to plant for dey
> garden. Work dem in moonlight nights en on a Saturday evenin.[13]

In spite of undertaking this heavy workload, the opportunity to provide
subsistence from gardening as well as the task system of labor enabled many
men and women to provide subsistence, clothing, and relative economic
security for their families and to establish a way of life that operated independently of the dominant culture.

Slaves who had garden plots cultivated a variety of vegetables, including
some they were already accustomed to in Africa, such as okra and benne seed
(sesame seeds). Other crops planted included: collard greens, turnip greens,
sweet potatoes, as well as black-eyed peas, cowpeas, kidney beans, lima beans,
and rice. According to Peter Wood, patterns of cultivation on these garden
plots did not change significantly from African farming practices, particularly
in the case of rice cultivation.[14] For example, he notes that the mortar and pestle
technique of processing rice, which became the accepted way of removing rice
grains from their husks, had a remarkably close resemblance to the traditional
West African method of pounding rice, a process normally performed by
women.[15]

Slave testimonies show that women passed on their knowledge of foods they
ate in Africa to their children and grandchildren, as stated in the recollections
of Shad Hall of Sapelo Island:

> Muh gran hestuh say she kin membuh de house she lib in in Africa. She say
> it wuz cubbuh wid palmetto an grass fuh roof, an duh walls wuz made of
> mud.——She membuh wut de eat in Africa too. Dey eat yam an shuguh cane
> an peanut an bananas. Dey eat Okra too. Dey dohn habtuh work hahd wid
> plantin deah. Jis go in woods an dig, an git big yam. Dey eat udduh roots
> too.[16]

According to Rosa Grant of Possum Point, Georgia, her grandmother used to
tell her that in Africa:

> dey plant berries an pumpkin an dey had tuh plant um ebry seben yeahs or
> dey die.[17]

Emma Hunter the wife of Charles Hunter of St. Simon's Island also said of her
African grandmother Betty:

> Now muh gran Betty she was African an she plant Benne seed. Once you
> staht plantin benne, you got tuh plant em ebry yeah aw yuh die.[18]

What is revealing in the above testimonies is the line of continuity linking the narrators with their African past. Although many of the fruits and vegetables mentioned such as peanuts, bananas, yam, pumpkin, and berries, were commonly known in the United States during the period of slavery, linking these crops with an African past presented these women with an opportunity to dispel negative images about their lack of history. In other words, they used this common knowledge to inform their children that their foremothers and forefathers had previously encountered these crops at another time and place and that their way of cultivating these crops was informed by that past.

Although certain items necessary to supplement their meager diets were not widely available to the slaves, their food culture was versatile enough to convert whatever they could procure to suit their particular needs. For example, slaves prepared specific foods from various items they could find, such as salt from boiled down dirt obtained from smoke houses, coffee from ground okra seeds and parched corn, and sugar from scraping the sides of old syrup barrels.[19]

The slaves' extensive knowledge of herbs and wild plants gathered from the woods was also used to prepare special foods with therapeutic qualities (healing foods) to treat the ailments of family and other community members.[20] The cultural knowledge of where and how to find and prepare these healing foods into teas and meals was safely protected within a family and was most often transmitted from mother to daughter. However most members of the family would be familiar with the uses of these herbs and plants.[21] Slave testimonies reflect this knowledge of family history and indicate that such knowledge was transmitted among family members. For example, Solomon Caldwell of South Carolina reported that:

> Ma would take fence grass and boil it to tea and have us drink it to keep the fever away. [She also] used branch elder twigs and dogwood berries for chills.[22]

And, Jack Waldburg of Tatemville, Georgia recalled that:

> —granmudduh, she from deah, [Africa] too, an she feah. She duh one wut lun me tuh make medicine frum root. She a midwife an tell me duh kine tuh use. I dohn make it no mo cuz I ain got a license.[23]

In the face of death, sickness and deprivation, the knowledge about plant roots, herbs and leaves of particular plants which had therapeutic powers and which could be prepared into special healing foods, was a crucial source of empowerment and resistance to dominant cultural practices. Enslaved women who practiced midwifery and men who were traditional healers were particularly able to sustain and validate this kind of knowledge because they were more able to practice it widely among the various slave communities in their area.

Knowledge of cultural traditions relating to the collection and preparation of wild herbs and plants as healing foods has persisted in the culture of present day Gullah communities in Georgia and South Carolina. For example, Velma Moore of Sapelo Island, Georgia, a key participant in my ethnographic study, informed me that in spite of the advancement and wider availability of modern scientific medicine, the use of wild herbs and plants as healing foods continues to play a vital role in the preventive and curative health care of Gullah people in her community. She explained that she was socialized into the concept and value of these practices when as a child she used to accompany either her father or mother for daily walks in the woods. From these experiences she learned where to collect particular plants and herbs, and how to prepare them into meals and teas to treat various ailments. She noted that life everlasting tea is still regularly used for colds, red oak bark tea is good for diarrhea, and the leaves of the mullien plant are good for fever and stomach trouble. Velma recollected that as a child, her mother would keep a variety of roots, leaves, and herbs in the kitchen, and would insist that in her presence a reluctant patient eat or drink a concoction she had prepared to treat a particular ailment.

Another way in which enslaved women and men exerted what limited control they had over their masters and mistresses, was that although many slaveowners would have preferred to control and centralize the distribution, preparation and consumption of food in the slave community, the slaves were able to insist that the preparation and consumption of food in the privacy of their own quarters was preferable.[24] Archaeological studies on plantations in Florida, Georgia, and South Carolina support this viewpoint and show that cooking was done primarily in domestic units and not communally.[25]

After returning to their quarters after a hard day's labor in the fields, women and men generally occupied themselves in work related to the well-being of their families, such as to tend the family garden plot, to make furniture and other household articles, or to try to earn some cash to provide for family needs. Such tasks were typically a male domain. Women were more likely to use the time and meager supply of food they had available to prepare distinctive meals for their families. Ash cakes, made from batter wrapped in leaves and cooked in hot ashes, highly spiced one pot meals, like Hoppin' John, which is prepared from rice cooked with peas–for example, cowpeas, black-eye peas, and red peas, were very popular meals that many former slaves fondly remembered. For example, Jack Waldburg recalls how his mother used to prepare ash cake for him and his siblings as children on the plantation:

Ma would make ash cake. She would mix duh cawnmeal, den open duh oak
ashes an spread in some hickory leaves, deen put duh cawnmeal on duh leabes
an cubbuh wid mo leabes, den put duh duh hot ashes on coals on duh top.
Wen it done, she take duh bread from duh ashes an rub it wid a rough clawt
aw brush an it would be pretty an brown. Dis, wuz bery fine wid fat meat aw
surup.[26]

Jack Waldburg's detailed description of how his mother made ashcakes,
indicates that attention to detail was a key lesson that enslaved women taught
their children in the privacy of their homes. Learning to observe closely and to
pay attention to detail were not simply ways to transmit African cooking styles,
flavors, and smells, intergenerationally; they were also critical rules of survival
under conditions were enslaved people were constantly in fear for their lives
and could not afford to make mistakes.

As an extension of the practice of cooking for the family, women were
probably expected to transfer this domestic role to the fields when there was a
lot of work to be done. At the Woodbourne rice plantation on the Waccamaw
in South Carolina, where midday meals were often prepared and eaten in the
fields, J. Motte Alston made the following observation about rice cooking in
the fields: "Uncover, as you walk along the banks of the fields, one of their little
three legged iron pots with its wooden cover, and try, if only from curiosity,
the rice which they have prepared for their midday meal."[27] One would assume
that women took responsibility for this activity, because rice cultivation
practices on plantations in the south eastern coastal region followed similar
patterns practiced in West African cultures.[28]

The cooking utensils and large open fireplaces used in slave homes were also
influenced by African cultural practices. Just as it was common for women in
West African households to make handmade earthenware bowls, pots, and jars,
and to prepare one pot meals and stews from open fireplaces, likewise, women
made similar use of these utensils in many slave households. For example, the
abrasion marks and charred remains of food found on colonware pots in South
Carolina and archaeological reports of inscriptions found on handcrafted pottery on plantation sites in South Carolina, indicate that these utensils were
made and used by slaves.[29] Studies of colonware pottery indicate that there is
a strong similarity in the design of these and prehistoric West African pottery
traditions.[30]

The above information is consistent with slave testimonies which show that
women used earthenware and wooden utensils in their homes and that their
children were acquainted with them. Shad Hall remembered some pots and
cups made of clay that his grandmother Hestuh told him were from Africa.[31]

Katie Brown also stated that her grandmother used funny words like 'mosojo' and 'sojo' when she was referring to a pot:

> She speak funny wuds we didn know. She say 'mosojo' an sometime 'sojo' wen she mean pot. Fuh watuh she say 'deloe' an fyuh she say 'diffy'. She tell us, 'tak sojo off diffy.'[32]

That only a few words and broken pots remain to tell the history of an African past is a testament to the destructive and annihilating force of slave society. Nonetheless, while Katie Brown's grandmother was no longer able to speak her original African language, her use of key words like 'mosojo' and 'sojo' was testimony of her will to keep the knowledge of her African background alive and to validate that heritage by transmitting it intergenerationally through dialogue.

In addition to the use of particular utensils and African words to express culture in slave homes, enslaved women also used food practices to transmit distinct religious traditions to their children. Although information about the relationship between food and the practice of religious rituals in slave family life is somewhat scanty, it is significant that in many of the narratives addressing this issue, much of what was remembered was recalled by women and transmitted by them to their children and grandchildren. In testimonies to the WPA interviewer, both Katie Brown and Shad Hall recalled that their grandmothers were practicing Muslims who observed Muslim fast-days and feast-days by wearing a Muslim head dress and preparing special foods for their families.[33] For example, Shad Hall, whose grandmother was a sister of Katie Brown's grandmother, recollected the special rice cake his grand-mother prepared every month, after the sun went down on a Muslim fast day:

> She make strange cake, fus ub ebry munt. She call it 'saraka.' She make it out uh meal an honey. She put meal in bilin watuh an take it right out. Den she mix it wid honey, and make it in flat cakes. Sometime she make it out uh rice. Duh cake made, she call us all in an deah she hab great big fannuh full an she gib us each cake. Den we all stands roun table, and she says, 'Ameen, Ameen,' an we all eats cake.[34]

Food rituals were also intertwined in the religious and spiritual customs associated with funeral ceremonies which tended to be long drawn out affairs in the slave community. Women played a central role in sustaining the continuance of African-derived food practices in these ceremonies, not only because of the special ritual foods they prepared, but also because of their conscious efforts to channel these traditions intergenerationally by constantly telling and retelling their children these stories.

The recollections of Jane Lewis of Darien, Georgia, show for example, how elaborate feasts were organized for mourners when a funeral occurred in the slave community:

> Yes'm, dey sho hab regluh feastes in dem days, but tuhday, at most settin-ups, yuh dohn git nuttn but coffee an bread. Den dey would cook a regluh meal an dey would kill a chicken in front uh duh doe, wring he neck an cook um fuh duh feas. Den wen we all finish, we tak wut victuals lef an put it in a dish by duh chimley an das fuh duh sperrit tuh hab a las good meal.[35]

Shad Hall's recollections from stories his grandmother told him about funeral rituals involving the sacrifice of a chicken are similar:

> Yes'm, Gran Hestuh tell me uh set-ups. Dey kill a wite chicken wen dey hab set-ups tuh keep duh spirits way. She say a wite chicken is duh only ting dat will keep duh spirits an she allus keep wite chicken fuh dat in yahd.[36]

Many other funeral rituals involving food described in slave testimonies, like that of leaving food and water out for the spirits of the dead, or to place spoons, cups, and other possessions on a new grave, were based on African cultural practices.[37] Bessie Reese of Brownville, Georgia, for example, mentions that she used to take food to her husband's grave on public holidays because she knew his spirit would be there to receive it, while Emma English, also of Brownville, recalled that her mother never used to allow them to go to bed at night without leaving some water for the spirits to drink. As each of them described it:

> I carry duh kine uh food we use tuh hab tuh eat on duh days he wuz off frum wuk. I take cooked chicken and cake an pie an cigahs—he like tuh smoke attuh eatin. I do dis cuz I know he will be lookin fuh me tuh bring it.[38]

> Muh mothuh nebuh would let us go tuh bed at night widout leabin plenty uh watuh in duh pails fuh duh spirits tuh drink wile yuh sleep. Ef yuh dohn leab no watuh dey wohn leh yuh res good.[39]

What was the significance of these food rituals in religious ceremonies in slave communities? How did the slaves make sense of these beliefs? On one level, these customs could be interpreted as providing a way to create a separate/alternative sphere of life from that which was imposed on the enslaved, and one in which they could maintain some sense of self-worth and control in expressing their way of life. In addition, these customs probably instilled a sense of group solidarity among slaves and fostered the continuity of a shared tradition. On a deeper level however, the observance of these practices by enslaved communities reflected the influence of African belief systems regarding death and afterlife.[40]

Enslaved women who cooked for these events were vital to the maintenance and transmission of these traditions, because they performed work which served as a symbolic and material link between the world of the living and the spiritual world. Because even after death the preparation of food and beverage was a necessary part of honoring ancestral spirits and sustaining the dead in their journey to the spirit world, women's preparation of special ritual foods constituted a sacred act in the expression of a shared religious tradition. As such, the preparation of food by women for religious rituals aided community centered institutions to become sites of cultural preservation and spiritual fellowship in the community of slaves.

Beyond the world of the individual slave household and community centered institutions the slaves created, the role of enslaved women as primary preparers of food permeated the world of the plantation master and mistress. According to John Egerton: "The kitchen was one of the few places where their imagination and skill could have free reign and full expression, and there they often excelled."[41] In these kitchens, the cooks who were more often women but could also be men, combined African with European, Native American, and other culinary styles to produce a variety of cuisines still popular among black and white southerners.

In the slave community, plantation cooks were well respected for both their culinary skills and the support they rendered to community members whenever it was necessary to do so. In other words, they tended to be influential members of their communities because they could often be counted on to provide information, steal food, and provide other forms of assistance when it was necessary to do so.

Most often the daughters of women who cooked for the household of the master and mistress apprenticed with them from an early age, because it was assumed that they would eventually take over from them or be ready to assume the same role in the newly wed homes of the children of these plantation owners. However, other young girls were also selected by the mistress of the household for training as cooks. Invariably, high standards were set for all, regardless of kinship ties to the cook.

African-derived methods of cooking were distinctive in the culinary styles of plantation cooks, although they were also influenced by other culinary traditions. As in Africa, plantation cooks prepared food with a variety of herbs, spices like hot pepper and ginger, and seasonings like sesame and smoked meats. Their habit of boiling and frying meats and vegetables was also consistent with West African cooking practices observed by Europeans in Africa, although some modifications were made as appropriate.

Thomas Winterbottom, a medical doctor employed by the Sierra Leone company in 1792 for example, noted that the art of cooking in Sierra Leone was confined to boiling and stewing and that baking or roasting were seldom used. He also noted:

> They use a kind of sauce to their meat, the boiled leaf of a plant somewhat resembling spinage. The okra, hibiscus esculentus, which enters into the composition of the celebrated pepper pot of the West Indies, is often used for the same purpose by the natives.[42]

William Bascom, later discussing the food of the Yoruba in the 1950s, also observed:

> Their manner of cooking is quite different from ours. They bake nothing, but all their food is boiled or fried in earthen pots. Various kinds of bread of corn and peas are fried in palm oil or tree butter. Sometimes they cook Indian corn in whole grains, like our "big hominy". Meat is always cut fine to be cooked. Sometimes it is stewed, but it is usually made into a palaver sauce which the Yorubas call obbeh, by stewing up a small quantity of flesh or fish with a large portion of vegetables, highly seasoned with onions and red pepper.[43]

To a large extent, southern cuisine maintained its distinctive character because of the influence of plantation cooks who introduced distinctive styles of flavoring and cooking methods into the southern household. For example, beans and peas were prepared into soups and stews by seasoning them with bits of salted or smoked meat and cooking them on a slow boil. Similarly, West African methods of preparing leafy green vegetables like spinach, sweet potato leaves, and turnip greens, into sauces seasoned with meat or fish, were modified into cooking green vegetables seasoned with pieces of smoked meat.[44] Hoppin' John, which is prepared from rice and peas, was also a popular African dish that appealed to both the slave community and the white plantation household. Less commonly known but also cooked in the plantation households were "Ground Nut Soup," made from peanuts, "Benne Soup," made from sesame, which originated in Africa, "Chickens Stewed With Tomatoes," "Okra Pilau," and "Tomato Pilau," all of which are popular West African dishes today.[45] That these African dishes were a part of the cuisine in plantation households, even among those who felt they were of a higher status in antebellum society, is evident from the fact that they were included among other European influenced recipes in prestigious nineteenth century southern cookbooks such as *The Carolina Housewife*.[46]

Notwithstanding that these African-derived cooking styles were appreciated and even incorporated in some cases into southern cookbooks, it must be noted that cooking was very laborious work and often performed under harsh and alienating conditions. As pointed out by Doris Smith, "Antebellum cooking was slave-labor intensive, and the fame of Southern cuisine is inarguably contingent upon a slave system in which human beings were forced to do that which technology had yet to render less backbreaking."[47]

Although little information exists about how women cooks fared with white mistresses with respect to how much control they could exercise over what was cooked, how it was prepared, and how much of their culinary knowledge they were willing to give away, many cooks were highly regarded in the homes in which they labored. Based on evidence from cookbooks of the period, it would seem that some wielded influence (even if limited) over what meals were prepared in the mistress's household. Much of this influence however, depended on the age of the mistress, her experience in household management practices, and perhaps the extent to which race and gender boundaries were enforced when the authority of the mistress was challenged, or the extent to which they expressed anger over the sexual encounters/liaisons their husbands initiated/forced on particular enslaved women.[48] On this basis it is clear that some mistresses were very cruel and asserted their authority by severely beating their cooks for simple errors, such as burning bread.[49] On the other hand, some mistresses did seek advice and even leaned on their cooks to supervise the management of the kitchen.

As African, European, Native American, and other culinary styles have developed or even combined to produce a distinctive southern food tradition, contemporary Gullah communities in the coastal region of Georgia and South Carolina have retained elements of African–derived cooking traditions in their daily food practices. Because of their daily involvement in cooking for the household, Gullah women are particularly conversant with stories and traditions about food and make a self conscious effort to encourage the practice of these traditions among their sons and daughters. As told to me by Velma Moore of Sapelo Island:

> They have folklore on rice down here. One of the things we grew up with for instance, after the birth of a child you wasn't given rice, no rice. Because rice is supposed to been too starchy for the newborn baby to digest through the mother's milk, and you wasn't given rice to eat at all.[50]

Some of the old folks believe that rice was also a cure for sick chickens, believe it or not. If your chicken were looking like they were kind of sick you was to feed them raw rice, and it supposed to make them feel better. So they will take raw rice and throw it in the chicken yard.[51]

I've known people to patch rice and make their coffee. Put it in the frying pan or something and you toss it lightly and keep shaking it lightly until it brown and you mix it and you can drink it and you put water and you make like coffee.[52]

Children are also socialized into eating traditional foods from an early age among present day Gullah. As explained by one woman:

When my baby gets about, I'd say five or six months, I start giving them you know, certain foods from the table. I give my baby grits and eggs. Sometimes I give them rice, but I have to make sure I cook it not too hard you know. And beans, I use the gravy on it. I've got a little baby 15 months old now. I've started her eating from the table, and that's the only food she will eat now. She loves soul food. I fed her rice and okra the one evening, and she loved okra and rice.[53]

The choice of seasonings used to flavor food is also distinctive to the culture. Although certain foods such as "Hoppin' John," "Red Rice," "Collard Greens," and "Shrimp and Okra Stew," are now popular southern dishes across ethnic lines, one way Gullah women try to control cultural boundaries in their way of cooking these foods, as distinct from other southern practices, is to assert that their style of preparation and type of seasonings used are different. Just as West African cooking is characteristically well seasoned with salt, hot pepper, onions, garlic, and smoked meat and fish, Gullah food is seasoned with a combination of seasonings such as onions, salt, and pepper, as well as fresh and smoked meats such as bacon, pigs' feet, salt pork, and (increasingly) smoked turkey wings, to reduce fat content. The views of Gullah women expressed in the following statements reflect some consistencies in the cooking practices of slave communities and present-day Gullah communities:

Question: As an African-American living in this area, what do you think makes the food you eat different?

Answer: Culture and what's available to you. I call it a make do society on Sapelo because you can't run to the supermarket to get things. We are plain cooking. We use salt, pepper, and onion, as basic additives. Our flavoring comes from the type of meat we put in it. Bacon is white folks food, pigs tails, neck bones and hamhock is what we use. Soul food is what other Americans call it, but we consider these to be foods we always ate. We never label ourselves or our food.[54]

Answer: Seasonings have a lot to do with it and the preparation is different. A lot of what we cook is seasoned with meat. Down here food is seasoned beforehand. It's not bland like the North.[55]

Answer: Um, on Sapelo you got things like red peas and rice. You know they cook the same things on that side over there too, but we assume that we have the strict monopoly on it, that nobody cooks it the way we cook it. You know, although they call it the same thing, the ingredients may be a little different that they use, or the taste is definitely different. So, it's considered Sapelo food. I mean very few places you go and they cook oysters and rice or they cook clam and gravy the way we do, and stuff like that. So, we got our way of cooking things. So we pretty proud of calling it Sapelo food. Yes.[56]

A final theme of this work reflects Rawick's statement that: "The slave community acted like a generalized extended kinship system in which all adults looked after all children and there was little division between 'my children for whom I'm responsible' and 'your children for whom you're responsible.'"[57] In the slave community, there were always older people and groups of women who rendered assistance with child care, care for the sick, as well as meal preparation, whenever it was necessary to do so. It was also common practice for white plantation owners to use women who were retired from work in the fields to care for children while their parents were at work. These circumstances gave those women who were so disposed, an opportunity to reminisce about the past, tell stories, prepare distinctive foods children would later remember, and ultimately, to take risks for the children's well-being.

In spite of the fact that typically many children were fed in troughs, some nurses did take good care of the children and some even took risks to steal food for these children. For example, the testimonies of Josephine Bristow, who grew up on a South Carolina plantation, show she was cared for by "de old lady" who boiled beans and made a lot of soup they ate with oven bread.[58] Ninety-seven-year-old Gus Feaster also recalled "Old lady Abbie" who prepared meat for them even when she wasn't allowed to do so:

De old lady, give us mush and milk fer breakfast. Shorts and seconds was mixed wid de mush; no grease in de morning a-tall. Twelve o'clock brug plenty cowpeas, meat, bread, black bread made frum de shorts. Jes' had meat at twelve o'clock, course 'sharpers' 'ud eat meat when master didn't know. Dey go out and git 'em a hog frum a drove of seventy'five er a hund'ed; dat one never be missed.[59]

In conclusion, while more overt forms of slave protest and rebellion have been well documented, examination of everyday activities such as cooking for the individual household, slave community gatherings, and white plantation household, has not received much analytical attention as a form of resistance to slavery. I have argued that analysis of how daily life was conducted by enslaved women and men can reveal much about how such groups used their own resources to resist the effects of an oppressive institution.

Through the daily activity of cooking which was primarily a woman's domain, enslaved women in the region of the Sea Islands of Georgia and South Carolina used ths sphere of activity to perpetuate cultural identity in their communities. The daily actions of these women was a form of resistance under slavery, because they helped their communities maintain a sense of self-worth, dignity, and group solidarity under very harsh conditions of oppression.

The slave testimonies show how women's knowledge of particular cooking practices and food rituals, their knowledge of therapeutic herbs and wild plants which were prepared into teas and meals to treat various ailments, and their role in preparing foods in observance of religious rituals, were essential to the cultural survival of families who were under a great deal of pressure to adapt to the harsh conditions of slavery and its dominant cultural institutions. Furthermore, their promotion of food traditions, although strongly reflecting African traditions, derived from a variety of culinary influences, and their use of common but resourceful strategies such as everyday practice, teaching by example, and constant recollections of the past through storytelling and other oral traditions, contributed to other forms of resistance against negative claims about the lack of history and tradition in the slave family and community. That these intentions were not eventually lost on their children, is befittingly expressed in the testimony of a woman who, when recollecting her memories of her mother, made the point of stating: "I is heered Maw tell it a thousand times, over and over."[60]

Cultural preservation through food preparation in the family and wider community (including the publication of cookbooks) has become a highly conscious act on the part of contemporary Gullah women, and is tied closely to their judgments about when to accept and when to resist change.[61] As a result, although present attempts to define and preserve the unique cultural tradition of these communities are threatened by the pace of economic development in the region, Gullah women have learned from their foremothers and forefathers that the observance and practice of the underlying principles of their traditions are vital to the survival and preservation of their culture.

~

NOTES

1. Katie Brown in Georgia Writers' Project (GWP), *Drums and Shadows: Survival Studies Among the Georgia Coastal Negroes* (Athens and London: University of Georgia Press, 1986, originally published 1940), 162.

2. Black feminist studies provide a framework for conceptualizing African cultural influences on black women's lives. These studies draw on the analytical constructs of an Afrocentric value system emphasizing self-reliance, women-centered networks, the use of dialogue and connectedness with community, spirituality, and extended family. For illustration see Cheryl Gilkes, "Together and in Harness: Women's Traditions in the Sanctified Church," in *Black Women in America: Social Science Perspectives*, eds. M. R. Malson, E. Mudimbe-Boyi, J. F. O'Barr, and M. Wyer (Chicago: University of Chicago Press, 1988); Patricia Hill Collins, *Black Feminist Thought: Knowledge, Consciousness, and the Politics of Empowerment* (Boston and London: Unwin Hyman, 1990); Bernice Johnson Reagon, "African Diaspora Women: The Making of Cultural Workers," *Feminist Studies*, vol. 12, (1986); Filomena Steady, *The Black Woman Cross-Culturally* (Cambridge, Mass.: Schenkman Publishing Co., 1981); R. Terborg-Penn, *Women in Africa and the Africa Diaspora*, (Washington, D.C.: Howard University Press, 1987).

3. More detailed discussions of the historical background and specific cultural influences of this area can be found in the following: Melville Herskovits, *The Myth of the Negro Past* (New York and London: Harper and Brothers Publishers, 1941); Lorenzo D. Turner, *Africanisms in the Gullah Dialect* (Chicago: University of Chicago Press, 1949); Peter H. Wood, *Black Majority: Negroes in Colonial South Carolina From 1670 through the Stono Rebellion* (New York: Alfred A. Knopf, 1974); Daniel C. Littlefield, *Rice and Slaves: Ethnicity and the Slave Trade in Colonial South Carolina* (Baton Rouge: Louisiana State University Press, 1981); R. Faris Thompson, *Flash of the Spirit: African and Afro-American Art and Philosophy* (New York: Random House, 1983); Charles Joyner, *Down by the Riverside: A South Carolina Slave Community* (Urbana: University of Illinois Press, 1984); Margaret Washington Creel, *A Peculiar People: Slave Religion and Community Culture among the Gullahs* (New York: New York University Press, 1988).

4. Critics challenge the utility of these narratives arguing that the informants were either too young at the time of slavery or were too old when interviewed for their recollections to be reliable and meaningful. Others argue that the informants were not scientifically representative of the former slave population, that the interviewers were not properly trained, that they were insensitive, and that they often produced biased interpretations of the interviews. Another criticism is that most of the narratives represented the experiences of men or were often recorded by male interviewers who portrayed conditions from a male perspective. These issues are addressed in more detail in the following: D. Sterling, ed., *We Are Your Sisters:*

Black Women in the Nineteenth Century (New York: W.W. Norton and Company, 1984); C. Van Woodward, "History from Slave Sources," in *The Slave's Narrative*, eds. Charles T. Davis and Henry Louis Gates Jr. (Oxford: Oxford University Press, 1985): 48-59; J. Blassingame, "Using the Testimony of Ex-Slaves: Approaches and Problems," in *The Slave's Narrative*, eds. Charles T. Davis and Henry Louis Gates Jr. (Oxford: Oxford University Press, 1985): 78-98; Mary Ellen Obitko, "Custodians of a House of Resistance: Black Women Respond to Slavery," in *Black Women in United States History*, ed. Darlene Clark Hine (Brooklyn, N.Y., Carlson Publishing Inc., 1990), 996; George P. Rawick, "Some Notes on a Social Analysis of Slavery: A Critique and Assessment of the Slave Community," in *Revisiting Blassingame's The Slave Community: The Scholars Respond*, ed. Al-Tony Gilmore (Westport, Conn.: Greenwood Press, 1978), 21; Melvina Johnson Young, "Exploring the WPA Narratives: Finding the Voices of lack Women and Men," in *Theorizing Black Feminisms: The Visionary Pragmatism of Black Women*, eds. Stanlie M. James and Abena P.A. Busia (New York: Routledge, 1993).

5. Ethnographic data is based on my field observations and semi-structured interviews conducted by the author with twenty two Gullah women in the Sea Islands and Neighboring mainland communities in South Carolina (Wadmalow, St. Helena, John's, Edisto, and Coosaw Islands) and Georgia (Sapelo and St. Simon's Islands, and Harris Neck) over several visits between 1989 and 1992. All names used in this article are pseudonyms.

6. See Larry Hudson, "'All That Cash': Work and Status in the Slave Quarters," and Mary Beth Corrigan, "It's a Family Affair: Buying Freedom In The District Of Columbia, 1850-1860," both included in this volume.

7. See Corrigan, "It's a Family Affair," for discussion on gender role specialization and mobility patterns of slaves.

8. Jacqueline Jones in *Labor of Love, Labor of Sorrow* 38, provides what limited evidence there is on this specific issue. She suggests that there were men who actively scorned work associated as women's work, such as cooking, and that some slaveowners took advantage of this reluctance by forcing some men to undertake these tasks in public, in order to humiliate them.

9. See J. Floyd Smith, *Slavery and Rice Culture in Low Country Georgia, 1750-1860* (Knoxville: University of Tennessee Press, 1985), 113; J.R. Dormon and R.R. Jones, *The Afro-American Experience* (New York: John Wiley and Sons, Inc., 1974), 159; E.J. Reitz, T. Gibbs, and T.A. Rathbun, in *The Archaeology of Slavery and Plantation Life*, ed. Theresa A. Singleton (Orlando: Academic Press, Inc., 1985), 166.

10. George P. Rawick, *The American Slave: A Composite Autobiography*, Vol. 1 (Westport, Conn.: Greenwood Publishing Co., 1972), 69; Floyd Smith, *Slavery and Rice Culture*, 113; see also Corrigan, "It's a Family Affair."

11. Hudson, "All That Cash."

12. Charlie Grant in Rawick, *The American Slave*, vol. 2, part 2, 172.

13. Sylvia Cannon in Rawick, *The American Slave*, vol. 1, part 1, 191.

14. See Wood, *Black Majority*, 61.

15. See Peter H. Wood, " 'It was a Negro Taught Them,' A New Look at African Labor in Early South Carolina," in *The Afro-American Slaves: Community or Chaos.*, ed. Randall M. Miller (Malabar, Fla.: Robert E. Krieger Publishing Co., 1981), 21.

16. Shad Hall in Georgia Writers' Project (GWP), *Drums and Shadows, 166.*

17. Rosa Grant in GWP, *Drums and Shadows*, 145

18. Emma Hunter in GWP, *Drums and Shadows*, 178.

19. See Federal Writers' Project extracts from "The Southern Negro," Box 38, File 22, Cuisine, Name: Odelia Anderson (Located in the University of Georgia Library: Hagrett Collection); Rawick, *South Carolina Narratives*, vol. 1, part 1, 138.

20. Wood, "*It Was a Negro Taught Them*" 17; for illustration on the healing powers of certain plant foods such as collard greens, see Verta Mae Grovesnor, *Vibration Cooking* (Garden City, New York: Doubleday and Co., 1970), xvi-xviii.

21. See Jones, *Labor of Love, Labor of Sorrow*, 257; Barbara Bush, "The Family Tree Is Not Cut: Women And Cultural Resistance In The Slave Family In The British Caribbean," in *In Resistance Studies In African, Caribbean, And Afro-American History*, ed. G.Y. Okihiro (Amherst: University of Massachusetts Press, 1986): 126; Peter Wood, "It Was a Negro Taught Them," 17.

22. Solomon Caldwell in Rawick, *South Carolina Narratives*, part 1, 171.

23. Jack Waldburg in GWP, *Drums and Shadows*, 68.

24. See Eugene D. Genovese, *Roll, Jordan, Roll: The World the Slaves Made* (New York: Pantheon Books, 1974), 574.

25. See F.W. Lange and J.S. Handler, "The Ethnohistorical Approach to Slavery," in T.A. Singleton, ed. *The Archaeology of Slavery and Plantation Life* (Orlando: Academic Press, Inc., 1985), 20.

26. Jack Waldburg in GWP, *Drums and Shadows*, 69.

27. J. Motte Alston, cited in Joyner, *Down By The Riverside*, 92.

28. As cited earlier, Wood, in *Black Majority*, makes reference to the fact that slaves generally followed the same cultivation practices they were familiar with in West Africa. Daniel Littlefield also discusses this issue in the context of a slave trader's observations of this same practice in Sierra Leone in the eighteenth century, in *Rice and Slaves*, 78-9. Although in either case it is not explicitly stated that women prepared this food, it is most likely that this would have been their responsibility within the division of labor. Kenneth Little, in *The Mende of Sierra Leone* (London and New York: Routledge and Kegan Paul, 1951), states the following in a discussion of the social organization of farming among the Mende:

> During the busy periods of the farming season, the household lives together communally. Food is prepared for the group as a whole under the direction of the big wife, who supervises its distribution. The women folk take it in turns to cook. (99)

Other supporting evidence comes from a nineteenth century account of Puerto Rican plantations, by George D. Flinter, *An Account of the Present State of the Island of Puerto Rico* (London: Longman, 1834), 248. He specifically noted that Puerto Rican slave women cooked for men and women working in the fields. This is cited in Morrissey's *Slave Women in the New World*, 50.

29. See Leland Fergusson, *Uncommon Ground: Archaeological and Early African-America, 1650-1800* (Washington, D.C.: Smithsonian Institution Press, 1992), 24. He reports that abrasion marks and charred remains of food were found on colonoware pots in South Carolina. He also mentions archaeological studies which report the inscribed initials of a young girl "MHD" found on handcrafted pottery on a plantation site in South Carolina.

30. See Leland Fergusson, "Looking for the 'Afro' in Colono-Indian Pottery," in *Archaeological Perspectives on Ethnicity in America*, ed. R.L. Schuyler (Amityville, N.Y.: Baywood Publishing Co., Inc., 1980), 20.

31. Shad Hall in GWP, *Drums and Shadows*, 166.

32. Katie Brown in GWP, *Drums and Shadows*, 162. In a personal communication with Lioba Moshi, a linguistics Professor at the University of Georgia, the following information which needs further research but which may have a possible connection to the word "mosojo" was conveyed to me:

    Msanjo/Msonjo (there could be phonemic variation): In Kichaga, a Bantu language spoken in Tanzania, this word is a food term. It is used to make reference to a special type of meal which is usually prepared for a guest or an important person. It is also used to refer to the marrow in bones. In many families, the bone with marrow is given to the head of the family who is usually a man.

33. Katie Brown, in GWP, *Drums and Shadows*, 167; Shad Hall, in GWP, *Drums and Shadows*, 167. Katie Brown and Shad Hall were descendants of a practicing Muslim family that had a strong sense of its ethnic and religious differences. Their great-grandfather was Bilali of Sapelo Island, Georgia, and before that of Timbo, in the Futa Jallon region of West Africa (probably present day Guinea). This information is drawn largely from Allan Austin, *African Muslims in Ante-Bellum America: A Source book* (New York: Garland Publishing, Inc., 1984).

34. Shad Hall in GWP, *Drums and Shadows*, 167.

35. Jane Lewis in GWP, *Drums and Shadows*, 147.

36. Shad Hall in GWP, *Drums and Shadows*, 167.

37. For comparable examples in West African cultures, see Kenneth L. Little, *The Mende of Sierra Leone* (London: Routledge and Kegan Paul, 1967); Melville J. Herskovits, *Dahomey* (New York: J.J. Augustin, 1938), 1, 356; Capt. R. Sutherland Rattray, *Ashanti Proverbs* (Oxford: The Clarendon Press, 1916), 37.

38. Bessie Reese in GWP, *Drums and Shadows*, 59.

39. Emma English in GWP, *Drums and Shadows*, 59.

40. Evidence suggests that in the Sea Island region of Georgia and South Carolina, dominant cultural practices among the slaves were largely derived from the Kongo-Angolan and Winward Coast regions of Africa. Although some of these African religious influences corresponded and coexisted with Christian doctrines, the underlying principles of African spiritual beliefs were present in the attitudes of slaves towards life and death. While Christianity is more individually oriented, African religious beliefs are community centered and involve a set of spiritual relationships involving God, the ancestors, other human beings, including those yet unborn, and other living and non-living species. Influenced by this world view,

the slaves believed that life continued after death and that death did not signify the end of life but the beginning of another journey into the world of the ancestors and the spirit world. They also believed in a tripartite division of the human being into body, soul, and spirit, and that after death the spirit survives the body and has the power to cause good and evil to a living person. For more detailed discussion see Margaret Washington-Creel, "Gullah Attitudes Toward Life and Death," in *Africanisms in American Culture*, ed. Joseph E. Holloway (Bloomington: Indiana University Press, 1990) 69-70; Patricia Jones-Jackson, *When Roots Die: Endangered Traditions in the Sea Islands* (Athens and London: University of Georgia Press, 1987), 24-8. A good background to African spiritual philosophy is John Mbiti, *African Religions and Philosophy* (New York: Praeger, 1969).

41. See John Egerton, *Southern Food: At Home, on the Road, in History* (New York: Alfred A. Knopf, 1987), 15-6.

42. Thomas M. Winterbottom, *An Account of the Native Africans in the Neighbourhood of Sierra Leone* (London: Frank Cass and Co., Ltd., 1969, originally published in 1803), 64.

43. William R. Bascom, "Yoruba Food," *Africa*, 21, no.1 (1951): 49.

44. Helen Mendes, *The African Heritage Cookbook* (New York: The Macmillan Company, 1971), 67-9.

45. For detailed information on comparable dishes in one West African society, see Pamela Greene, *Favorite Sierra Leone Recipes* (Freetown: Commercial Printers Company Limited, n.d.).

46. Sarah Rutledge, *The Carolina Housewife, or House and Home* (In facsimile, with introduction by Anna Wells Rutledge, Columbia, S.C., 1979. 2nd edition., 1851; 3rd edition, 1855; an undated 4th edition). This book is cited in Karen Hess, *The Carolina Rice Kitchen:The African Connection* (Columbia, S.C.: University of South Carolina Press, 1992), 102-3. What is interesting about the *Carolina Housewife* is that it was probably written for the use of white women of upper class southern society. Information collected for the book was based on recipes used by friends and acquaintances of Rutledge. This is the only information I have come across that groundnut soup and benne soup, which are West African dishes, were well established meals in the homes of plantation owners. Groundnut soup especially, is a dish served with rice, originating from the Sene-Gambian region of West Africa.

47. Doris Smith, "In Search of Our Mothers' Cookbooks: Gathering African-American Culinary Traditions," *Iris*, (Fall, 1991):24.

48. Some aspects of this issue are discussed in Elizabeth Fox-Genovese, *Within the Plantation Household*, (Chapel Hill: University of North Carolina Press, 1988), 160; Hess, *The Carolina Rice Kitchen*, 48; Marietta Morrissey, *Slave Women in the New World: Gender Stratification in the Caribbean* (Lawrence: University Press of Kansas, 1989).

49. The complex relationship between the plantation mistress and women slaves, and the harsh treatment imposed by some of these mistresses is discussed in some detail in Catherine Clinton's, "Caught in the Web of the Big House: Women and

Slavery," in *Women and the Family in a Slave Society*, ed. Paul Finkelman (New York: Garland Publishing, Inc., 1989) 21; Morrissey, *Slave Women in the New World*, 4, 149-150; Deborah White, *Ar'n't I a Woman? Female Slaves in the Plantation South* (New York: W. W. Norton, 1985).

50. Interview with Velma Moore, Sapelo Island, 1991.
51. Ibid.
52. Ibid.
53. Interview with Bernice Brown, St. Helena Island, 1989.
54. Interview with Velma Moore, Sapelo Island, 1991.
55. Interview with Sandra Parker, Wadmalow Island, 1989.
56. Interview with Vanessa Buck, Sapelo Island, 1989.
57. Rawick, *The American Slave*, vol. 1, 93.
58. Josephine Bristow in Rawick, *South Carolina Narratives*, vol. 1, part 1, 99.
59. Gus Feaster in Rawick, *South Carolina Narratives*, vol. 2, part 2, 44.
60. Rawick, *South Carolina Narratives*, vol. 3, part 3, 75.
61. For more discussion on the preservation of African-American culinary traditions in published cookbooks, see Doris Smith, "In Search of Our Mothers' Cookbooks."

~

CONCLUDING REFLECTIONS

Stanley L. Engerman

Each generation of historians has had somewhat different concerns in the understanding and interpretation of the nature of slavery. In the U.S., scholars have interested themselves in different aspects of southern life and with different members of the southern population. These studies have often utilized different types of primary sources and methods of analysis, although some of the major reinterpretations have developed from using familiar sources in a different manner. While, at times, the changes may seem to point to quite different interpretations, these may be primarily shifts in focus and emphasis as to what are regarded as the most significant issues.

Slavery has always been a difficult subject to write about, because of our moral concerns. The attempts at southern or northern justifications for past and present behavior, the difficulties posed by the race issue to both blacks and whites, and the desire to make history usable for the present-day, have all served to make the examination of slavery a rather heated scholarly (and non-scholarly) battleground. This problem can be seen quite clearly in the attempts to describe the interactions between slaves and masters, determining how these patterns varied with crops produced, plantation size, and location, as well as how they changed over time as conditions within the South changed. Since masters had the legal power in the South, as well as the control of other means of domination, including arms, they could determine what the slaves were allowed to do, but to do so they would have to have been willing to pay any economic and psychological price. If slaves were given the "space" that is described in many of the essays in this volume, we should ask why this was so and what was the reason that the masters accepted this course of behavior. In the views of Stanley Elkins, where cruel masters meant psychologically destroyed slaves, and in the descriptions of Herbert Aptheker, where slavery and harsh masters meant perpetually rebellious slaves, we find discussions of master-slave interactions that, however inaccurate, made psychological sense and provided for a believable pattern of mutual behavior. Present views of slave space, and the examination of what slaves did with it, therefore, pose important questions for understanding the masters as well as the slaves. In a 1967 article in *Civil War History*, dealing with "Resistance to Slavery," George Fredrickson and Christopher Lasch argued, with what may now seem some overstatement, that slavery as a system resembled a "maximum-security prison," which operates by "a system of compromises, an uneasy give-and-take which gives prisoners a limited leverage within the system." It was then argued that "this adjustment limits the power of the guards, [and] a corruption of authority takes place." The Fredrickson and Lasch essay was among the first answering the questions of slave psychology posed by Elkins, and it helped point to a new direction in slave studies. This approach is seen most influentially in the 1974 study by Eugene D. Genovese, *Roll, Jordan, Roll*, but the post-Elkins reaction can be seen in almost all writings on slavery of the past three decades.

The starting point for studies of slavery must be that slavery was immoral because it meant a severe reduction of the human rights of the enslaved. Examination of other questions, such as material treatment, economic performance, and demographic behavior, should not in any way contradict this moral indictment. Rather, these questions provide much important information about the nature of slave life and of southern society. We should remember that the actualities of slavery are often quite difficult to generalize about. There were many masters and many more slaves in the South during the time slavery existed, and there were important changes over time, in addition to variations in methods of slave control and behavior by crop produced and plantation size, among a number of important factors. There were, no doubt, combinations of motives on the part of both masters and slaves, and these caused not only particular patterns of behavior, but often they could come together, in some psychological admixture, to explain any one set of actions. Moreover, individual behavior could itself be highly variable. Nevertheless, despite these complexities, scholars have seldom been stopped from generalizing about slavery, and such generalizations have long characterized historical writings, past and present. Once the immorality of the system is accepted, we frequently return to questions requiring the quantification of qualitative behavior patterns: how many behaved or were treated in one manner? how many in another? This type of question is also critical when using one of the major sources for examining slavery, the southern law codes. It is obviously essential to study laws, since they reflect what people believed to be important and also because they do influence what can happen, but laws may not themselves provide the best guide to the actual range and frequency of different varieties of master and slave behavior. Events that the law prohibited may have occurred with some frequency while the absence of a legal permission need not mean certain actions did not occur. Actual behavior patterns could have been either better or worse than the law specified.

The present essays fit into, and extend, the recent analysis of United States slavery, with obvious implications for the study of slavery elsewhere as well as for the examination of lower classes in most societies. There are two key aspects of the interpretations presented in these essays. First, attention has been shifted from the masters to the study of the slaves, and to their actions and reactions within the slave system. This is referred to as regarding the "slave as actor." Second, attention is now given to what are regarded as the positive accomplishments of slave life and culture, rather than the previous emphasis on the negative impacts upon the slaves of master behavior and of the slave system. Descriptions of the slave family, their religion, their community life, even their economic behavior, now detail a richness of slave accomplishments within the slave regime, as the slaves used the space they were provided with to obtain, as best was possible, their desires and demands.

These two points, the "slave as actor" and the positive accomplishments within slavery, are central to the most recent work on slavery, but they need not have been linked together. To discuss the "slave as actor," with attention to the constraints imposed by the master and the overall slave system, could lead in a different direction; the slave's reactions leading to those destructive and "dehumanizing" aspects argued for by contemporaries, both proslavery and antislavery, and by some subsequent scholars. Such impacts the slaves dealt with as best they could, but with quite limited positive accomplishments. Earlier writers on slavery had, in a sense, also discussed the impact of slavery upon the slave and the slaves responses to their circumstances. This was true, for example, of those claiming the slaves had undergone psychic destruction and infantilization, or lived in a state of constant anger and hostility. What is most recent, however, is the discussion of the human dignity and self-esteem of the slave, and the contention that slavery (and the "Middle Passage" from Africa to America) need not have been "dehumanizing." And, if we recognize the "slave as actor," we should also recognize that so was the master, and that it is necessary to look at both individuals in studying their interactions and their outcomes.

Some of these issues of slave belief and behavior had been a focus of debate before World War II, with a major distinction between those pointing to the intensity of African carryovers and those arguing that the slaves had been "completely stripped" of their African background before arrival in America. Few would hold either of these extreme positions today. In most studies of the dynamics of slave adjustment to white and black society in the South, focus is on the interaction of the different sets of forces coming from Africa and from America. Studies point to some African carryovers in slave belief and behavior, as well as situations in which African patterns re-emerged after a time, in response to changing situations. It is now possible to examine the slaves without necessarily implying, as some argued earlier, that only pure African carryovers could demonstrate the "humanity" of the slaves. It is this process of dynamic adjustment that these papers describe, demonstrating the different influences upon the slaves and the masters.

The essays in this volume contribute to our understanding of slavery by their discussions of several different aspects of slave life, including the slaves production of foodstuffs for themselves on garden plots, the buying and selling of goods in their internal economy, and the accumulation of cash and other forms of wealth, arising from working for themselves, with sales and trades with their masters or with other slaves and free people. They demonstrate how these influenced the slave family, work, patterns of manumission, and other aspects of slave life. Also of concern here is the impact upon what the ex-slaves brought into the era of emancipation in regard to beliefs about the family, economic behavior, and other matters. Freedom was obviously a dramatic step, but the nature of responses to it were greatly influenced by what had happened to the African Americans, and how they perceived it, in those preceding centuries of slavery that are examined in these essays.

In some ways the findings about slave production for themselves, their trading transactions, and their ability to accumulate some assets, are not new to slave historiography. Many previous writings had commented on them. They were, however, then considered to be relatively minor or even aberrational aspects of the system of slavery. Now they have become more the center of analysis, reflecting shifts in focus in the study of slavery, with greater attention to the actions of the slaves, and an increased desire to see how these acts fit into the broad context of slavery.

The findings and interpretations of these essays reflect the use of an extremely wide variety of primary and secondary sources. The new interpretations do not arise from a dependence on only one particular type of material, but come from the drawing of implications from a number of quite different sources. There are various government and legal documents, relating to masters and slaves: census data, court records, land deeds, tax records, wills and probate records, laws, manumission registers, and records of the Freedmen's Savings Bank, the Southern Claims Commissions, and the Freedmen's Bureau. There are familiar master documents containing information about slaves, including account books, letters, farm and personal journals, and diaries. In regard to slaves and ex-slaves there are also numerous sources, including the WPA narratives, slave and ex-slave autobiographies, novels, cookbooks, folktales, and interviews with the present-day descendants of slaves. In addition, several essays draw upon archaeological methods, examining the remains of plantations and artifacts, in order to obtain information about slave life. Yet this very richness of data can only take us so far, since the information needed to describe individual reactions and psychological beliefs is never as complete and precise as desired. There is thus a need for historians to imaginatively reconstruct these beliefs and psychological conditions using the various sources available.

The analysis of plantation records for the early period of settlement in Virginia indicates that it was possible that a slave community developed rather quickly, since many of the arrivals had come from the same areas within Africa. We do know that, after arrival, the situation for slaves was quite different in the U.S. than in most other slave societies of the New World. The U.S. had a lower number of African imports, permitted by the unusually favorable demographic experience of U.S. slaves. There was a relatively early ending of the international slave trade. U.S. slavery was influenced by the smaller size of cotton and tobacco plantations, relative to those in the Caribbean and elsewhere growing sugar, and there was greater number of whites compared to blacks in the population of the U.S. South relative to slave areas elsewhere in the Americas. The U.S. slaves experienced rather disruptive conditions again, after nearly two centuries of settlement, when the westward movement accelerated at the start of the nineteenth century. The importance of earlier patterns of settlement and of mobility (or lack of it) in influencing slave culture are suggested by the greater frequency of continued African patterns on the Gullah Coast of South Carolina and Georgia resembling more those of, e.g., the Caribbean islands than those in the rest of the U.S. South.

The dynamics of the adjustment of family patterns posed problems, particularly given the initial unbalanced sex ratio in the transatlantic slave trade. While such excesses of males over females characterized most other migrant groups, being quite dramatic for indentured servants, the involuntary movements of slaves into an area dominated by members of a different culture meant that the initial changes were more challenging for Africans. Certain patterns known in Africa, such as polygamy and prolonged lactation, generally disappeared, the former relatively quickly. There may have been some master encouragement to family formation, whether to reduce the numbers of runaways, to provide for better feeding and care, to encourage reproduction, or because masters regarded this as morally necessary. Nevertheless, the master's ability to provide for family stability was limited, as was demonstrated by the frequency of estate sales, gifts to offspring, or sales in times of financial difficulty. Yet by at least the middle of the eighteenth century a pattern of nuclear families with extensive kin networks had developed, and these played a major role in the slave community and economy. This pattern was to persist, even after the start of a large-scale westward movement.

There has long been debate about the relative roles of slave parents and kin and the master and his family in influencing slave children. To W.E.B. Du Bois, for example, the absent father was not one physically absent but rather one forced to play a different role in raising his children than was a father in a free society. While acknowledging the ultimate power of the master, studies point to the importance of slave parents and relatives in educating and disciplining children, while the examination of production on slave garden plots and of slave marketing demonstrate a rather stronger family unit than had been earlier suggested. To some extent, fathers did provide for their families and influenced the material well-being of their children and other family members. Patterns of family formation and behavior may have differed somewhat in slavery and in freedom. With emancipation the master's influence disappeared, leading to important changes in the roles and functions of children and of men and women within the black family. The basic two-parent, nuclear household continued after emancipation, but with changes in its inner dynamics as well as in its relations to the external world.

Several essays deal with the issues posed by slave production for themselves and the market exchanges that these often led to. There were exchanges, of goods and money, between masters and slaves, as well as between slaves on the plantation and also with slaves and others outside the plantation. These forms of production and exchange go back a long time, but it is only recently that their importance within the U.S. South has been recognized. We have been taught by Sidney Mintz that these opportunities were important in the West Indies, influencing conditions under slavery and then freedom, but their role in the South had not previously been accorded similar attention. It was up to the master to provide the slaves with garden plots and the poultry and small livestock with which to produce food and other goods, although this allowance may have been forced by the slaves' desires. There were some benefits to the masters, particularly in reducing the needs to purchase or produce food for the slaves. There were, however, distinct costs to the master, with the threat of a loss of output on a loss of control. The slave laborer could adjust the numbers of hours worked and working intensity to be more productive on his own plots than when working for the master. Also to the extent that slaves recognized the relation between their individual input and the output of their plots, their sense of the injustice of the system could be magnified.

Moreover, the study of the role of cash in the slaves' internal economy shows that slaves could develop a market-like mentality, as seen in their transactions as well as in their seeking to obtain more consumption by working for themselves. Slaves could adjust the time and intensity of their own work, leading to some social and economic differentiation within the slave community, based upon abilities and preferences as to consumption (whether of necessities or of what might seem to be luxuries) and leisure. This income opened opportunities for intergenerational transfers via inheritance, possible if families had stayed together for long periods. Thus the slaves' own production, to obtain cash or other considerations, led to a quite different set of attitudes towards production and of exchange after emancipation, than earlier works had suggested.

The market-like considerations that were present in rural areas were probably even more extensive in urban areas, where forms of labor market behavior such as self-hiring permitted slaves to choose their own working and living arrangements. The funds earned, over the amounts paid to their masters, could be used for various purposes, including the purchase of freedom for members of their family and kin. The process of manumission, whether paid for by slaves or, no doubt, more frequently by free blacks, meant a need to accumulate savings over time and this would have required some legal or non-legal ability to store money as well as to have an acceptable means of enforcing the use of partial payments.

Many have broadened the concept of resistance to include actions that did not directly threaten the system. Was any independent action of a slave for his or her own reasons to be seen as an act of resistance, since the slaves themselves selected their behavior rather than having it imposed by the master directly or influenced by him? Slaves utilized the space provided them in manners of their own choosing. In some cases slaves are seen to have behaved almost like free laborers, in threatening the withdrawal of labor to get better working and living conditions from the master. Even with these threats, however, slavery long persisted and, to some, these actions were to be regarded less as resistance than as a form of co-option in that it did not, at least as of 1860, bring the system down. In this regard, the analysis of slave resistance is similar to that of lower class free labor, where some forms of resistance meant that there were economic gains but no overthrow of the existing order. While actions by slaves forced master adaptation, their ultimate threat to the system is less clear. It is, however, quite clear that the slaves did not wish to live in slavery, as was demonstrated by the departure of slaves from the plantation with northern advances during the Civil War and the failure to reintroduce the plantation afterwards.

Where do we now stand in slave studies? These essays demonstrate the rather dramatic changes that have occurred in our understanding of masters, slaves, and slave societies over the past several decades. While it has been the U.S. South that has been most studied, many of these reinterpretations have been found applicable to other slave societies in the New World and elsewhere. In many ways the previous sharp distinction between slavery and other forms of labor institutions, including what is regarded generally as free labor, has been eroded. While slavery obviously remains at one end of a spectrum, it is now seen to have many characteristics and effects similar to other types of societies. Actual patterns of behavior do not always neatly follow from legal constructs.

In its economic aspects, slavery has been found to be consistent with profitability to masters, long-term viability, and, by the standards of the times, reasonably rapid growth. Perhaps the southern economic situation could have been better, at that time or in the future, but that is not the same as arguing that the economy was backward, stagnant, and declining. Southern growth was aided, of course, by the growing demand for cotton and tobacco, but the accomplishments required that masters were not unconcerned with making profits, devised new methods and technologies for producing and distributing outputs, and, further, were concerned with the design of measures to encourage labor to produce and not cause too many problems. The actions of masters were influenced by the slaves' desires and expectations, and these became important considerations of the slaveowners.

The recent analysis of slavery has pointed to the space allowed the slaves, allowing them to make choices within the slave system. As workers, slaves were able to bargain with their owners, threaten to limit their work input and, in general, negotiate with them, though not as equals, to obtain better working and living conditions. Slaves, wherever possible (and it now seems to have been possible more often than earlier believed) lived in two-parent nuclear households, lived with parents and with grandparents often present, and formed their own communities, all with limited white presence, although probably not without some considerable white influence. Religion was a central point of the lives of slaves, and, as in other aspects of their behavior, there was a mixture, of varying and uncertain magnitudes, of African, European, and American influences. Harsh the laws of slavery, and many masters, were, but the slaves were not "dehumanized" - psychologically destroyed, infantilized, or left bereft of their own cultural and social beliefs. As with most lower classes, discontent with their situation did not lead directly to an overthrow of the system. But, within the major constraints imposed by the system, slaves had an ability to create their own beliefs, to make their own choices about marriage, income, and consumption patterns, and to seek means to achieve more favorable working and living conditions. All this is to describe a slavery quite different from the portrayal prevalent until recent decades.

This new understanding of the slaves and of the southern economy and society is important not only for the examination of the antebellum era, but also in providing a better basis for analyzing the transition to freedom during the Civil War and after 1865. If the slaves now appear to have been different than earlier believed, so should the freedmen. We can, therefore, anticipate that the reinterpretations of the black slaves will soon be followed by new examinations of the freed blacks during and after emancipation. This, in turn, will re-open many questions about the pace and pattern of changes in the postbellum southern society, with its new demands for work and labor, with perhaps reinterpretations of freedom as dramatic as those that have recently emerged for slavery.

CONTRIBUTORS

JOSEPHINE BEOKU-BETTS is a member of the Sociology Department at the University of Georgia. Educated in Sierra Leone, England, and the U.S.A., she has written several articles on women in Africa.

KENNETH BROWN teaches in the Department of Anthropology at the University of Houston. His "Structural Continuity in an African-American Slave and Tenant Community," co-authored with Doreen C. Cooper, appeared in *Historical Archaeology*.

JOHN CAMPBELL is a Research Associate at the University of Minnesota, and Adjunct Professor of History at Winona State University. He has published articles on slavery in The Journal of Interdisciplinary History and Slavery and Abolition, and is completing a book on slave property and market participation.

DR. CHERYLL ANN CODY is an independent researcher living in Houston, Texas. She has published essays on naming practices and the familial lives of enslaved people, and has a forthcoming study of the demographic and family history of the Ball family slaves.

MARY BETH CORRIGAN is a Ph.D candidate at the University of Maryland at College Park. She is completing her dissertation entitled "The Transformation of the African-American Family in the District of Columbia, 1850-1865."

STANLEY ENGERMAN is Professor of History, and John Munro Professor of economics at the University of Rochester. He is the author of several articles on slavery and abolition.

244   WORKING TOWARD FREEDOM

SHARON ANN HOLT is Program Officer at the Pennsylvania Humanities Council in Philadelphia. Her article, "Making Freedom Pay: Freedpeople Working for Themselves, North Carolina, 1865-1900," appeared in the May 1994 issue of *The Journal of Southern History*.

LARRY HUDSON teaches in the Department of History at the University of Rochester. His book, *Work and Slavery: The Slave Family in South Carolina, 1820-1860* will be published by the University of Georgia Press.

WILMA KING is Associate Professor in the Department of History at Michigan State University. Her most recent publication is an edited work entitled *A Northern Woman in the Plantation South: Letters of Tryphena Blanche Holder Fox, 1856-1876* (Columbia, University of South Carolina Press, 1993).

ROBERT OLWELL teaches in the department of History at the University of Texas at Austin. He is completing a book on slavemasters and social order in the South Carolina Lowcountry, 1739-1784.

LORENA WALSH researches at the Colonial Williamsburg Foundation. She is co-author of *Robert Cole's World: Agriculture and Society in Early Maryland* (Chapel Hill: University of North Carolina Press, 1991).

~

INDEX